ROMANCING THE CATHEDRAL

ROMANCING THE CATHEDRAL

Gothic Architecture in
Fin-de-Siècle French Culture

ELIZABETH EMERY

State University of New York Press

Published by
State University of New York Press, Albany

For information, address State University of New York Press,
90 State Street, Suite 700, Albany, NY 12207

Production by Dana Foote
Marketing by Patrick Durocher

Library of Congress Cataloging-in-Publication Data

Emery, Elizabeth (Elizabeth Nicole)
Romancing the cathedral : gothic architecture in fin-de-siècle
French culture / Elizabeth Emery.
p.   cm.
Based on the author's thesis (Ph. D.—New York University, 1997)
presented under the title: Reconstructing the cathedral.
Includes bibliographical references and index.
ISBN 0-7914-5123-2 (alk. paper)—ISBN 0-7914-5124-0 (pbk. : alk paper)
1. French fiction–19th century—History and criticism.   2. Cathedrals in literature.
3. Arts, French.   4. Arts, Modern—19th century—France.   5. Cathedrals in art.
6. France—Civilization—19th century.   7. Zola, Emile, 1840–1902—Criticism and
interpretation.   8. Zola, Emile, 1840–1902. Trois villes.   9. Huysmans, J.-K.
(Joris-Karl), 1848–1907—Criticism and interpretation.   10. Huysmans, J.-K.
(Joris-Karl), 1848–1907. Durtal.   11. Proust, Marcel, 1871–1922—Criticism
and interpretation.   I. Title.

PQ663 .E54 2001
843′.809357—dc21

2001034869

10 9 8 7 6 5 4 3 2 1

CONTENTS

ILLUSTRATIONS

Introduction

Cathedrals impressed a devout Catholic of the seventeenth
century much less than they do an atheist of the twentieth.
—Marcel Proust, *Le Côté de Guermantes* (1920)

Fin-de-siècle France was swept by a furor for all things medieval. In the 1880s and
1890s, administrators voted to incorporate medieval literature into the secondary
school and university curriculum; the government passed its first laws to protect
historical monuments; *La Revue des Deux Mondes,* the most widely read periodical
of the time, published lengthy, multivolume essays about the Middle Ages, and
student groups mobilized the Latin Quarter to re-create medieval celebrations.
Symbolist writers and poets sang the virtues of the Middle Ages; the Louvre opened
a department devoted to medieval and Renaissance studies; and artists like the
Nabis envisioned themselves as medieval monks, fashioning tapestries, stained-
glass windows, manuscripts, and liturgical objects. The medieval climate of this
time was so thick that the young Paul Valéry described its influence as "life considered through a stained-glass window."[1]

While the romantic infatuation with medieval themes is well-documented,
the French Gothic Revival of the 1880s and 1890s is little known and rarely discussed.[2] The turn-of-the-century interest in medievalism was not a direct continuation of the eighteenth-century "troubadour genre" begun by Sainte-Palaye, Mil-
lot, and Tressan, in which authors glorified courtly love, worshiped chivalry, and
praised old French. Nor did it resemble the "gothic furor" of the romantics.[3] During the first Gothic revival, Musset's *Rolla* and Chateaubriand's *Le Génie du Christianisme* both evoked nostalgia for a time of pure faith, while Hugo's *Odes et ballades* and *Notre-Dame de Paris* conjured up visions of knights errant, troubadours,
and enthusiastic crowds as well as scenes from the Gothic novel: corpses hanging
from gibbets; night terrors; and the mysterious activities of evil priests in the vein
of Claude Frollo. Authors of the fin de siècle continued to refer to these themes,
yet they also began to represent the Middle Ages and medieval art as worthy of scientific study.[4]

By the end of the century, the Gothic cathedral, with its mixture of art, music, scripture, and ceremony, had become the most appreciated figure from the
Middle Ages.[5] In 1870 Michelet called the cathedral of Strasbourg "the entire Middle Ages, the entire accumulated history of the world and of Strasbourg."[6] An 1880
sonnet from Paul Verlaine's *Sagesse,* in which the poet travels to his dream

1

Middle Ages via the wingèd and passionate cathedral, illustrates the extent to which it was associated with this period.[7] Editors published books from all over the world, in which writers as varied as John Ruskin, Albert Robida, Emile Mâle, Henry James, and Henry Adams described their pilgrimages to medieval French cathedrals.[8] By World War I the image of the Gothic cathedral had permeated French social and artistic life to such an extent that, as Proust remarked, an early twentieth-century atheist attached more value to cathedrals than a devout seventeenth-century worshiper. The cathedral had become *un lieu de mémoire,* a treasured part of French heritage.[9]

Despite its great popularity now, Gothic architecture was not always admired; in fact, it had long been maligned. Most French writers and artists from the sixteenth to the nineteenth centuries linked Gothic architecture to the Dark Ages and dismissed it as "misshapen," "inept," or "monstrous."[10] The term *Gothic* was first widely applied by Giorgio Vasari, who associated the style with the Barbarians in his 1550 *Vite.* The derogatory term spread throughout Europe and was applied indiscriminately to all nonclassical architecture from the sixth to the fifteenth centuries.[11] Françoise Choay argues that France's negative consideration of Gothic architecture stemmed largely from exposure to and embrace of classical architecture during the sixteenth-century wars with Italy. The shift in attitude is striking when compared to the English, who never stopped appreciating the Gothic style.[12] It was only in the aftermath of the French Revolution, as church property was transferred to the state and as vandals came under criticism for their excesses, that the French began conceiving of medieval structures as worthy of consideration. At this time, architects and art historians devoted their attention to medieval constructions, which had so long been neglected. In fact, their knowledge of it was so rudimentary that they had to create parameters with which to evaluate it; the vocabulary to describe medieval architecture did not even exist in French. Arcisse de Caumont's *Essai sur l'architecture du moyen âge,* the first well-researched book about medieval architecture published in France, did not appear until 1824.[13] Even eighty years later, while composing *Mont Saint-Michel and Chartres,* Henry Adams remarked that "the French have been shockingly negligent of their greatest artistic glory."[14] Much of the serious scholarship about the Gothic cathedral in French dates from the early years of the twentieth century.

This book traces the cathedral's rise in popularity during the nineteenth century by examining the cultural context that built it into a cherished figure: nineteenth-century literature, newspapers, essays, interviews, and correspondence all discuss the Gothic style. I focus primarily on the period known as the fin de siècle, the 1880s and 1890s, when the cathedral became a figure of predilection.[15] While the early nineteenth century struggled to categorize medieval monuments and to preserve them, by the end of the century the importance of Gothic architecture was undisputed. It took nearly a century for architects and art historians to understand the cathedral's form, function, and symbolism, but, by 1900, the cathedral, and the Middle Ages in general, underwent a boom of scholarly and scientific study that culminated in the field we know today as medieval studies.[16] This period of concentrated interest in the past created many of the organizations, publications, and laws we rely on today in the study of the Middle Ages.[17] The cathedral had developed from a popular literary theme into a multifaceted symbol of French sprit.

The Cathedral and the Fin de Siècle

One of my major goals in this book is to shed light on the fin-de-siècle period as a decisive juncture for medieval studies, and particularly for the cathedral. Interest in philological and positivist approaches to art and literature, craving for spiritual fulfillment, and worries about the industrialization of art, produced a climate particularly hospitable to a rich symbolic figure like the Gothic cathedral, which could be interpreted on many levels. The late-nineteenth-century fascination with the cathedral grew out of an attraction to the history and spirituality of the Middle Ages, before settling into contemporary issues of politics, religion, and art.[18] In fact, the late nineteenth century progressively detached the cathedral from its medieval context to consider it from different angles: as a historical monument from the Middle Ages, as a house of worship, and as a sublime work of art. Its semantic flexibility allowed it to be claimed by different groups, all of whom embraced it as the embodiment of their conflicting ideals.

The rise of tourism and the creation of museums in the late nineteenth century also contributed to the cathedral's popularity. As increasingly affluent members of the bourgeoisie found the time and the means to travel, they sought out new aesthetic pleasures. Théophile Gautier, for example, complained about the "cathedral indigestions" brought on by his prolonged excursions.[19] A wealth of guidebooks to picturesque monuments and European museums began appearing in the late nineteenth century; they catered to this tourist class. Among them were the Baedeker guides, Robida's *La Vieille France* series, John Ruskin's guides to England, France, and Italy, and Emile Mâle's studies of French cathedrals. The public visited museums—the Musée des monuments historiques and the Musée de Cluny were both institutionalized in the mid-nineteenth century—and cathedrals in order to study and sketch medieval art. It was during these years that the cathedral began to break away from the Middle Ages to gain significance in its own right, as an admirable work of art. It is no coincidence that even Victor Hugo, the early nineteenth-century champion of the cathedral and the Middle Ages, would declare in the 1870s that he loved the cathedral, not the Middle Ages.[20]

Images of the Gothic cathedral and its component arts flourished in the 1880s and 1890s, independently of the Middle Ages. Claude Monet painted his modern impressions of the Rouen Cathedral from 1892 to 1894; his 1895 Paris exhibit of them had to be prolonged to accommodate public interest. Popular newspapers and journals like *Le Courrier Français, La Plume,* and *Le Rire* were full of images of and articles about cathedrals. The organizers of the 1889 World's Fair even created a cathedrallike interior for an exhibit of Catholic treasures; they commissioned six stained-glass windows for the display.[21] The cathedral was also behind the "vitromanie"—the stained glass craze—that led to the foundation of the Musée du Vitrail, and created a passion for placing medieval tapestries and windows in domestic interiors.[22] As the fashion for all things medieval slowed down in the first years of the twentieth century, however, the cathedral began to develop into a symbol of its own, an image that could be claimed by all walks of society. It is ironic that this period, notorious for the political, religious, and aesthetic turbulence that culminated in the Dreyfus Affair, the separation of Church and State, and the publication of numerous works about the country's spiritual and aesthetic "degeneration," would praise the Gothic cathedral, an inherently sacred Catholic structure.[23] The cathedral was considered not only a place of worship, but also a space of nationalistic and artistic inspiration.

Recent scholarly studies have begun to explore the nineteenth century's fascination for architectural monuments as both historical markers and models for literature, yet few of them identify the end of the century, which was heavily influenced by positivism and the secular politics of a Republican government, as inherently different from the rest of the century.[24] In addition, few recognize the rich historical, spiritual, and aesthetic aspects of the cathedral as distinct from other architectural structures.[25] A notable exception is Françoise Choay, who, influenced by the work of Austrian art historian Aloïs Riegl (1858–1905), identifies the end of the century as a crucial period for the development of the modern conception of the historical monument. Riegl believed that the "use value"—a monument's continued performance of the task for which it was originally created—causes us to weigh religious architecture differently from empty, unused, or purely aesthetic monuments.[26] I agree. At a time of increased secularization, diminishing Church power over society, and abandonment of churches, the Gothic cathedral—a 600-year-old structure still functioning according to the beliefs for which it was created—exerted a fascinating attraction for people worried about social fragmentation, disappearing beliefs, and vanishing traditions. Today's French laws concerning the conservation of monuments were passed in 1887 and 1913, largely in order to protect churches that lost funding after the separation of Church and State in 1905.[27] Because scholars have tended to subordinate the religious functions of the cathedral to its architectural or artistic components, it has been underestimated as a symbolic figure in fin-de-siècle France. This study will show how, by the end of the century, the cathedral had paradoxically come to represent not only the spiritual integrity of the Catholic Church, but also the history of a secular French nation, and redemption through art.

The Cathedral and the Novel

Although architects, Parliament, art historians, and the clergy played important roles in the recognition and preservation of monuments in the nineteenth century, writers and artists provided the critical mass that brought the cathedral to the attention of the public. It was no coincidence that novelists Charles Nodier, Victor Hugo, and Prosper Mérimée led efforts to publicize and advocate the medieval heritage of their country, the first with *Voyages pittoresques et romantiques dans l'ancienne France* (1820–1878), the second with *Notre-Dame de Paris* (1831) and essays against vandalism, and the third with his work as General Inspector of Historical Monuments. The predilection for the Gothic cathedral in France emerged almost entirely from literature and art: architects and art historians of the nineteenth century were profoundly influenced by these works, which served as the catalyst for preserving French monuments.[28]

This book elucidates the ways in which major French novelists of the end of the century—Emile Zola, J.-K. Huysmans, and Marcel Proust—carried on this early nineteenth-century tradition by reflecting and responding to their contemporaries' obsessions with cathedrals. Zola, Huysmans, and Proust were the first French novelists since Hugo to include long descriptive passages about *real* Gothic houses of worship—Notre-Dame de Chartres, Notre-Dame d'Amiens, Notre-Dame de Paris—in their fiction. Although others—Maurice Barrès, Léon Bloy, and Paul Claudel, to name a few—wrote extensively about cathedrals in their nonfictional work, they did not tend to do so in the novel.[29] Zola, Huysmans, and Proust insist on the ways in which disparate elements such as architecture, symbolism, liturgy, and music come together to produce a powerful spiritual effect.[30] They do not simply glorify Gothic architecture in these novels. Instead, they place their churches in contemporary urban contexts where the cathedral exerts its influence on the city around it.

In *Les Trois Villes* (*Lourdes, Rome, Paris*), the Durtal cycle (*Là-Bas, En route, La Cathédrale, L'Oblat*), and *A la recherche du temps perdu*, the cathedral serves as a point of reference for each protagonist as he attempts to understand his place in society. Zola's Pierre Froment, a priest who has lost his faith, hopes to rekindle his belief in Catholicism by visiting Lourdes, Rome, and Paris; Huysmans's atheist, Durtal, stumbles on the Church through his love of art and sanctifies his resulting conversion by living in religious communities; and the encounters of Proust's hero with the Gothic architecture of Combray, Balbec, and Venice help him renew the faith in art that he had experienced as a child. All three series of novels are essentially realist: they are set in 1890s France and Italy; their plots concern quests undertaken by characters with well-documented social classes, professions, and family lives; and the protagonists describe details of everyday life from articles of clothing to political discussions. The main characters of these series of novels are fascinated by their society. They observe morality in the world around them, from corrupt politicians to decadent sexual mores; they reflect on the links between past and present, social order and disorder; and they search for spirituality, in the beauty of a perfectly performed sonata or in the sacrifice of an individual for the ideals of his community.

Les Trois Villes, the Durtal cycle, and *La Recherche* resemble such contemporary novel series as *Le Culte du moi* (1888–1891, Maurice Barrès), *L'Histoire Contemporaine* (1897–1901, Anatole France), or *Jean-Christophe* (1904–1912, Romain Rolland), which also figure single protagonists who comment on contemporary values, yet the novels of Zola, Huysmans, and Proust differ from these works in their central focus on aesthetic concerns and spiritual evolution. *Les Trois Villes,* the Durtal cycle, and especially *La Recherche* can be considered variations on the *Bildungsroman* or *Künstlerroman;* the reader follows the protagonist's artistic and spiritual evolution. Moreover, the explicitly religious vocabulary and imagery used by the characters to describe their journeys in *Les Trois Villes,* the Durtal cycle, and *La Recherche,* coupled with the prominent space given to descriptions of houses of worship, links them to an even older tradition: the pilgrimage. The characters' travels from cathedral to cathedral evoke this medieval practice, which was renewed in the nineteenth century by appearances of the Virgin Mary in France and encouraged by clergy hoping to make reparations for the sins of nineteenth-century French society.[31] A form of tourism (the two were often conflated), a pilgrimage was ostensibly driven by devotion to God. The churches in the novels of Zola, Huysmans, and Proust mark each step of the characters' journey toward different kinds of spiritual enlightenment. After numerous false starts and wrong turns, all three protagonists discover solutions to their problems: Pierre Froment invents a religion of science; Durtal finds solace in God; and Proust's hero discovers a religion of art. The cathedral serves as a guide and a mirror; its description in the text illustrates the spiritual progress made by these characters.

Throughout this book I use the word *religion* in the broad terms used by nineteenth-century thinkers to refer to communication with a superior force. They often employed the words "worship," "faith," and "resurrection," vocabulary traditionally associated with Christian traditions, to refer to secular experiences. The definition of religion proposed by Larousse confirms the nineteenth-century tendency to associate it with communication with some kind of divinity. Larousse identifies the Latin etymology as *religio,* "which signifies link, link with the soul" and *religare,* "from re, prefix, and from *ligare,* to link."[32] For Larousse and his contemporaries, the term *religion* could thus be applied to a broad range of beliefs extending from the positivist systems of Auguste Comte to traditional sects such as Catholicism or Judaism.

In the years following the Revolution, French society witnessed the growth of a great number of secular cults, created with the intent of reforming or replacing Catholicism, which was seen as incapable of responding to the needs of modern believers. Even the most seemingly anticlerical thinkers as Michelet believed that religion was an essential aspect of society: people needed a firm belief to keep immorality in check and to guide themselves through the perplexities of the modern world. Although most of these "secular religions" or religious reforms varied in their scope and aims, many of them relied on traditional Christian vocabulary to express their aims. Accordingly, many of these religions described themselves as a "new Christianity" or a "true Christianity." They claimed that they would bring a Golden Age or a new world order, that they would result in utopian civilizations where society would return to the social harmony of an idealized primitive Christianity.[33]

By the end of the century, after numerous shifts in political power, the defeat of Sedan, the 1892–1894 anarchist attacks in Paris, and the Dreyfus Affair, much of the century's early social optimism had been replaced by pessimism, cynicism, and individualism, especially in the wake of the 1893 French translation of Max Nordau's *Degeneration* (*Entartung*). The "cults" discovered by the protagonists of Zola, Huysmans, and Proust respond to their characters' needs, yet they also provide ideal solutions for the readers of their books; they suggest links to a communal belief that will reunite and reinvigorate society. Instead of reproducing the pessimism that marked the conclusion of novels by Bloy, Bourget, and Barrès, Zola, Huysmans, and Proust show their readers that they, too, can find values that will help them surmount the seeming crises of their time. The Gothic cathedral, the structure that guides their protagonists in their travels, stands at the center of these novels as a stable and optimistic reminder of strength. It has withstood hundreds of years of natural disaster, war, and political upheaval, and will continue to do so.

The Cultural Context

Until the late nineteenth century, the cathedral stood primarily as a vestige of the Middle Ages, a time whose image was manipulated in the political and literary discourse of the nineteenth century in order to rationalize varying national or spiritual concerns. The Middle Ages, like the cathedral, were claimed by both Catholics and Republicans. The conflicting symbolic meanings attributed to the cathedral thus placed it at the center of the arguments that tore apart the decade preceding the separation of the Catholic Church and the French State. Yet despite and perhaps because of the fact that Republicans, Catholics, and artists all claimed it as a representation of their own convictions, by the end of the century the cathedral was universally admired. Zola (an anticlerical positivist), Huysmans (a Catholic convert), and Proust (a Jewish aesthete raised as a Catholic), were separated by their philosophical and religious differences, yet they all embraced the cathedral.

Although it seems contradictory that the cathedral could be claimed as a figure of the Republican state, as a house of worship, and as a marvel of art, all at the same time and by diametrically opposed factions of society, it is precisely this multifaceted nature that led to the cathedral's consecration in the French collective consciousness. In his 1903 *Der moderne Denkmalkultus* (*The Modern Cult of Monuments*), Aloïs Riegl, an Austrian art historian and museum conservator, categorized the conflicting attitudes of his time toward historical monuments in an attempt to develop a theory that would assist art historians in the future conservation of monuments. In this valuable essay, he provides an overview of the shifting attitudes toward art in the nineteenth century. Riegl divides the consideration of monuments into two major and conflicting categories: "of recollection" (*Erinnerungswerte*), which addresses issues dealing with posterity and conservation, and "of contemporaneity" (*Gegenwartswerte*), which pertains to modern or contemporary reactions to the monument. Within the category of recollection he distinguishes between "the age value," which glorifies the exterior marks of time and refuses conservation or modification; "the historical value," which appreciates a monument for its ability to reflect its original state and seeks to keep it from further decay; and "the value of intentional recollection," which actively attempts to immortalize a monument by restoring it to its presumed original state. These three values, which are based on aesthetic, historical, and conservatory goals, enter into conflict with values that praise a monument's role in contemporary life, its "use value." This category is especially important for religious architecture, whose function as house of worship overwhelms its value as antiquity. Even when a monument is appreciated for conflicting reasons, Riegl argues, it is still considered important and more valuable than other structures.

The cathedral is such a monument. Because of the complex web of conflicting social and aesthetic discourse linked to it in the late nineteenth century, it is important to consider literary and artistic descriptions of cathedrals against the context that produced them. Zola, Huysmans, and Proust, for example, were all involved in the major social, literary, and artistic crises of the time: Zola and Proust publicly defended Colonel Dreyfus; Huysmans worked for the French Ministry of the Interior, where he participated in the implementation of France's domestic policies; and all three wrote essays and articles about contemporary art and literature. Zola and Huysmans collaborated until 1884; Proust read, wrote, and critiqued the works of Zola and Huysmans.[34] These authors did not live in a vacuum; they could not help but participate in the political, literary, and artistic battles shaping the world around them. *Les Trois Villes* and the Durtal cycle are all but forgotten today, yet Zola and Huysmans's novels were best-sellers that galvanized readers. The Charpentier press sold all 88,000 first-edition copies of each of Zola's *Trois Villes,* while Huysmans's Durtal novels averaged 15,000 copies each in the first two weeks of sales. These works have vanished from the literary canon, yet the readers, journalists, and critics of the fin de siècle devoted hundreds of pages of commentary to them.[35]

Zola, Huysmans, and Proust represented the cathedral as a highly symbolic edifice for a divided French nation. They describe it as a total work of art that establishes harmony in diversity. The decision to incorporate existing buildings in a work of fiction corresponds to what Philippe Hamon calls the nineteenth-century fascination with the "semaphoric properties of certain architectural objects." He argues that the atmosphere we attribute to a building is the sum of the discourses pronounced in or about it. Accordingly, describing real churches in literary texts serves as a way for authors to refer to or to rewrite underlying or implied intertextual referents—myths or legends—surrounding individual edifices.[36] As Zola, Huysmans, and Proust focus on Parisian and Venetian churches—the Sacré-Coeur basilica and Saint Mark's basilica, for example—they draw on their readers' collective consciousness about the political, spiritual, and artistic controversies surrounding these real places. *Romancing the Cathedral,* the title of this book, thus derives not only from the authors' emotional and aesthetic attraction to the cathedral—Henry Adams referred to "wooing" the cathedral during his study of Chartres—but also from their incorporation of Gothic architecture into novels (*romans*) in which they extrapolate on its accepted meaning in order to convince others of its merits.[37]

In a time in which critics Ferdinand Brunetière and Paul Bourget were criticizing literature that contributed to the degeneration of society's value systems, all three of these writers returned to the technique employed by Victor Hugo in *Notre-Dame de Paris:* they used a fictional narrative to focus on specific symbolic structures in order to present their didactic message about social and artistic renewal. Only a few years after Hugo's death (1885), they continued and renewed his vision of the novel as an instrument of social change. These three writers left Hugo behind, however, as they added to his myth of the cathedral by presenting it as a structure that has continued to survive into the modern world; in *Les Trois Villes,* the Durtal cycle, and *La Recherche,* the cathedral incarnates harmony in diversity. It becomes a figure for the nation to emulate.

Chapter 1, "The Synthesis of France," traces the cathedral's transformation from medieval image to French myth. I broadly outline the early-nineteenth-century conception of Gothic architecture before focusing on the period between the inauguration of the Sacré-Coeur and World War I, a turbulent time preceding the French separation of Church and State (1905), during which the cathedral underwent its most serious modification in the public imagination. How, by the end of the century, had the French perpetuated or modified traditional myths about cathedrals? What—at this point in time—was the catalyst that caused Zola, Huysmans, and Proust to choose the Gothic style as a descriptive locus of their work? How does each of their novels reflect contemporary understanding of the cathedral?

Chapter 2, "'The Immense Cathedral of the Future World': Zola and the Religion of Science," examines Zola's paradoxical use of the cathedral in his late novels. Although he was known as the Father of naturalism, and constantly de-

nounced Catholicism in his works, he changed tack sharply after finishing his
Rougon-Macquart series. In subsequent works he abandoned the scientific method
he had promoted since the early 1870s in order to create an idealistic dream for
humanity, a "religion of science" that would give his readers the faith to face the
crises of the fin de siècle. The cathedral lies at the heart of Zola's contradictory relationship to religion and science, past and future, as it did for many Republican
contemporaries. Although their secular sentiment led them to advocate the destruction of the political power of the Catholic Church, they also admired the
Gothic cathedral as a perfect democratic structure in which all factions of society
cooperate.

Centered on former naturalist J.-K. Huysmans's extremely public and con-
troversial conversion to Catholicism, chapter 3, "'The Soul of Arches': Huysmans
and the Medieval Church," explores the cathedral's relationship to issues of faith
that motivated Catholic writers as varied as Léon Bloy, Paul Claudel, Charles
Péguy, and François Mauriac. Huysmans profited from his literary renown to publicize the medieval faith of the Church contained in Gothic cathedrals.

The final chapter, "Perpetual Adoration: Proust and the Art Spirit," explores
the memorial and symbolic value that the cathedral gained between the separation
of Church and State and World War I. Beginning with an examination of the newspaper articles and essays Proust dedicated to the defense of churches from
1900–1906, it traces the role played by the cathedral in his development of an aesthetic theory crucial for *A la recherche du temps perdu*. The cathedral itself serves as
a privileged artistic figure for the hero of the novel as for many of his peers.

Unlike Philippe Hamon, whose primary focus in *Expositions* is a semiotic
and rhetorical analysis of the relationships between literature and architecture (architecture as both metaphor for literary composition and as an element that provides a realistic effect for fictional narratives), I analyze the ideological and historical context behind the fin-de-siècle fascination for the Gothic cathedral. I examine
Les Trois Villes, the Durtal cycle, and *La Recherche* as "mirrors" that reflect and re-
fract the images of society presented by their authors, thus questioning the ways
in which Zola, Huysmans, and Proust responded to the conflicting political, religious, and aesthetic ideology of their time by reconfiguring it in their novels. By
exploring the ways in which these three authors present the cathedral, I also reveal
the influence they exerted in shaping turn-of-the-century conceptions of Gothic
architecture and the novel. Victor Hugo's *Notre-Dame de Paris* provoked widespread public outcry against the destruction of national monuments in the 1830s.
The fin-de-siècle novels of Zola, Huysmans, and Proust proposed a more intangi-
ble vision of the cathedral: a space of cooperation, a national treasure that, by 1914,
was universally admired as the "synthesis" of the French nation.

ONE

The Synthesis of France

> The cathedral is the synthesis of the country. I repeat: rocks,
> forests, gardens, northern sun [. . .] all of our France is in our
> cathedrals [. . .]
> —Auguste Rodin, *Les Cathédrales de France* (1914)

How, by 1914, had the French come to consider a structure built for worship by
the medieval Church as "the synthesis of the country"? How could a society that
passed laws against monastic orders, Catholic education, and religious services glorify the cathedral as the ultimate symbol of the modern French nation? It is imperative to analyze the connotations the nineteenth century attached to the cathedral before examining fictional representations of cathedrals and reactions to them.
This chapter thus traces the cathedral's status in the nineteenth-century consciousness before focusing on the social turmoil that transformed it into a unifying symbol of the French nation.

The Romantic Cathedral

The French appreciation of the Gothic was a nineteenth-century phenomenon,
begun primarily by romantics Chateaubriand, Nodier, and Hugo, who published
works about the Middle Ages and Gothic architecture in the early years of the century. The French vogue for the Middle Ages developed out of the European attraction to Gothic architecture that accompanied the romantic movement; it was
an inherently international phenomenon, spread by writers, art historians, and
artists—Horace Walpole, William Beckford, Madame de Staël, Chateaubriand,
and the Schlegels, to name a few—who traveled throughout Europe for pleasure
or as émigrés from revolutionary France.[1] The Gothic was prized for its alleged
sensitivity to nature, beauty, spirituality, and asymmetry, in opposition to the regulated structures and rationality of classical art.[2]

Eighteenth-century England experienced the first "Gothic Revival," a period
that produced homes and buildings modeled on those of the Middle Ages.[3] Capitalizing on this vogue, Gothic novelist Horace Walpole built Strawberry Hill,
which he furnished in the medieval style; Walpole's taste for the Gothic probably
began during his travels through France and Italy with the poet, Thomas Gray
(1739–1741).[4] William Beckford, the eclectic writer and art collector, had also

traveled extensively throughout Europe, notably in Holland, Germany, Italy, and France. Impressed by Walpole's construction, the author of the Gothic novel *Vathek* (1782) had his own Gothic abbey designed and built at Fontville, England, from 1796 to 1800.[5] The affinity between tales of horror, picturesque ruins, and buildings based on them spread throughout Europe and led to the construction in France and England of a number of English gardens with Gothic ruins.[6]

In Germany, a parallel movement of appreciation for the Gothic style occurred from a distinctly historical and aesthetic angle. Johann Wolfgang von Goethe was one of the first writers to give serious impetus to the revival of interest in the Gothic by attributing an origin to it. His passionate 1772 essay, "Von Deutscher Baukunst," written on the twenty-one-year-old writer's arrival in Strasbourg, produced what Alain Erlande-Brandenburg has called a "veritable resurrection of the Middle Ages" in Germany.[7] Goethe's awestruck praise of the cathedral's "grandeur" and its effect on his soul, his comparison of its vertical stretch to that of the "tree of God," and his reverence for the "Babel-like vision" of its architect constitute an unequivocal tribute to the Gothic style and its German origins.[8] Goethe's study of the Strasbourg cathedral gave impetus to the notion that Gothic art was German, a nationalistic view that culminated in the century-long project to complete the Cologne cathedral.[9]

Goethe's passion influenced prominent writers and thinkers like August Wilhelm von Schlegel, whose lectures at the University of Berlin considered the origins of the Gothic style. His brother, Friedrich, was also influential, especially in what would become the movement to rebuild Cologne Cathedral. He met Sulpiz Boisserée, a champion of Gothic architecture, in Paris in 1803, and the two authors' enthusiasm for the cathedral led to Boisserée's discovery of the original designs. The rest of his life was consecrated to completing the plans, to publishing them, and to rebuilding the cathedral.[10] Boisserée's *Histoire et description de la cathédrale de Cologne* was published in France and Germany in 1823, and was widely disseminated throughout Europe to great popular acclaim; it gave credence to the conception of the Gothic style as inherently Germanic.[11]

The Schlegels's collaboration with "le groupe de Coppet," centered in Coppet, Switzerland, at the home of Madame de Staël, would further spread ideas about the Middle Ages. Madame de Staël, daughter of Jacques Necker, the French statesmen, welcomed writers and thinkers from all over Europe; she would continue the tradition during her exile from Napoleonic France. Her influential *De l'Allemagne,* begun in 1802 and published in 1810, would revolutionize literary circles in France by introducing the French to the theories of Goethe, Lessing, and Schiller—notably by publicizing their belief in Christianity as the root of modern genius and by describing their admiration of Gothic architecture for the religious sentiments it inspires—and by championing medieval themes as a way to renew modern French literature.[12] One of the leading French authors who influenced and was influenced by Madame de Staël and her friends, was Chateaubriand.

The French Context

In France, commentary about Gothic architecture had never truly vanished; it was simply rare and generally negative.[13] Renewed interest in the Gothic in France developed during the French Revolution, notably through the efforts of Alexandre Lenoir, who as guard of the warehouse established in the former Petits-Augustins convent, salvaged many religious artifacts from the wrath of the Revolutionaries. He later displayed his collected material (1794–1816) and developed it into what would eventually become the Musée des Monuments historiques, an edifice that preserved bits of history—tombs, cathedral statuary, stained glass—for Parisians. Jules Michelet was one of the many writers and artists to credit Lenoir for allowing them to discover the past, notably the Middle Ages.[14]

In France, writers—Nodier, Chateaubriand, and Hugo—created the symbolic registers that would remain attached to the cathedral throughout the century. Charles Nodier, a writer and literary critic, collaborated with Baron Isidore Séverin Justin Taylor and Alphonse de Cailleux to produce the twenty-five volumes of *Les Voyages pittoresques et romantiques dans l'ancienne France* (1820–1878). This work, which was amply illustrated, was one of the first to use extensively new lithographic techniques. It drew the public's attention to the aesthetic value of ruins. Nodier's enthusiasm for French architecture, which he championed in popular periodicals, notably the *Journal des débats* and *La Quotidienne*, led Victor Hugo to consider him the author who had most convinced his contemporaries to appreciate France's heritage.[15] Nodier brought attention to ruined cathedrals; Chateaubriand fueled the French obsession for the cathedral as an aesthetic marvel that inspires spiritual reflection; and Hugo began an opposing myth of the cathedral as a democratic stone book that preserves French history.

In *Le Génie du Christianisme* (1802), Chateaubriand devoted a chapter to "Des églises gothiques," which he glorified for the "vague feeling of divinity," the "shiver" they evoked in the visitor.[16] His haunting lyricism lingers on the cathedral's ability to "transport" us to the "magical" early years of Christianity. For Chateaubriand, whose goal in *Le Génie du Christianisme* was to prove that the fine arts flourished because of Christianity, the cathedral was a symbol of the Middle Ages—"the age of magic and enchantment"—an idyllic time in which life was regulated by a naive yet powerful faith.[17] This piety, he felt, inspired the construction of Gothic cathedrals and monasteries, which were modeled on the forests in which the primitive Christians had worshiped. He thus saw Gothic cathedrals as an attempt to re-create the experience of worshiping in nature: the Gothic vaulting reproduced the natural lines of intertwined branches, while the addition of organ music and ornamentation re-created the murmurs, winds, and thunder of nature. "The centuries recalled by these religious chords project their ancient voices from the heart of the stones, and sigh from corner to corner of the vast basilica."[18]

Chateaubriand's nostalgia for the artistic and spiritual purity of this lost

Golden Age—captured in Gothic cathedrals—spread throughout the century through his writings and numerous illustrated editions of them. His influence can be seen in the works of authors as diverse as Montalembert, Verlaine, and Proust. At the end of the century, art historian André Michel credited Chateaubriand with having created the myth of the Gothic cathedral as a forest, a "sentimental and poetic fantasy" that was taken as "archeological doctrine" by French artists and the general public.[19] Chateaubriand realized the impact his *Le Génie* had exerted over his contemporaries. In 1837 he took credit for having renewed interest in medieval religious architecture. "It is from this work that the present day taste for medieval buildings derives: it was due to my prompting that the people first came to admire these old churches."[20] Chateaubriand's legacy continued to thrive in the writings of Catholics like Charles de Montalembert, whose admiration for the "passion" of Gothic architecture would lead him to embrace the restoration movement wholeheartedly, and in the efforts of Dom Guéranger, who nearly singlehandedly restored the Benedictine order in France and reintroduced plain chant.[21] L'abbé Gaume inspired a new "Querelle des Classiques" that pitted supporters of the Middle Ages against classicists with his 1851 pamphlet, *Le Ver rongeur des sociétés modernes.*[22] For many Catholics, the cathedral, the monarchy, and the Church came to constitute an inseparable block.[23]

Chateaubriand's influence could still be felt by the end of the century in the works of poets like Paul Verlaine, who, in *Sagesse* (1880, dated 1881), wrote poems expressing the desire to return to the purity and stability of the Middle Ages and the cathedral: "It is toward the enormous and delicate Middle Ages/That my wounded heart must navigate/Away from our days of carnal spirit and sorry flesh/[. . .]/High theology and solid morals/Guided by the unique folly of the Cross/On your wings of stone, oh wild Cathedral!"[24] Verlaine's Catholic poems, which praise the cathedral as a space of moral support and Christian folly, exerted great influence over the Catholic artists of the end of the century, many of whom advocated abandoning reason for faith. Charles Morice went so far as to call *Sagesse* "a thirteenth-century Gothic cathedral" because of the depth of its lyricism and the brilliance of its versification.[25] The spiritual honesty of Verlaine's poems would provide a model for Catholic poets Péguy and Claudel.[26]

Chateaubriand began the nineteenth-century vogue for an idyllic Middle Ages by reattaching the cathedral to its medieval Christian roots, yet even more of the nineteenth-century adulation of the Gothic style stemmed from Victor Hugo's extremely secular *Notre-Dame de Paris* (1831). While Chateaubriand used the cathedral as one of many manifestations of "the genius of Christianity," Hugo focused on Notre-Dame de Paris. He represented this church as a symbol of the French nation's democratic and artistic heritage in order to spur his contemporaries to action: he protested against the "vandalism"—both demolition and restoration of old architectural structures—that he felt was destroying France's past. Between 1824 and 1832, Hugo published inflammatory poems and articles entitled "La Bande noire," "De la destruction des monuments en France," and "Guerre aux démolisseurs!" in order to discourage such activities. He specifically mentioned churches Saint-Germain-l'Auxerrois and the Sainte-Chapelle in Paris, which had been damaged in order to accommodate roads and government buildings or to enlarge markets.[27] These articles, however, received paltry attention compared to the effect he achieved by using the novel to focus on the plight of Notre-Dame, the cathedral at the heart of Paris. The 1831 *Notre-Dame de Paris* continues Hugo's vituperation against "vandalism," but inscribes it within a fictional narrative set in 1482. Hugo was able to spread his message about the dangers of destroying historical monuments by using his novel to publicize his beliefs.

Hugo's didactic project to preserve French monuments appears from the beginning of the book with his somber meditation on the word 'ΑΝΑΓΚΗ, an inscription allegedly left by a medieval visitor to the cathedral's tower and erased by the time of publication of *Notre-Dame de Paris*. This example of the ephemerality of creation—the writing, its author, and the cathedral itself—provides a succinct summary of the didactic message of the book: without active attention to documenting and conserving works of the Middle Ages (as Hugo attempts to do in what he calls the "fragile souvenir" of his book), France is in danger of seeing its past crumble away. Hugo dispenses this wisdom throughout the book; however, he does so primarily in small, easily digestible morsels of didacticism tucked into an engaging plot with an abundance of local color.

Hugo introduces the bulk of his message about the importance of the cathedral in the third book of *Notre-Dame de Paris*, a chapter entitled "Notre-Dame," which interrupts the development of plot to describe the modern Notre-Dame de Paris, a "majestic and sublime edifice" that has fallen victim to the ravages of time and vandalism. By breaking away from the medieval story to comment on the nineteenth century, Hugo drew his readers to an edifice they knew well, thus allowing them to see for themselves how much had been lost since the Middle Ages. He reserves his highest praise for the cathedral as a cultural construct, a reflection of the spirit and society of the time in which it was built. Later, in the chapter entitled "Ceci tuera cela," he insists even further on the cathedral as a historical marker, the equivalent of a modern book.

Hugo thus subtly encourages his readers to appreciate the cathedral by linking it to the values they esteem in the nineteenth century. By labeling architecture the precursor to literature, he inextricably links Notre-Dame de Paris to the national patrimony, thereby making it impossible for his contemporaries to condone destruction of the cathedral. Hugo presents the "beautiful architectural pages" of "stone books" as the medieval equivalent of the nineteenth century's printed paper books. Accordingly, throughout the novel he refers to the cathedral as a book written by the architect-poets of the past.

Philippe Hamon has described the relationship of literature and architecture as an "epistemological collaboration" that allows both fields to define themselves.[28]

Hugo took full advantage of such metaphoric symbiosis in evoking cathedral as book and book as cathedral. Both structures—architectural and literary—served the same function for him: they were the media through which humanity attempts to represent its spirit. Dante, he argues in *Notre-Dame de Paris,* built a Romanesque church, Shakespeare a Gothic cathedral, and Byron a mosque. Each stone of a monument tells a story about the history, science, and art of the society that constructed it.[29] The metaphor of the cathedral as a stone book, which stems from Horace's *exegi monumentum,* would lie at the heart of the nationalistic and literary connotations the late nineteenth century attached to medieval religious architecture.[30]

Hugo assigned a parallel function to architecture and literature, yet he favored the printed page because he felt it had triumphed over architecture. In "Ceci tuera cela," the transition from sculpture to writing becomes a survival of the fittest: each generation replaces its ancestors' form of expression by choosing a new medium in which to present its own ideas. Eventually, we forget how to interpret the old forms and abandon them. Hugo's theory is summed up in the words of his character, Claude Frollo: "Ceci tuera cela: la presse tuera l'église." From the vantage point of 1482, Frollo predicted that the printed book would "kill" the stone book and replace it as privileged form of human expression.

Although he began *Notre-Dame de Paris* by proclaiming the superiority of architecture, Hugo ended it by glorifying the written word. Similarly, although he purported to preserve Notre-Dame de Paris from vandals by portraying it in his novel, his book reflects the phrase "ceci tuera cela": *Notre-Dame de Paris* replaces the medieval cathedral in the novel with an imaginary cathedral of paper.[31] While Hugo reanimated the cathedral known to his contemporaries by portraying it in its medieval context, the Notre-Dame he preserves in his work is not the Notre-Dame of his readers. The fictional Notre-Dame resembles Hugo's lugubrious drawings. It is a terrifying edifice haunted by shadows: "fantastic," "supernatural," "horrible," and "monstrous," his description emphasizes the barking of dogs and the disturbing, ever-preying gargoyles.[32] Although Hugo had purported to preserve the cathedral by portraying it in his work, he did not. If the edifice had been destroyed, its literary counterpart would have resembled the original in name alone. Ironically, neither his polemics against vandals nor his decision to preserve Notre-Dame in his novel were what eventually saved the cathedral from the nineteenth-century vandals he wanted to criticize. Hugo's ultimate accomplishment was to use the novel, a popular form of literature, to disseminate a message of social activism to his readers.

Hugo's influence on his contemporaries cannot be underestimated. The scientific and theoretical aspects of *Notre-Dame de Paris* were among those most praised by reviewers of the novel, and exerted such influence that readers wrote to Hugo with questions about conservation of monuments. The book spawned innumerable illustrated editions and sparked huge popular debates about the unscrupulous projects of the "bande noire," a group that bought valuable old properties in order to tear them down and sell the materials for scrap. It also led to one of the most influential public manifestations in support of conservation, Montalembert's March 1, 1833, "Lettre à M. Victor Hugo," in which the young politician castigated such "vandals" at length, while praising Hugo for being "the first to unfurl a flag that could rally all selfish souls to save the monuments of ancient France."[33] Even Balzac joined in the fray, publishing in *La Caricature* a piece entitled "L'Eglise," a meditation on the beauty of Saint-Gatien of Tours and on the purity of the artists who built it. He dated it February 1831, the month that vandals broke into Saint-Germain l'Auxerrois during a funeral service and demolished much of the structure and its art. Such vocal defense of churches gave support to the administrative projects of François Guizot, then Minister of the Interior, and enabled him to win funding for committees and an *Inspecteur général des monuments historiques*. From 1830 to 1837 these new organizations grew to encompass a *Commission des Monuments historiques* (devoted to physical restorations) and a *Comité des arts et monuments,* to which Hugo was named. Hugo served this group— responsible for publicity and ideology regarding the protection of monuments— for thirteen years (1835–1848). Even after he left to pursue a political career, he continued to correspond with architect and conservator friends until his death in 1885. He assisted in the conservation of monuments throughout Europe.[34]

In order to fully understand the extent to which Hugo's enthusiasm for Gothic architecture influenced his contemporaries, it is not enough to discuss the emphasis he placed on conserving monuments; in *Notre-Dame de Paris* Hugo also elaborated architectural theories that had a tremendous impact on nineteenth-century conceptions of the cathedral.[35] Hugo's identification of *Notre-Dame de Paris* as a democratic structure stems from his belief in architecture as the reflection of the culture that erected it. Since each new form expressed a generation's liberation from its ancestors— "this will kill that"—formal innovation was the result of historical movements: "The greatest products of architecture are less individual works than social works; more the offspring of the working people than the effusion of a man of genius; the deposit left by a nation [. . .]"[36] The ogive, or arch, manifest in Gothic architecture, is the formal element that signals this new social order for Hugo. While the "somber style" of Romanesque architecture embodied the tyrannical priesthood that he envisioned as controlling the early Middle Ages, he felt that the Gothic style represented a move toward freedom from this repressive system: "free political symbols, capricious and unleashed." Notre-Dame is especially valuable for Hugo because of its transitional style: "It is no longer a Romanesque church, it is not yet a Gothic church. This edifice does not fit a type." Hugo understands this hybrid nature, in which the cathedral reflects both Romanesque and Gothic forms, as indicative of a shift from one regime (theocracy) to another (democracy). He reads, in each idiosyncrasy of the cathedral, a page of France's changing history.[37]

For Hugo, the Crusades were the historical catalyst that unleashed the new form. He saw this period as a great popular movement in which the medieval nobles asked to share power with the Church and the people asked to share power with the nobles. As a result, the cathedral came under the power of the bourgeoisie:

> The cathedral itself, once such a dogmatic edifice, henceforth invaded by the bourgeoisie, by the commune, by liberty, escapes from the priest and falls under the power of the artist. The artist builds it at his will. Goodbye mystery, myth, law. Here are fancy and capriciousness.[38]

Hugo transforms the cathedral into a secular French monument. Quasimodo, the popular "Pope of Fools," is much more a part of the cathedral than Claude Frollo, the church's clergyman, and religious ceremonies are strikingly absent from the novel. Frollo never performs mass in the cathedral, which he uses to conduct experiments in alchemy. It is Quasimodo who provides the structure's soul; he rings the bells, wanders the cathedral's towers, and defends it against the invading crowds from La Cour des miracles. His animating popular presence replaces the church's spirituality.[39]

Throughout *Notre-Dame de Paris,* the cathedral is, as Hugo says, a skeleton. He describes neither its interior nor the ceremonies celebrated in it.[40] The action of the novel takes place in the cathedral's peripheries: towers, staircases, and bells. In an 1879 article about the novel, Emile Zola—who would compose his own work about a cathedral a few years later—criticized Hugo's lack of interest in the cathedral's interior decoration and religious ceremonies:

> Have you noticed? The novel, which has the pretension of restoring Notre-Dame to the fifteenth century, takes place only among the gargoyles of the church. Not a single interior ceremony, not a scene in the nave, in the chapels, in the sacristy. Everything takes places up there, on the galleries, in the tower stairwells, among the gargoyles [. . .] It is surely for the gargoyles that the book was written, since the soul of the church—the chancel with its votive candles, its canticles, its priests—is absent [. . .][41]

For Zola, Hugo's attempt to resurrect the Notre-Dame of the fifteenth century was a failure: he had simply replaced spirituality with spectacle.

In fact, Notre-Dame does seem to be a giant stage on which the major characters play. Just as the mystery play that opens the novel ends in farce, so religion, in the novel, has been replaced by popular theatricality. Quasimodo's heroic rescue of La Esmeralda becomes a parody of a curtain call, as he holds the gypsy over

(1852–1893), the first cathedral to be commissioned in nearly one hundred years—who advocated the supremacy of neoclassical forms over the Gothic.[49] This eclectic group of writers was composed of those affiliated with liberal neo-Catholics (Didron, Montalembert, Lassus, Pugin), who believed that medieval architecture could only thrive with a return to the Middle Ages and its religious context, and those who saw the restoration of Gothic architecture as a largely national or patriotic venture (Mérimée, Viollet-le-Duc). As a group, they were held together by their belief in the importance of preserving Gothic architecture, an activity Lassus referred to as the sacred duty of Frenchmen. Their attacks on its detractors are represented by a number of writings championing the Gothic style, works that culminated in Viollet-le-Duc's decision to write a *Dictionnaire raisonné de l'architecture* (1854–1868) in which he would respond to criticism of medieval architecture.[50]

Viollet-le-Duc added to Hugo and his colleagues' image of the cathedral as "national architecture" by describing it as a "national monument," "the symbol of French nationality," a structure erected because of cooperation between monarchy and Church. He, too, insisted that Gothic architecture was the result of a bourgeois protest against the feudal order and its representative, the castle. Although he grudgingly admitted that the cathedral was a religious monument, like Hugo, he emptied it as much as possible of theological signification, thus focusing on the economic and political motives behind its construction. "Of course cathedrals are religious monuments," he wrote in *Le Dictionnaire raisonné de l'architecture française,* "but they are above all national edifices."[51] For Viollet-le-Duc, the Gothic cathedral was "the Parthenon of French architecture," a national ruin that had been nearly emptied of the religion that originally inspired it.

Viollet-le-Duc exerted an enormous influence on subsequent conceptions of Gothic architecture, largely because of his important position in French society; he was a personal friend of the imperial family and the architect in charge of important nineteenth-century cathedral restorations (Vézélay in 1844, Notre-Dame de Paris in 1845). His prolific writings, especially *Le Dictionnaire raisonné de l'architecture française* (begun in 1854) and *Le Dictionnaire du mobilier* (1858) were published and debated throughout the century. The theories of Hugo and Viollet-le-Duc succeeded in rescuing the cathedral from post-Revolutionary vandalism, while forming the backbone of the Republicans' misinformed adulation of a secular cathedral, a product of France's first democratic movement.

Viollet-le-Duc's advocacy of Gothic architecture as a national style stemmed primarily from the fact that its value was not yet universally recognized. In fact, as Barry Bergdoll has remarked, the importance of Gothic style caused a rift in the *Commission des Monuments historiques;* neoclassicists and "Gothicists" argued over its importance for modern architecture. Neoclassicists Albert Lenoir and Léon Vaudoyer disputed the preeminence Viollet-le-Duc and his friends, Didron and Jean-Baptiste Lassus, had attributed to the Gothic style. In their history of French architecture, published from 1839 to 1852 in the journal *Le Magasin Pittoresque*, they clearly took aim at the "Gothicists" and their idolization of medieval architecture: "What? Gothic is our national art! And we should thus renounce all of the progress that has been made since! What? these are the limits imposed on French genius, and since the fifteenth century our art has lost all originality, all character!" Beulé, a professor at the Académie des Beaux-Arts devoted an entire lecture (6 January 1857) to proving that Gothic architecture was neither "national" nor "religious." "I ask Gothic cathedrals what thought inspired them and I see nothing that belongs to French genius!"[52] For this group, French architecture had evolved constantly over time; they did not dispute the importance of the Gothic style, but felt the neoclassical developments that followed the Renaissance showed an evolution in architectural styles, and should thus serve as the most important model for modern architecture.[53] These two groups battled each other over every major restoration project and every new construction project of the century, in France and abroad. The ferocity of the argument can be gauged by an 1851 article published in *Les Annales archéologiques* by Carl Schnaase, a German correspondent, who attempted to distinguish between German and French reactions to the architecture of the Middle Ages: "We do not have this conflict between the academic school and the Christian and French school that occurs on French soil [. . .] no school here attempts to expunge the memory of one or the other from today's art."[54] Administration, Church, and nationalists all conspired to further their own beliefs about the Gothic style and its importance, while categorically denying opposing claims. The cathedral had not yet become a figure of compromise.

The Cathedral in the Literature of the Second Empire

The cathedral occupied an ambiguous position in the national consciousness during the Second Empire: like the Middle Ages, it was alternatively praised or condemned in accordance with political or religious belief. While Catholics claimed the cathedral as a representative of Chateaubriand's myth of medieval religion, secular members of society either criticized this vision as "feudal," or, in the tradition of Hugo and Viollet-le-Duc, praised it as an example of an early democratic movement. Janine Dakyns traces much of the anti–Middle Ages rhetoric of this time to the Catholic revival of the 1840s. Because both the growing religious right and Louis-Napoléon began to champion the cathedral as a symbol of the Church and Christian genius in art, and because the emperor decided to reward the Church for its political collaboration by financing church restorations, religious architecture became—for many Republicans—the ultimate symbol of the oppression and decadence of the Middle Ages, the values they saw reflected in Louis-Napoléon's Second Empire. When the new emperor claimed the Middle Ages and chivalry as symbols for his reign, he further alienated Republicans.[55] Literary representations of the cathedral at this time paralleled the architectural battles about Gothic and neo-classical styles.

Jules Michelet's writings embody the nineteenth-century tendency to link the cathedral to shifting conceptions of the Middle Ages. In the 1835 edition to his *Histoire de France,* he praised the Middle Ages as "this long miracle," "this marvelous legend whose traces fade each day." Early in his career he considered the Middle Ages a wonderful and magical time whose legacy was vanishing, and whose representative was the cathedral: "this purity, this sweetness of soul, this marvelous elevation to which Christianity bore its heroes."[56] He praised Gothic architecture as the culmination of medieval faith, as the physical incarnation of medieval piety—its prayers and tears—and as a human attempt to embrace a higher power: "Precious tears, they ran in limpid legends, in marvelous poems, and drifting up to the sky, they crystallized in gigantic cathedrals that wanted to reach the Lord!"[57] Caught up in the Gothic fervor of the 1830s, Michelet visited churches all over France and Germany and discussed religious architecture with his friends, many of whom were archeologists and art historians.[58] Michelet emulated Hugo in his praise of the cathedral, which he presented as the place of the people—"The Church is, itself, the people"—and a construct of their faith. Michelet's early glorification of the eleventh and twelfth centuries caused a generation of readers to believe in a golden age of religious democracy, the beginning of French national identity.[59]

By 1861, however, Michelet had expunged most positive comments about the cathedral from his new edition of *Histoire de France.*[60] In *La Sorcière* (1862) and *La Bible de l'humanité* (1864), he transformed the poignant tears of the Middle Ages into the sobbing of a martyred people, oppressed by the Church. After praising this time for its piety, he criticized it for its suffering. The representation of medieval religious architecture parallels his shifting conception of the Middle Ages.[61] In *La Renaissance* (1857), one of the works that most harshly attacks Gothic architecture, he depicts the cathedral as a symbol of the oppressive time period that erected it: the title of this section is "L'Agonie du moyen âge." In another section, "L'architecture rationnelle et mathématique—La déroute du gothique," he presents the Gothic cathedral as Romanesque architecture's "fragile neighbor": it is poorly constructed—"sickly" and "spindly"—a kind of "lame art" eternally surrounded by a host of doctors (masons).

Michelet's condemnation of Gothic architecture was largely, as Jean Pommier and Laurence Richer have suggested, a result of the severe ideological stance he took against Catholicism in 1843, when he published *Les Jésuites* and became an anti-Catholic, antimedieval crusader. Where Michelet had originally enjoyed the Middle Ages as a nostalgic period from the past, his contemporaries' focus on reinstating medieval Catholicism in the nineteenth century infuriated him. As Richer suggests, he felt violated by the fact that priests were stealing "his" cathedrals.[62] Her detailed studies of Michelet's journals reveal his conflicting feelings toward cathedrals. Despite his criticism of the way they were being used, he remained attracted to them. "I love them all," one journal entry notes. During this time, Michelet began arguing against the restoration of cathedrals, which would contribute to the Catholic Church, arguing that it was more important to achieve secular goals: "With the cost of two restorations of Notre-Dame one could have founded a church more vibrant and more in accordance with God: primary schools, the universal education of the poor."[63] By the end of his life, in *La Bible de l'humanité* (1864), Michelet encouraged readers to embrace progress by turning their backs on both the cathedral and the period it symbolized: "We must make an about face [. . .] turn our backs on the Middle Ages, on this morbid past [. . .] Let us forget and walk on! Let us walk toward the life sciences, to museums, to schools."[64] Yet even as he advised his readers to forget the Middle Ages, Michelet continued to dream of building his own kind of cathedral: "Let us, too, build, not the cathedral of stone, but the cathedral of science, build all night long; we will rest during the day!"[65]

Like Michelet, Ernest Renan had a shifting conception of the cathedral and the Middle Ages. In his youth, he dreamed nostalgically of the Middle Ages as a time of heroism, monasteries, and faith, the antithesis of the vulgar modern world. For him, cathedrals were "gigantic monuments of ancient faith," the only form of art that attracted one's eye.[66] In 1862, however, he published "L'Art du moyen âge et les causes de sa décadence" in *La Revue des Deux Mondes,* an article that attacked the late Middle Ages and their crumbling symbol, the cathedral: "an embroidery of stone, which, as Vasari says, seems to be made of cardboard."[67] Dakyns suggests that this attack on Gothic architecture is, like Michelet's, an "oblique censure of the Empire" and its oppression of the media.[68] Although Renan had always loved Greek monuments, after an 1865 trip to Athens he began using them to prove the immeasurable superiority of Greek architecture to the fragility of the Gothic style: "The Parthenon surpasses in grandeur our most gigantic Gothic churches."[69] All of his subsequent writings, including the 1876 *Prière sur l'Acropole,* continued in this vein, which pitted the dark ages of the cathedral against the age of reason represented by the Parthenon.

Michelet's lugubrious vision of the cathedral and its corruption and disintegration under Second Empire rule and Renan's advocacy of classical architecture were shared by a number of their contemporaries, who also criticized Gothic architecture. Edgar Quinet, Michelet's friend, proposes a tragic view of the cathedral in *Ahasvérus,* in which the cathedral of Strasbourg speaks—evoking its misery through a lengthy, but imaged monologue—only to introduce and comment on a dance of death taking place inside it. This haunting passage is composed of questions and interjections that build an image of a troubled cathedral seeking its Master. Quinet lavishes detail on the cathedral and its component arts and gives it a sympathetic voice, but also paints its fatigue and bewilderment in the modern world. Other writers, like Louis–Xavier Ricard, Hippolyte Taine, and Louis Ménard, inspired by Michelet and Renan, present the cathedral as spindly and degenerate, ready to crumble with the first sign of change; in fact, these cathedrals do vanish, replaced by reason and classical architecture. Janine Dakyns calls such representations "versified Michelet"; the cathedrals are dead or dying, killed by a Catholicism that sucks the life from them.[70]

Michelet and Renan incarnate the shifting intellectual reaction to the cathedral in the middle of the century: it was inseparable from the Middle Ages and the Catholic Church. Depending on the political affiliation of the person describing it, the cathedral was alternatively represented as an idealized utopian space of faith, a product of French nationalism, or a decadent feudal structure. While Catholics Montalembert, Gaume, and Veuillot carried on Chateaubriand's tradition of representing the cathedral as a product of Catholic faith, those, like Viollet–le–Duc, who were associated with the Emperor, used it as a symbol of the French past. Others, such as Michelet and Renan, rejected the cathedral as a menacing symbol of an oppressive time, a structure built to frighten the medieval populace and doomed to collapse. By the end of the Second Empire the cathedral had become an embattled figure used to illustrate the ideas of either the Catholic-supported Empire or the minority Republicans.

The Franco-Prussian War and the Commune

The debate between the spiritual legacy of Catholicism and the rational beliefs of Republicanism spans the nineteenth century only to explode in the Third Republic after the Franco-Prussian War and the bloody civil revolt of the Commune.[71] The war, France's first military loss since Napoléon, delivered a crushing blow to national pride and resulted in a weighty reconsideration of the country's stability. The four-month occupation of Paris by Germans, the loss of the provinces of Alsace and Lorraine to the German Empire, and the five billion gold franc ($1 billion) reparation were perceived as the ultimate degradation, so much so that Ludovic (Louis) Vitet, former Inspector of Historical Monuments and member of the Académie Française, evoked the defeat as "an abyss of agony and shame."[72]

Much of the immediate debate about the defeat made use of biological rhetoric to present the loss as an illness from which France could recover. Such arguments reopened discussion of French origin and the country's debt to the Germanic invasions of the fifth century. From the sixteenth century, one of the most popular theories about French origin had held that the aristocracy descended from energetic, pure-blooded Germanic invaders, while the common people were products of the weak, mixed-race Gallo-Romans.[73] Despite widespread disagreement about such theories, the Germanic invasions were seen as a primarily positive aspect of French culture; they had allegedly infused the Gallo-Romans or Celts with the strength and courage of German blood. After the Franco-Prussian war, blame for the loss corresponded, once again, to this binary system. Catholics and Royalists blamed the degenerate and mixed-race nonnoble rulers of France for defeat, while Republicans interpreted France's weakness as a result of interference with the Revolutionary project.

Soon after the war, historian Fustel de Coulanges, who had lost his professorship in ancient history when Strasbourg was conceded to the Germans, began to realize that such incorrect attitudes about the past were a major point of contention for contemporaries. In an 1871 article for *La Revue des Deux Mondes,* he insisted that understanding the Middle Ages, a stable time of "simple and just ideas," would help the country rebound from the war:

> Understanding the Middle Ages—the exact, scientific, and sincere understanding of them without bias—is, for our society, a concern of the highest order. It is the best way to put an end to the insane regrets of some, to the empty utopias of others, to the hatred of all. To reestablish calm in the present it is not un-useful to begin by destroying prejudices and errors about the past. History imperfectly observed divides us; it is by better understanding history that the work of reconciliation must begin.[74]

Fustel's concern for the correct interpretation of history was shared by Ludovic (Louis) Vitet, who, in a book review that appeared in the periodical a few months later (May 15, 1872), argued that "At this time the false interpretation of the past is the most dangerous of poisons."[75] Both scholars worried about the warring factions in French society and attempted to propose theories that would reconcile them.

Fustel went on to publish major multi-installment articles for *La Revue des Deux Mondes,* the most widely read periodical of his time, in which he argued that one of the most glaring falsehoods about the Middle Ages was the myth of the Germanic invasions of the fifth century; it was an erroneous yet foundational element in the story of French identity. He showed, using sources from the Middle Ages, that Germany never subjugated France. In his essays, Fustel categorically undermines the theory of French reliance on German blood, while creating a new, powerful history of stability for the French nation.

Fustel's new interpretation of medieval French history became a rallying point for French patriots: writers, historians, teachers, and government officials expunged German influence from French literature and history, and argued for the inherent "Frenchness" of ambivalent medieval figures like Joan of Arc and the Frankish Roland.[76] The Gothic cathedral was swept up in this postwar surge of French nationalism. Cologne Cathedral, which early nineteenth-century Germans had vociferously claimed as "German to the core [. . .] a national monument in the fullest sense of the word" and whose reconstruction writer Josef Görres had billed as "the symbol of the new empire that we are trying to build," had led to

dominates Paris by casting his web over it, then drawing it into his bloody clutches (Figure 1.1). A similar image was displayed on the cover of the anticlerical bulletin, *La Lanterne,* which portrayed the Sacré-Coeur with a demonic priest perched above it and the words "Voilà l'Ennemi!" at its base (Figure 1.2). Instead of accepting the basilica as a necessary step to recovering from the Franco-Prussian War, the Republic interpreted its construction as an act of war. In a series of counterstrikes, it passed anticlerical measures, including the 1882 laws forbidding teaching by members of the clergy, the 1902 dissolution of monastic orders, and the 1905 Separation of Church and State.

Republicans were not alone in interpreting the Sacré-Coeur as the symbol of the corrupt modern Catholic Church. Paray-le-Monial, the site of Marie Alacoque's visions of the sacred heart, was one of the most popular pilgrimage sites in France after the Franco-Prussian War, yet the sentimentality and garish materiality of the Cult of the Sacred Heart disgusted conservative Catholics and clergy for whom the true Church was that of the Middle Ages. *Le Ralliement,* Pope Leo XIII's attempt to reconcile the Catholic Church with the Third Republic in the hopes of calming France's rampant anticlericalism, only exacerbated conservatives. His project backfired as Republicans mistrusted the Vatican's intent, and conservatives accused liberal Catholics of betraying faith for political conquest. Such conflicts extended to the planning of the Sacré-Coeur basilica. Many Catholics wanted a Gothic design and thus rejected architect Abadie's proposal for a domed structure. To them it seemed too "foreign" (Roman) and "pagan."[86] The Sacré-Coeur provided these believers with a tangible image of the modern Church, whose interests lay in foreign politics and economics. Conservative Catholic Léon Bloy propagated such associations by accusing clergy of using the Sacré-Coeur to sell the Catholic faith for political and financial gain: "The Sacré-Coeur basilica is more a work of vanity than a work of faith [. . .] everything must be paid for there [. . .] it is the heart of Jesus transformed into a boutique."[87] For both Republicans and conservative Catholics, the Sacré-Coeur had become an emblem of the modern Catholic Church of *Le Ralliement,* an organization in which religion was tainted by foreign politics and money.

The Gothic Cathedral: "The Synthesis of France"

In reaction to the Sacré-Coeur and the unstable and contaminated modern values it represented, conservative Catholics and Republicans alike began to promote the Gothic cathedral as the true image of the French nation and its faith. The Catholics embraced the cathedral idealized by Chateaubriand: for them it represented the purity of medieval belief, the social harmony of French worshipers, and beauty of art dedicated to God. Republicans, too, claimed the cathedral; they adopted

Figure 1.1. *La Vision de Victor Hugo,* 1802–1902. *L'Assiette au Beurre,* no. 47, February 26, 1902. Photomechanical. Jane Voorhees Zimmerli Art Museum. Rutgers, The State University of New Jersey. Norma B. Bartman Purchase Fund. Photo by Jack Abraham. 1987.0458.

Figure 1.2. *Voilà l'Ennemi! La Lanterne,* 1902. Eugène Ogé. Color lithograph. Musée de la publicité, Paris.

Hugo's vision of a democratic Middle Ages in which a primitive Republic inspired religious belief. Once again, each faction claimed the cathedral for its own purposes.

At the end of the century, novelists Emile Zola and J.-K. Huysmans, a Republican and a Catholic, respectively, presented the cathedral as a symbolic compromise between the religious myths begun by Chateaubriand and the democratic myths disseminated by Hugo. Describing real architectural structures in their novels allowed them to play on the symbolic attributes their contemporaries had attached to churches in Chartres, Lourdes, Paris, or Rome. Their descriptions of the Sacré-Coeur and the religious architecture at Lourdes refer to and rewrite contemporary discourse about these structures.

In *Les Trois Villes* and the Durtal cycle, which are set in the 1890s, Zola and Huysmans reconstructed the public image of the Gothic cathedral by emphasizing its artistic superiority and its inherently communal nature, aspects they saw as overshadowing petty conflicts about its history. Instinctively, they responded to Fustel de Coulanges's call for a compromise in the understanding and representation of French history. Though both authors use the image of the cathedral for their own purposes, they also evoke it as a space of pure faith in which the social and political differences of the Middle Ages were reconciled as members of society came together to build it. Such praise creates a unified myth of the cathedral, a positive alternative to the Sacré-Coeur, which represents politics, civil war, and commercialized art.

These authors return to the Middle Ages to understand the motivations that prompted the building of Gothic structures. This is certainly the case for Huysmans, who provides one of the most striking examples of his contemporaries' tendency to contrast the "good" Gothic cathedral with the "bad" Sacré-Coeur. As Huysmans's protagonist, Durtal, studies the symbolism of Notre-Dame de Chartres in *La Cathédrale,* he remembers a thirteenth-century manuscript that described the spiritual and democratic mobilization responsible for constructing the cathedral:

> What remains incredible and is nevertheless certified by all of the documents of the time, is that these hordes of elderly and children, of women and men, disciplined themselves in a flash; and yet they belonged to every class of society [. . .] divine love was so strong that it obliterated distinctions and abolished castes [. . .] the spirit of the multitude must truly have been admirable [. . .].

Huysmans's description focuses on unity in diversity. Despite the disorder caused by the reunion of thousands of people of varying classes, harmony reigns supreme. One of the most unusual elements of this passage is Durtal's willingness to accept at face value this story recounted by a Latin manuscript from the Vatican. He wants to believe in a better France, a nation in which faith brought together all members of society and made them forget their prejudices. The Frenchmen of his imagination worked for a higher cause: the artistic construction of the cathedral of Chartres. He goes on—in the same passage of the novel—to contrast the good faith of this process, marked by the "divine love," "piety," and "miracles" to the corruption inherent in the building of the Sacré-Coeur:

> We build temples much differently today. When I think of the Sacré-Coeur of Paris, that gloomy, ponderous construction built by men who have inscribed their names in red on every stone! [. . .] Oh! the good crowds of the past [. . .] they would never have considered exploiting their love, linking it to their need for ostentation, to their hunger for lucre![88]

Durtal loathes the Sacré-Coeur and its commercial bourgeois foundation. He longs for the days in which people volunteered their time and energy to erecting a monument that served as a testimony to their belief. This nostalgia for the purity of the past is a direct response to the disparate and self-serving goals of nineteenth-century engineers and architects, whom Durtal accuses of prostituting the Church by buying redemption. And although Durtal mentions the stained-glass windows of Chartres that record the trades of bourgeois donors, he never equates this medieval portrayal of benefactors to that of his contemporaries' acknowledgment of donations (inscribing names on bricks); he wants to believe in the purity of his dream. The tensions between faith and greed, democracy and commerce, observed by Durtal in the construction of the Sacré-Coeur, echo his contemporaries' criticism of the modern French nation and the industrial art it sponsored.

France was reeling from its defeat at the hands of the Prussians when a series of Republican scandals spun the country further out of control. In 1887, the public discovered that generals and senators had been peddling influence and selling government awards. Soon after, General Boulanger, a war hero, won the popular elections, only to abandon his responsibilities by fleeing France with his mistress. In 1891–1892 the Panama Canal Company collapse crushed many small investors and revealed the illegal activities of hundreds of Republican politicians. At the same time (1892–1894), bombs began to explode in Paris as anarchist workers demanded to be freed from oppression by their wealthy employers, and as the general population worried about the effects of industrialization. President Carnot was assassinated in June 1894. All of these events pitted Catholics against Republicans, while undermining public confidence in the government's ability to stabilize the country. When Max Nordau published *Dégénération* (*Entartung*) in French (1893), his condemnation of modern French society only exacerbated the finger-pointing. France persuaded itself that it was characterized by social, moral, and artistic degeneration.[89] The Dreyfus Affair, which had begun in 1894, exploded in 1898, and literally tore France in two.[90]

Huysmans's characters, in *La Cathédrale,* depict a harmonious and simplified medieval France. Durtal feels that in the Middle Ages, France reigned over other countries because of the "supremacy" of its medieval architecture and faith, but that this architectural and political predominance has long vanished.[91] The Middle Ages and medieval faith, the historical root of the powerful French nation, remain, however, in the image of the cathedral, a structure in which science, religion, and art exist in harmony. In contrast to the politics and propaganda that surrounded the religion and art of the Sacré-Coeur, the Gothic cathedral provided a myth about an art created on a pure spiritual base. In *La Cathédrale,* Huysmans reminds his contemporaries of the artistic feats of which the French nation is capable when its people work toward a unifying goal.

Emile Mâle shared this vision of the cathedral as a place of harmonious diversity. The great twentieth-century art historian's doctoral thesis, the 1898 *L'Art religieux du XIIIe siècle en France,* published four months after Huysmans's *La Cathédrale,* also portrays the cathedral as a synthesis of conflicting nineteenth-century images of the cathedral. He painstakingly traces the medieval theological science of symbolism, yet includes what he calls Hugo's theory of "genius," the concept of the cathedral as a stone book. Mâle's work also demonstrates the extent to which fin-de-siècle scholars had tempered romantic views with a more systematic approach to the Middle Ages. At the end of his thesis, he criticizes Hugo and Viollet-le-Duc for creating a myth of the Gothic cathedral as a democratic structure and as an early example of "freedom of the press." The Middle Ages, he argues, did not revolt against feudal rule in building cathedrals, nor did they prefigure the French Revolution. He represents Gothic sculpture as inherently religious. Although the cathedral is clearly a national monument, he writes, it is, above all, a didactic work of art that teaches theological conceptions to the masses through its symbolism: "To the Middle Ages art was didactic. All that it was necessary that men should know [. . .was] taught to them by the windows of the church or by the statues in the porch."[92]

Both Huysmans and Mâle's works, published in the middle of the Dreyfus Affair, illustrate the extent to which the turn of the century's "Gothic furor" differed from that of the 1830s. The romantics promoted the myth of an idealized spiritual or democratic secular cathedral, according to political or religious belief, while their children—Catholic and Republican—admired Gothic architecture for the ways in which its art combined both spirituality and erudition. Huysmans, for example, praised the romantics for having brought Gothic architecture to the public's attention by calling it an "encyclopedia of stone," yet he blames them for having begun "monumental materialism" and "architectural positivism." He accuses them of having ignored the cathedral's soul: "They saw only shell and skin; they became obsessed with the body and they forgot the soul."[93] He similarly criticizes Chateaubriand for attaching too much importance to nature instead of focusing on the Christian inspiration evident in the cathedral itself.[94] Both romantic and fin-de-siècle myths about the cathedral developed from the French nation's social troubles, but while the 1830s admired it for either body or soul, the 1890s were fascinated by the combination of the two. They were attracted to what Hegel had called the "reconciliation of differences into a single unity."[95]

Such views regarding the the cathedral's artistic superiority gained currency in the years leading up to the 1905 decision to separate Catholic Church and French State. The ideas of Huysmans and Mâle were adopted by others, notably Marcel Proust, whose 1898–1906 series of articles about John Ruskin and Gothic architecture were published in *Le Figaro* and *Le Mercure de France,* leading periodicals of the time. As the government proposed a law to end the state subsidy of church services, Proust wrote an article entitled "La Mort des cathédrales," in which he defended religious ceremonies as the soul of French churches and of the French tradition. He described the cathedral as "the highest and most original expression of French genius." Like Huysmans, he praised the cathedral as humanity's ultimate accomplishment: "This artistic achievement was the most complete because all of the arts collaborated in it; it derived from the greatest dream to which humanity ever aspired."[96] Proust championed the cathedral for its art, which superceded conflicts of religion or politics. By 1909, when he began to write *A la recherche du temps perdu,* there was no longer any question that the cathedral had become the ultimate symbol of France's artistic tradition. It had grown into a figure of compromise and unity in diversity: it had become "the synthesis of the country."

"Crise de vers"/ "Crise du roman"

But why would Zola and Huysmans, prominent naturalists of the 1870s, whose literary ideology was based on using historical or scientific data to present general laws about human behavior, have chosen to describe religious architecture and its spirituality at great length in their novels of the 1890s? Isn't faith—an invisible, irrational phenomenon—the antithesis of scientific belief, which is dedicated to the observable and explainable? Although many nineteenth-century realists had described fictional churches in their novels, very few had devoted more than cursory space to describing real French cathedrals, and even then such passages served primarily to provide local color.[97] Balzac's *Le Curé de Tours,* for example, is set in and around the cathedral of Tours, yet the reader learns nothing about its interior, nor do we ever see its facade. In *Maître Cornélius* and *L'Elixir de longue vie,* he provides brief impressions of the cathedral of Saint-Gatien in Tours. These passages, in which the narrator witnesses a mystical "dance of stones," are mere echoes of an earlier sketch, "La Danse des pierres," originally "L'Eglise" and later fictionalized as the Couvent de la Merci in "Jésus-Christ en Flandres."[98] Flaubert also devotes a passage of *Madame Bovary* to Emma and Léon's encounter in Notre-Dame de Rouen, yet he too uses the cathedral as a backdrop.[99] Even Zola had only described one nonfictional French church at length in his Rougon-Macquart series: l'église Saint-Eustache in *Le Ventre de Paris*.[100] In 1891, why did both Zola and Huysmans suddenly decide to begin writing works that served as mirrors of fin-de-siècle France and its spiritual concerns while devoting extensive descriptive passages to real houses of worship?

First of all, literature, and especially the naturalist novel, was implicated in the turn of the century's sense of political and social crisis.[101] France was seen as insecure and sick, nauseous from the abundance of conflicting political, philosophical, and artistic theories circulating throughout society.[102] Naturalism, as the leading literary "school," came under attack for its seemingly pessimistic analysis of the sordid details of modern life; it was considered an extension of the Republican dedication to science and pragmatism.[103] Catholic and nonnaturalist authors, led by Paul Bourget and Ferdinand de Brunetière, pronounced naturalism "bankrupt," incapable of giving society an ideal that would help it reform.[104] These writers felt that the novel should serve as an escape from daily life, not as an affirmation of the sad facts of reality. They craved the stability of a great, synthetic vision that could consolidate and control the proliferation of contradictory messages: "The day when an artist with a profound understanding of spiritual things appears, much darkness will dissipate, and pessimism will be followed by a period, not of happiness—this fin de siècle is too tragic for that—but of moral bravery."[105] The death of Victor Hugo, in 1885, was yet another setback; he was just such a leader.

In this period of pessimism, naturalism became the scapegoat for everything wrong with literature: depressing subject matter; no attempt to please the audience; lack of happy endings. In 1887, Zola's former disciples publicly renounced his methods as superficial and scientifically unsound in "Le Manifeste des Cinq," an open letter to *Le Figaro*. They accused him of falsifying his research, of trying to become the new Hugo, and of actively seeking pornographic subjects; attacks against naturalism continued to multiply in the next few years.[106] Tensions came to a head in 1891, when most of the literary establishment, including Huysmans, rejected Zola's theories. The year began with the serialization of *Là-Bas* on February 16; the first installment included a two-page invective rejecting naturalism's materialism, its commercialism, and its lack of interest in the ideal. *Là-Bas* gained even more publicity because it was published in the same review—*l'Echo de Paris*— and at the same time as a provocative series of interviews conducted with leading French authors.[107] Journalist Jules Huret purposefully created a sensationalist atmosphere; his questions pit writers against one another. He asked each interviewee what he thought about the death of naturalism and about the literature of the future. His leading questions produced the results he wanted: nearly everyone criticized naturalism, and Zola is the person most often mentioned in the collection. The survey was a phenomenal success, read by all of Paris, and Huret published the interviews in August as *L'Enquête sur l'évolution littéraire*.[108] It is a book that provides invaluable testimony to these authors' belief that they are experiencing a social and literary crisis.

The interviews reveal the prevailing notion of literature—and particularly the novel—as an instrument of social change; according to these authors, the novelist has a responsibility to react to his readers and their tastes. Indeed, all of the nonnaturalist writers agree that Zola's form of naturalism is dying because it does not take into account the contemporary hunger for optimism and idealism. Edouard Rod states the case clearly: "I believe that naturalist literature, without having come to term, is past its prime [. . .] it was the literary expression of a particular positivist and materialist movement that no longer responds to contemporary needs."[109]

L'Enquête sur l'évolution littéraire parallels the polemic battles that divided contemporary France and that would culminate in the virulence of the Dreyfus Affair. Huret presents his book—with literary evolution in its title—as a kind of survival of the fittest, "the battle of Psychologists against naturalists, of symbolists against Parnassians." The other interviewees, he felt, served only to illustrate the wealth of contemporary literature.[110] Although he interviewed each writer individually and almost everyone rejected association with a school, when Huret published his interviews, he classified writers by the labels they had refused: "Les Psychologues," "Les Mages," "Les symbolistes et Décadents," "Les naturalistes," "Les Neo-Réalistes," "Les Parnassiens," "Les Indépendants," and "Les Théoriciens et Philosophes."[111] He thus gave the impression of organized theoretical battles among groups. The wording of his preface, with its insistence on "combat," "battle," "combative morals," as well as his decision to include appendices in which authors insult each other, furthered the illusion of all-out war, in which compromise was elusive. Huret borrowed Hugo's conception of literary evolution as "ceci tuera cela": he shows that the psychologists and symbolists were killing naturalism.

Huret's tidy classification of writers simplifies the elements at work in the literary battles. Even though the naturalists claimed that the symbolists were poetic dreamers, disconnected from the real world (Zola insulted the work of Moréas and Morice as "poetry from a jar"), and although the symbolists accused the naturalists of excessive materialism in their long works (Morice called the naturalist dedication to representing reality the work of "a mercenary who picks up a stone on one side of the road to deposit it on the other side"), neither group was as Manichean as the other made it out to be. Each "group" distanced itself from the others largely by refusing to acknowledge the core similarities—finding general laws about human behavior, exploring the working of the human mind, or evoking emotional states—of their literary projects. Such divisive polemics produced what was perceived as a crisis in the novel. As Michel Raimond's *La Crise du roman* argues, symbolist poets and playwrights implicated the novel as they criticized positivist techniques. These literary feuds began a devaluation of the novel that profoundly disturbed established novelists like Zola and Huysmans, while prompting Proust to hesitate before deciding to become a novelist. Writing should have been a unifying force, yet Huret's interviews perpetuated the public conception that irreconcilable differences separated writers and genres.

All of these authors returned over and over again to the need for unity, for a single aesthetic that would bring harmony to their discussions. Among the interviewees, Stéphane Mallarmé rises above the fray. In the 1886 "Crise de vers," published the year after Hugo's death, Mallarmé had already shown that he understood his contemporaries' craving for stability, for a single voice to organize all the dissenting ones. Although he recognized this impulse, he argued that an imposing artistic vision such as that of Hugo—"he was, personally, verse"—crushed new developments. Hugo's death thus liberated hundreds of individual artists. With "Crise de vers," Mallarmé showed the positive aspects of the literary crisis: "Literature here suffers an exquisite crisis, fundamental."[112] In his interview with Huret, Mallarmé would return to this concept. Despite the fear instability produced in his contemporaries, he saw it as good for literature in a way that the early nineteenth century had not been: artists became more individualistic; they breached the formal and generic rules imposed by tradition. Although his peers craved a single and powerful voice, Mallarmé accepted that the crisis was "exquisite": it was an absolutely necessary step toward literary innovation. Mallarmé's nuanced view demonstrated that reassurance could be found by optimistically embracing disparity. Unlike his contemporaries, he did not separate literature into genres and schools, nor did he see naturalism as dead. Mallarmé reconciled conflicting visions of literature by returning to the concept of versification, which he presented as the foundation of all attempts at style, in both verse and prose.

Spiritual Naturalism: A Compromise

Why then did Zola and Huysmans become attracted to the cathedral and begin to represent it in their works? Given the public outcry against naturalism and the novel in general, after 1891 they increasingly sought ways of addressing spiritual or supernatural phenomena. The topics they chose for their next novels—satanism, pilgrimage, and religious conversion—reform naturalism according to their contemporaries' demands, while plunging their characters into religious worlds where cathedrals are familiar figures.

In their interviews with Jules Huret, both Zola and Huysmans acknowledged that, in order to survive, naturalism would have to cater to its readers by referring to spirituality. They both defined naturalism as a research-based study of

characters and their interaction with a milieu. For them, naturalism did not pre-
clude analysis of the psyche. Both writers were open to modifying the naturalist
novel. Huysmans proposed a "spiritualistic naturalism" that would "blend" body
and soul, while Zola mentioned a "classicism of naturalism" that would "capture
the soul of modern society." Unlike many of their detractors, they were willing to
embrace diversity by including different kinds of subject matter in their novels.

The similarities in the two responses reveal Zola's admiration for the
younger writer,[113] but also provide an explanation for what scholars have often
considered the sudden and disturbing shift to idealism that occurs in Zola's *Les
Trois Villes*. Almost as an aside to his discussion of literature's future, Zola quietly
told Huret that he would do what "they" [his readers] wanted, given the time.[114]
This admission is particularly striking given his repeated claims, only a few months
earlier, that he would retire after finishing the Rougon-Macquart series in order to
profit from the rest he felt he had earned.[115] Although he had been under attack
for twenty years by authors like Brunetière, the events of the first months of
1891—Huysmans's defection from naturalism and the Huret interview—gave
Zola the impetus to change the focus of his work and to continue writing. He
promised to give his contemporaries the idealism they requested and he found his
topic—the Lourdes pilgrimage—only four months later.

Although Zola and Huysmans effectively stopped corresponding with each
other after the publication of *Là-Bas*, in this three-month period they both came
to the decision to open naturalism to a scientific examination of body *and* soul in
order to respond to criticism about its materialism and pessimism.[116] *Les Trois
Villes* and the Durtal cycle, with their increased emphasis on depicting the contemporary world and incorporating religious themes into their novels, thus
emerged from a double reaction to literary arguments about spirituality and science. Not only did they want naturalism to satisfy their contemporaries' desire for
idealism—for a positive representation of the modern world—but they also
wanted to valorize their own form of literature in the eyes of the critics that declared it obsolete.

The Cathedral-Novel

Bourget had called for someone whose idealism could stabilize the conflicting ideology of the fin de siècle and Zola and Huysmans took up the challenge. Instead
of escaping into their work like prominent writers Flaubert, Goncourt, or Mallarmé, after 1891 Zola and Huysmans took advantage of their position in the public eye by attempting to affect society through their art.[117] The public was fascinated by the personal lives of writers, as we are by celebrities today. In fact, one of
the reasons for the great success of *L'Enquête sur l'évolution littéraire* was, as Huret
noted, reader interest with the authors.[118] Zola and Huysmans's trips to visit

cathedrals created a great deal of scandal and speculation about what these "porno-graphic" naturalists could be doing at religious sites; journalists followed them and published stories about their activities; and leading religious, political, and artistic figures argued over the meaning of their voyages. Zola's trips to Lourdes and Rome, for example, were heavily covered by the French, Italian, and Russian press, while Huysmans's interest in satanism and his conversion and retreats in Trappist monas-teries were widely discussed and challenged.[119] Both received enormous quanti-ties of fan mail from readers all over Europe. Like Hugo, Zola and Huysmans used the novel as a bully pulpit to present their research and theories to contemporaries. Unlike Remy de Gourmont, Jean Lorrain, or Maurice Barrès, whose characters condemn society as irremediably sick, Zola's and Huysmans's semiautobiograph-ical heroes attempt to find ways to come to terms with their time. Like Gothic churches, whose religion brought together entire communities, their hybrid nov-els provide models for social reconciliation.

Writing in 1914, Charles Morice attributed his contemporaries' growing fondness for the cathedral to the rise in idealism of the 1880s, the same movement that pressured Zola and Huysmans to transform naturalism.[120] Inspired by Ver-laine's *Sagesse* and Villiers's *Axël,* many artists longed for an ordered and dreamy Middle Ages of cathedrals and chivalry, the opposite of the modern world. The key words of this time became "soul" and "dream." Reviews such as *Le Saint-Graal, Durendal,* and *La Trêve,* and groups of artists including the Nabis and Péladan's new order of chivalry "La Rose+Croix, le Temple et le Graal," thrived on repro-ducing "medieval" communities in the fin de siècle. The French discovery of the English Pre-Raphaelites and the Italian, Flemish, and French Primitives, as well as the Benedictine revival of medieval liturgy and plain chant sparked interest in me-dieval mysticism and its links to art. Symbolist and decadent painters and poets Edmond Dulac, Henri Pille, Paul Verlaine, and Jean Lorrain portrayed the cathe-dral as the symbol of the Middle Ages, a structure in which religion and art were fused, a place where one could escape from the commercial artistic values of the turn of the century.[121] Writers Jean Moréas, Pierre Quillard, Saint-Pol-Roux, Gus-tave Kahn, and Maurice Maeterlinck attempted to reproduce the Middle Ages in their works, prompting others, such as Heredia, to declare that symbolism was es-sentially a return to the Middle Ages.[122] Throughout this medieval revival, the op-erative image of the Middle Ages was the cathedral. Like the romantic period, this 1880s vogue for the Middle Ages focused mainly on an irretrievably lost France of prayers, shared values, and order, to which the fin de siècle could only return in dreams.

In *Les Trois Villes* and the Durtal cycle, Zola and Huysmans capitalized on their contemporaries' interest in the cathedral as an ideal of art and religion by re-activating its original significations and by adding new meanings to it. According to George Duby, emphasizing the unity of the congregation was one of the major goals of the medieval priests responsible for the design of Gothic architecture:

By altering the structure of the vaults, [Suger] was able to open up bays, re-place separating walls by pillars, and so realize his dream: that the coherence of light be used to extract the essential oneness of liturgical celebration; that all of the officiants be gathered in unison by the semicircle itself and, still more, by one unifying source of light; that within that radiance their simultaneous gestures harmonize like voices raised as one voice in the plenitude of choral singing; that the parallel rites of the liturgy, all bathed by the same light, come together to form one unanimous celebration.[123]

Zola and Huysmans called on such unifying ideas about the cathedral to evoke stability in a troubled time. Gothic churches, structures built during what was considered the infancy of the French nation, existed all over France and served as visible testaments to perseverence and community cooperation. Despite natural disasters, revolutions, and vandalism to which they had been subjected, they still stood, just like France herself.

The structuring principle of Emile Mâle's *L'Art religieux du XIIIe siècle*—the concept of the cathedral as a *speculum* or "mirror"—is a helpful model to keep in mind while reading *Les Trois Villes,* the Durtal cycle, and *A la recherche du temps perdu,* because these books seek to guide or instruct the reader by portraying the society of their time. The medieval mirror, as its name implies, reflects the person looking at it. But unlike a true mirror, in which one sees things as they are, medieval *specula* showed things as they ought to be. One was expected to see oneself in the mirror, but also to absorb and emulate the positive examples inside it. Emile Mâle linked the didacticism of *specula* to both books and cathedrals. In the novels of Zola, Huysmans, and Proust, each character interacts with members of society who serve as examples of good and bad behavior. It is only in reaching the conclusion that one discovers a theory—religion of science, medieval theology, religion of art—that reveals that the protagonists' earlier adventures were lessons. The books do not so much seek to reflect society, as to propose models for successfully functioning within it.

This allegorical system also provides a conceptual structure for hybrid novels: it provides an overarching message that reunites seemingly unconnected or fragmented passages. As Zola and Huysmans responded to the crisis in the novel by opening naturalism to analyses of the tensions between body and soul, they also tinkered with the form of the naturalist novel. Interior monologue, dialogue, and didactic exposition overwhelm plot; extended discussions about science, religion, and art weigh down action in *Les Trois Villes* and the Durtal cycle. Like novels such as Flaubert's *Bouvard et Pécuchet,* in which the two main characters' quest for knowledge constitutes the plot, Zola's and Huysmans's novels adopt what Janell Watson has called "catalog form," in which descriptions or *enumeratio* take over an increasing amount of space. The expansion of static scenes often frustrates readers.[124] *Rome,* for example, was dismissed by critics as a "giant guidebook included in a romantic melodrama," and *La Cathédrale* as "less a novel than a guide, an enthusiastic Baedecker [sic]."

Proust, too, struggled with the novel's form, attempting to write *Jean Santeuil,* the long work that he finally abandoned in 1899. His frustration with balancing fiction and documentation caused him to compare himself to the husband of Dorothea Brooke in George Eliot's *Middlemarch:* Casaubon spent his life wading through documents in his attempts to find a key to all mythologies.[125] Ten years later, Proust was able to overcome his discouragement by incorporating his studies into *La Recherche,* yet the resulting form still confused readers. E. M. Forster, for example, complained about its dispersion, in which fragments seemed to have no relationship to the whole; he described it as "chaotic, ill constructed, it has and will have no external shape."[126]

The novels of Zola, Huysmans, and Proust are more, however, than strangely organized repositories of information: the salvation each of their characters finds at the end of the series casts a retrospective light over everything that has preceded much as religious belief gives everything in the cathedral a function. All three narratives are driven by their characters' inability to reconcile reason and faith; the reader sees the world from their uncomprehending perspective. Yet by the end they have succeeded in their quests and better understand the world: Pierre discovers a religion of science; Durtal finds solace in Catholicism; and Proust's hero experiences salvation in a communal spirit fostered by art. Unlike Bouvard and Pécuchet, who return to copying documents at the end of Flaubert's novel, Pierre Froment, Durtal, and Proust's hero find effective spiritual resolutions to their questions.

Mâle's use of the concept of the great mirror—the *Speculum majus*—to structure *L'Art religieux du XIII siècle,* came from Vincent de Beauvais, who attempted to collect all of human knowledge into what we would now call an encyclopedia. Vincent de Beauvais himself had taken the concept of mirrors from medieval theologians, who, in turn, had based their concept on the plan of God as presented in the Scriptures. Mâle thus blurred the distinction between book, cathedral, and theology by presenting Gothic architecture to his readers as a visual representation of the theologian's invisible "intellectual cathedral." He argued that the genius of the cathedral builders was like that of educators: they created a "Bible for the poor" in which "the simple, the uneducated" are able to grasp a bit of the theologians' erudition, their "invisible cathedral." Mâle chose this "logical order" to structure his own book, whose chapters correspond to the four mirrors of the Middle Ages—Nature, Science, Morals, and History—the categorization most used by medieval thinkers.

In their attempt to represent fin-de-siècle society in their novels, Zola, Huysmans, and Proust also collect real characters, politics, places, and beliefs. Despite the seemingly fragmented, guidebook or catalog aspects of these novels, the pieces do find unity in the overarching "intellectual cathedral," the theoretical message revealed at the end. *Les Trois Villes,* the Durtal cycle, and *La Recherche* are not catalog-novels: they can be considered cathedral-novels, where the encyclopedic collection of information presented to the reader through art goes hand in hand with the revelation of a spiritual system that creates order out of seeming confusion. Each of their series disseminates a message about a positive spiritual force in the fin de siècle, from a secularized religion of science to Catholicism or a cult of art. Although Zola, Huysmans, and Proust adopted the image of the cathedral as a model for social unity within their novels, it also serves as a metaphor for a kind of art that brings science and religion—the concepts at the heart of the conflict between naturalists and symbolists, the novel and poetry—into harmony. Zola, Huysmans, and Proust rewrote the image of the cathedral in their novels according to their own "theologies," yet each of them dwelled on the ways in which the Gothic style was produced by the collaboration of science, religion, and art. Its unity in diversity became the model not only for society, but for their hybrid novels. Unlike Hugo, who was interested in Gothic architecture primarily as a monument from the past, Zola, Huysmans, and Proust champion the cathedral in the present as the perfect model for a new kind of living "stone book." It provides an ideal model for their own eclectic novels, which attempt to make sense of the conflicting ideologies of fin-de-siècle France.

Both Proust and Romain Rolland equated their multivolume works (*A la recherche du temps perdu* and *Jean-Christophe*) to cathedrals in the early years of the twentieth century. They could make this association because the scientific, mystical, and artistic connotations attached to Gothic architecture by this time evoked not only the temporal, spiritual, and didactic intent of their works, but also the brilliant structural design of the cathedral itself. The cathedral was no longer a theme attached to the Middle Ages, as much as a complex symbol representing harmony in diversity. By World War I the cathedral served as the perfect model for both social accord and for hybrid art that combined didacticism with virtuosity. Championed by all groups of French society as the French nation's ultimate artistic achievement, the conflicting symbolic claims on the cathedral did not diminish its stature; instead, they contributed to it, elevating it to the highest ranks of nationalism, spirituality, and art. The numerous ideals attached to Gothic architecture resulted in the turn of the century's paradoxical vogue for the cathedral. Despite a growing aversion to religious orders, Catholic education, and religious services, by World War I the cathedral had become a national French myth: "the synthesis of the country."

Two

"The Immense Cathedral of the Future World": Zola and the Religion of Science

> [Pluchart's] speech focused upon the greatness and advantages of the International [. . .] He explained its goal, the emancipation of workers; he showed its imposing structure—on the bottom, the commune, higher up the province, higher still the nation, and at the summit humanity. His arms moved slowly, piling up the floors, erecting the immense cathedral of the future world.
>
> —Emile Zola, *Germinal* (1885)

Emile Zola, father of the "experimental novel" and champion of science and technology, does not, at first glance, appear to have much in common with Chateaubriand or Paul Verlaine, who promoted an idealized image of the "enormous and delicate" Gothic cathedral. A self-proclaimed defender of technological advances, Zola chastised contemporary writers—especially romantics, Parnassians, and symbolists—for their tendency to hide in "medieval cities" instead of contemplating the wonders of the modern world.[1] In a June 3, 1870 article for *La Cloche,* he also criticized the Parnassian school's lack of enthusiasm for new discoveries: "Young poets thought that the locomotive would hiss at poetry. And so they shut themselves in their ivory tower [. . .] With hatred for the future, for modern life, they threw themselves into the past, into death."[2] Despite his vociferous public disdain for the escapism of many of his contemporaries, Zola's fiction reveals that he, too, was obsessed by the past, especially as manifested in religion and religious architecture. In his novels, Zola presents the Gothic cathedral as an artistic reflection of the enthusiastic spirit of primitive French people.

The cathedral lies at the heart of Zola's contradictory views about progress: although he criticized it as a structure from the past, he also adopted it in his novels as a model for the future.[3] In *Germinal,* for example, Zola uses the cathedral as a symbol of tomorrow's accomplishments. When he describes the speech of Pluchart, the socialist labor organizer, Zola equates the character's impassioned presentation of the expansive social goals of the International Workingmen's Association to building "the immense cathedral of the future world."[4] Etienne

Lantier becomes a similarly prophetic figure as he "preaches" to the masses in the forest, a scene reminiscent of *Le Génie du Christianisme* in which Chateaubriand attributed the development of Gothic cathedrals to worship under tree arches. Etienne, the "apostle," inspires the workers to "religious exaltation," as his powerful vision "reconstructs" the "future humanity." Zola's description transforms scenes of highly modern social activism into religious tableaux from an unidentifiable past. The nineteenth-century workers, equated to "primitive Christians," are transported by their "dream" into an idealized time in which hope springs eternal.[5] Etienne and Pluchart, perched on their "pulpits," are the "apostles," converting their followers to a "new religion."[6]

Comparing a social ideal to a "primitive" Christian setting is at the heart of Zola's ambiguous representation of progress: although his journalism explicitly identifies science as the path toward bettering humanity, his fiction constantly describes the results of such goals in terms of religious models from the past. Although he glorifies science, the values Zola praises as the basis of a better future—faith, truth, justice, fraternity, and peace—are those that he evokes when he describes the religion practiced in Gothic cathedrals during the Middle Ages. He criticized his contemporaries for hiding in their ivory towers, yet he, too, sought inspiration in the past.

Les Trois Villes: The Duel between Science and Religion

The tensions Zola saw between religion and science and past and future form an undercurrent of the Rougon-Macquart series, but they explode in the 1890s, with the publication of *Les Trois Villes* (*Lourdes, Rome, Paris*) and *Les Quatre Evangiles* (*Fécondité, Travail, Vérité,* and the unfinished *Justice*), novels in which Zola attempted to respond to society's demands for spirituality in literature by becoming the prophet of a new faith, a "religion of science," to be practiced in "the immense cathedral of the future world." In the late 1880s and early 1890s, Zola and naturalism had become the scapegoats for society's pessimistic outlook on the future. In reaction to science's rational and often depressing presentation of social problems—like the brutal working conditions exposed in *Germinal*—contemporaries called on naturalist writers to portray positive or inspirational models in their work. Zola responded to such criticism by composing *Les Trois Villes,* a series in which he wanted to paint the duel between science and religion before proposing a "dream" that would reconcile them.

Zola's notebooks for *Les Trois Villes* show the extent to which the project emerged in reaction to contemporary criticism. He wrote nine pages of these notes only one month after the publication in book form of *L'Enquête sur l'évolution littéraire,* the series of interviews in which almost all of France's leading writers agreed that naturalism was dead. He discovered Lourdes in 1891, during the national pilgrimage, which, as he told his friend, Henri Céard, had inspired him: "Oh! what a fine book could be made with this extraordinary city! It is haunting me; I spent a night building the outline."[7] Zola's feverish night of writing produced the preparatory file for *Lourdes*.[8] This manuscript, conserved at the Bibliothèque Méjanes in Aix-en-Provence, gives the project's parameters: in the wake of society's condemnation of science and naturalism in favor of religion and symbolism, he wanted to evoke these conflicts in a novel that would paint the "duel" between science and the need for the supernatural.[9] The city of Lourdes provided Zola with the perfect setting in which to explore the relationships between positivism and idealism, the issues that troubled him after Jules Huret's 1891 interviews. Zola would end *Lourdes* by depicting the optimism his contemporaries craved: he would create "the dream of a single people," a term that echoes Pluchart's utopian vision of "the immense cathedral of the future world." Both ideals valorize a united society that places humanity above all.

Gothic architecture provided Zola with a perfect unifying symbol because it reconciled science (the technological marvel of its architecture) with religion (the spiritual function of the edifice), the two forces that he saw as "dueling," as splitting contemporary France in two: "[. . .] France cut in two [. . .] two classes, two enemy races in continual war."[10] Unlike the Rougon-Macquart novels, which are set in the Second Empire and are generally driven by the ways in which characters respond to political, financial, or amorous situations, the *Trois Villes* series is set in 1890s France and focuses on a single protagonist, Father Pierre Froment, who attempts to reconcile contemporary attitudes toward religion and science. His name, which blends the contradictory images of rock and wheat, sterility and fertility, summarizes his personal conflicts: his life has been torn between the pious religious inclinations inherited from his mother and the productive rational legacy of his scientist father. Pierre became a priest to please his mother, a devout Catholic who wanted to offer Pierre to the Church in expiation for the death of her atheist chemist husband. On his mother's death, however, Pierre fell gravely ill. While recovering, he discovered his father's writings, thus awakening his dormant reason. Suddenly Pierre no longer trusts his innate belief in the dogmas of the Church. His quest to reconcile religious and scientific beliefs, both for himself and for others, thus provides the subject matter for *Les Trois Villes*. Instead of continuing to pit science against religion as did the contemporaries interviewed by Jules Huret, Zola created a character who tries to bring them together through his art: his optimistic dream for the future.

Pierre is the architect of Zola's "cathedral of the future world." He firmly believes that religion and science can and should peacefully coexist. He attempts to rekindle his own religious faith by making pilgrimages to Lourdes, Rome, and Paris, three of the centers of fin-de-siècle religious activity. Throughout his travels his idealized vision of the medieval cathedral—a shelter in which humans come together for the common good—provides him with a model for the perfection he seeks in his own time. Pierre contrasts this mythical cathedral to the commercialized or politically inspired houses of worship he encounters in his quest: the basilica in Lourdes, Saint Peter's in Rome, and the Sacré-Coeur of Paris. But unfortunately, each leg of his journey also persuades him that the Christian virtues of faith, hope, and charity have vanished from the modern Catholic Church.

At the end of *Paris*, Pierre abandons the Church, and in the tradition of Saint Peter, his namesake, he builds a new (secular) church. Pierre marries and becomes the first evangelist of "the religion of science," a belief in science as the path to social salvation. Each of the subsequent *Quatre Evangiles* traces the way in which Pierre's four prophet sons disseminate their father's religion in the twentieth century: Mathieu spreads a message about the dangers of abortion and the effectiveness of scientific farming techniques in *Fécondité;* Luc uses technological advances in a steel foundry to build a Fourierist community in *Travail;* Marc's dedication to secular teaching overcomes the tyranny of Catholicism's hold over a town in *Vérité;* and Jean was to have argued for the elimination of war in *Justice* had Zola not died while composing this novel. In the 1890s, Zola imitated Pluchart by using his art to erect a dream church, a symbol of the future perfection of society.

This chapter examines the ways in which Zola's shift from literary scientist of the Rougon-Macquart series to evangelical builder of the cathedral of the future in *Les Trois Villes* and *Les Quatre Evangiles* was not, as one critic has called it, a dilution of the aging Zola's mental faculties.[11] Instead, it was a conscious attempt to reconcile his precarious position in the ideological rifts of his time. But while he repositioned himself, Zola also discovered his unconscious nostalgia for an idealized past represented by the cathedral. Within *Les Trois Villes*, Zola the romantic battles Zola the naturalist thus creating hybrid and difficult novels in which lyrical descriptive passages alternate with summaries of political and religious theories.

In *Zola et son temps: Loudes, Rome, Paris,* René Ternois comprehensively examines Zola's relationship to the social and literary theories of the fin de siècle, yet he barely considers the novels as fiction. This is unfortunate, because the most fascinating aspect of *Les Trois Villes* is the way in which Zola used *literature* to explore and influence his contemporaries. Zola's often inaccurate representation of political or religious ideology in *Les Trois Villes* (Ternois calls the religion of science "pure gibberish") pales in comparison to Pierre Froment's dreams, his optimistic visions of the future.[12] By using Pierre's point of view to describe characters and settings, Zola vests them with physical attributes that reflect their ideology. Through description, Zola creates symbolic entities that summarize the narrative's tensions between religion and science. Modern Catholic churches thus become dens of iniquity while medieval architecture, and notably the cathedral, is held up as a symbol of French unity. Pierre sees Christian faith as the ideal that the Catholic Church has betrayed since the Middle Ages.

This chapter begins by examining descriptions of religious architecture throughout Zola's work. It questions the ways in which the social and artistic crises of the late nineteenth century caused Zola to bring the cathedral myth to the fore-front of his work as a symbol for French social unity. The second section explores Zola's use of the cathedral myth to overcome the conflicts between science and re-ligion that haunt non-Gothic structures in *Les Trois Villes*. Where most of his churches serve as the intersection for temporal conflicts between past and future, religion and science, Gothic architecture towers over these battles as a positive sym-bol of the French nation's potential for social and artistic harmony. The final sec-tion questions the effects of Zola's idealism and social evangelism. As he became progressively interested in using the novel to give his contemporaries an ideal, he created a new kind of novel that, like a Gothic cathedral, uses its art to edify those who study it.

Le Rêve: Zola's Dream Cathedral

Churches appear over and over in Zola's Rougon-Macquart series, from *La Con-quête de Plassans, La Faute de l'abbé Mouret, La Joie de vivre,* and *La Terre* to *La Débâcle.* Yet it was only in the late 1880s, during the beginning of the heated conflicts between symbolists and naturalists, that the cathedral began to play a cen-tral role in his work. In 1888, Zola pleasantly surprised his readers by publishing *Le Rêve,* a fairy tale novel with an all-powerful, personified twelfth-century cathe-dral at its heart. L'Eglise Sainte-Marie, which Zola modeled on Notre-Dame de Paris, structures the novel as it does the town of Beaumont-l'Eglise: "She is the mother, the queen [. . .] She beats at the center; each street is one of her veins; the city has no breath but hers."[13] Although this novel, like *Les Trois Villes* and *Les Qua-tre Evangiles,* has traditionally been poorly represented in the critical commentary devoted to Zola, *Le Rêve* exemplifies Zola's contradictory use of the cathedral to respond to his contemporaries. He wanted to confront his detractors on their own terms by satirically embracing idealism, yet in the end his own fascination for me-dieval religious architecture negated his critical message.

Placing a cathedral at the center of a novel was a new tactic for Zola, who, as a staunch Republican, tended to portray churches as symbols of Catholicism and its antiquated goals. Zola's scientific and democratic beliefs stem from his up-bringing: he was extremely proud of his engineer father's scientific background and showed an early ambivalence to organized religion.[14] Colette Becker suggests that his tenure at the liberal and anticlerical Librairie Hachette (1861–1862) pro-foundly influenced him and was a primary factor in his early decision to join the ranks of the Republicans. Zola embraced his employer's ideals of liberty and progress while rejecting what he saw as the authoritarian control and retrograde values of the Church.[15] Like Michelet and Renan in the Second Empire, Zola en-visaged Catholicism as the enemy of the Republic and the root of contemporary society's economic, religious, moral, and political problems.[16] In accordance with such views, he tended to portray religious architecture as the enemy of social progress. From the early *Mystères de Marseille* to his last novel, *Vérité*, churches haunt Zola's work as symbols of Catholicism and the oppressive, antiquated traditions it represented for him: they incarnate death, domination, ostentation, and sexuality.

Jean Borie is one of the few scholars to examine religious architecture in Zola's works; he points out the preponderance of caves and steeples, castrating matrices and dominating phalluses.[17] While his reading is a brilliant meditation on Zola's oedipal conflicts, Borie does not venture far beyond a Freudian explication of Zola's mythology of churches, thus neglecting the biblical myths attached to religious architecture and overlooking the importance of churches in the overall structure of Zola's oeuvre. While churches do provide interesting insights into the orphaned Zola's ambivalence about his dead father, religious architecture must also be considered in the context of Zola's animosity for the modern Catholic Church. His descriptions of monstrous churches most often directly condemn the people who built them.

Dungeons and tombs, these churches stand out in modern society as antiquated monuments from the past, as oppressive figures that separate their inhabitants from the living and impede progress. They are silent, empty, full of shadow, and marked by damp chill, much like ruins in a Gothic novel.[18] Albine links churches and tombs in *La Faute de l'abbé Mouret* as she shows Serge the "crushed walls" of his church. "You are in a grave," she says, "You cannot stretch your arms without skinning your hands on the stone [. . .] it is so small that your limbs are stiffening as if you were laid out alive in the earth."[19] Zola links these stifling structures to the feudal system by portraying churches, even modern constructions, as fortified castles whose steeples and domes dominate the landscape. While Albine describes the interior of Serge Mouret's church as a tomb, its exterior becomes "a formidable fortress that nothing will overthrow."[20] Continuing in this feudal vein, which echoes Hugo's theories about form and function, the domed "crowns" of churches such as Saint Peter's in *Rome* and the Sacré-Coeur in *Paris* are linked to the oppressive powers of God and king.

Ceremony transforms these dominating figures into dens of opulence. In *Une Page d'amour*, Hélène and Jeanne, mother and daughter, go to church only to succumb to the dream produced by the overwhelming light of candles and torches, the heady perfume of incense mixed with flowers, and the sparks thrown by the gold, silver, and crystal reflected in these flames. Angélique, in *Le Rêve*, is similarly dazzled by the abundance of candles, flames, torches, and chandeliers— "as bright as two suns"—that remind her of a blazing tabernacle.[21] Such displays of pageantry evoke temples where women and idolatrous crowds are seduced by priests.[22] The pontiffs of this cult are dedicated to filling their coffers with gold and to worshiping pagan gods. They belong to the time before Christ banished merchants from the temple.[23]

Zola generally suppresses religion from his representation of churches; they have lost their religious character as they have become everything else: "stables," "wheat markets," "waiting rooms," "museums," and "train stations" are a few of the terms Zola uses to describe churches.[24] Most often, however, he portrays them as theaters or brothels, where the public seeks pleasure. One of the most comic of such secular transformations occurs in *Pot-Bouille,* where workmen manhandle statues as l'abbé Mauduit works to transform the church into a theater: "Just imagine the effect [. . .] the plain and simple drama in this darkness of a tabernacle, beyond the mysterious night of the stained-glass windows of these lamps and golden candelabras. Eh? I think it will be irresistible."[25] Like Stendhal, who often represents churches as places where his heroes meet and seduce women, Zola cultivates the image of sacrilegious houses of worship that attract and corrupt the people, especially women. L'abbé Faujas, in *La Conquête de Plassans* is the prime example of such a calculating priest. In choosing stables, train stations, museums, and theaters as equivalents for churches, Zola secularizes and perverts religious spaces by converting their sacred values into commercial and sexual equivalents.[26] In Zola's novels, churches no longer serve the spiritual needs of their congregation; instead, they cater to the political or libidinal goals of clients.[27]

Zola's negative representation of churches conforms to the nineteenth-century Republican *topos* of identifying clericalism as the public enemy (Figure 1.2). Yet in 1888, Zola suddenly broke with his own tradition by glorifying medieval religious architecture in *Le Rêve.* He portrayed l'église Sainte-Marie as a mother and queen, and placed it at the heart of his fictional city, Beaumont-l'Eglise. Everything in this fairy tale occurs under the watchful protective eye of the cathedral, who embraces the town as if it were "a brood sheltered from the cold by her wings of stone."[28] This positive representation of the church is surprising given Zola's history of condemning churches and the Catholicism behind them. But this church is also different: it is a medieval cathedral, modeled on Notre-Dame de Paris.

L'église Sainte-Marie is omnipresent, from the first page of the novel when Angélique, the orphan heroine, seeks refuge from the snow under a statue, to the last page, in which she dies after leaving the cathedral's shadow. Adopted by the Hubert family, artisans who live in a fifteenth-century house attached to the cathedral and who embroider chasubles for its bishop, Angélique grows up hearing stories about medieval saints and reading about them in a 1549 edition of *The Golden Legend.*[29] She models her comportment on the piety and good deeds of the saints whose stories are represented in the medieval book and in the cathedral's statues and stained glass. As an adolescent Angélique falls in love with a young stained-glass artisan who resembles the Saint George portrayed in the cathedral's windows, only to discover that he is a marquis, the son of the cathedral's bishop, and a descendent of the town's prominent medieval family. Their courtship takes places in and around the cathedral, the theater of their desire and an accessory to their illicit relationship: Angélique first sees Félicien working on the cathedral; they meet in its enclosure; and the scaffolding around it allows Félicien to climb into Angélique's room. Against their families' wishes, the two marry in the cathedral, but as Angélique leaves its medieval shadow to enter the real world she drops dead.

Despite the nineteenth-century setting, Angélique's transformation from Rougon-Macquart offspring to noblewoman seems to be taken from *The Golden Legend.* Her life, like her dream of marrying a prince, comes to an end as she leaves the shadow of the cathedral to kiss her new husband on the sunny town square. Zola, however, perverts the storybook ending by killing his heroine. His narrator adds the words, "All is but a dream," a phrase that raises a number of questions about Zola's intent in the book. To what does the "all" refer? Does the narrator insinuate that life is only a dream? or does he mean to criticize Angélique's life and the events of the novel? What does this statement mean for the cathedral, which structures Angélique's experiences and serves as the ultimate symbol of her reveries? Zola himself was close-mouthed about his novel, allowing readers to interpret it as they pleased. Some of his intentions become clearer, however, when we place the book's focus on dream and Gothic setting into its ideological context.

Rêve (dream), along with *âme* (soul), was the key word of the psychological and symbolist backlash against naturalism expressed in the Jules Huret interviews of 1891.[30] Contemporaries Bourget, Brunetière, and Moréas had criticized Zola's lack of dreams and his dedication to physical observation, especially after the 1887 publication of *La Terre,* whose detailed descriptions of procreation and childbirth subjected him to charges of pornography. Zola's preparatory notebooks reveal that his choice of topic in *Le Rêve* was a reaction to such criticism. He planned the book as a slap in the face of the people who claimed he was incapable of creating psychology. Zola's goals in the novel were twofold: to surprise his contemporaries by giving them what they wanted—an idyll—in a form suitable for all readers; and to force the public to recognize that he could treat the supernatural through naturalism.[31]

His objectives for *Le Rêve* are striking because they reveal the extent to which, in the 1880s and 1890s, Zola began responding to reader comments while writing his novels. He did not adopt a dream as the topic of *Le Rêve* because it fit his plans for the Rougon-Macquart series, but rather because he wanted to answer critics. Zola was irritated by literary battles that broke artists into separate camps by purposefully misinterpreting the coded words of the other side: *rêve, âme, psychologie.* Instead of defending himself by identifying previous works in which he truly had explored psychology—*La Faute de l'abbé Mouret, La Conquête de Plassans,* or *Une page d'amour*—Zola decided to modify his approach to include the vocabulary and techniques of his critics. He fulfilled his adversaries' demands by creating an idyll catered to their tastes.

As we saw in the introduction, a medieval revival was in full swing by 1888. A curious historical personage named Mérovak came to incarnate the symbolists' fascination with medieval interiors and the creation of neomedieval art in the nineteenth century: he could be considered Angélique's spiritual brother. In the 1890s, this artist lived in one of the towers of Notre-Dame de Paris and traveled from cathedral to cathedral selling his drawings of religious architecture or playing the piano to survive. He was nicknamed "man of the cathedrals" by the press, and his extravagant appearance—long black beard and black cape—endeared him to the symbolists who admired him as a *primitif,* a neomedieval artist devoted to his Catholic art and unconcerned by commercial gain. The term *primitif* was used, at this time, to refer to medieval religious artists who dedicated their work to God; it was an aspiration of artists such as the Nabis. By association, the term was attached to medieval worshipers, whom they described as primitive Christians.[32]

Le Rêve, which features an artist heroine who lives in a fifteenth-century house attached to a twelfth-century cathedral, caters to the symbolist artists' predilections for medieval domestic interiors and medieval artists. The town of Beaumont-l'Eglise, circumscribed by the cathedral, has not changed since the Middle Ages: "A special stationary population lives here, leading the existence that their ancestors have followed from father to son for the last five hundred years. The cathedral explains everything, gave birth to everything and conserves everything." Zola created an escapist, dreamy world where characters are devoted to the piety and spirituality of the past, incarnated by a cathedral that dominates every action of the town: "Hence this soul of another age, this religious torpor in the past, this cloistered walled city that surrounds it, redolent of an old perfume of peace and faith."[33] In *Le Rêve,* Zola recreates the Parnassian "ivory tower" he had once criticized.

Zola's focus on Angélique, whom he calls "a primitive Christian," and on the Huberts, a pious couple whose family has embroidered religious ornamentation for the cathedral since the Middle Ages, also capitalizes on the symbolists' equation of artisans to primitive Christians. This family lives in the cathedral (their house is attached to it) and devotes itself to religious art. It is no coincidence that two years later Zola's publishers capitalized on the symbolist tenor of the book by having it illustrated by Carlos Schwabe and Lucien Métivet, well-known symbolist artists who frequented Joséphin Péladan's Rose+Croix circle. The book is full of hearts and doves, flowers and perfume, and images of traveling spirits (represented as ghosts or smoke), as is evident on the book's cover artwork (Figure 2.1).[34] The novel was so popular that it inspired a lyrical drama that ran for ninety-three performances after its debut in 1891.[35] Immediately following the publication of the book, poems and drawings of Gothic cathedrals began appearing in journals like *Le Rire* and *Le Courier Français* presenting the cathedral as Zola did l'église Sainte-Marie: Gothic churches were transformed into guardians and mothers, benevolent figures watching over and protecting their cities (Figure 2.2).

Readers were giddy with enthusiasm about the idyll Zola had created: "This book is a poem of grace," wrote one reviewer of the work.[36] Others also remarked

the lyricism, the spiritual imagery, and the medieval themes, but above all the public was delighted by the elevated tone of this book, which differed from what they saw as Zola's traditional focus on base aspects of reality. They complimented him for a fairy tale well done: "*Le Rêve* is, after the symphony, the melody, a tune for the flute—not heroic but mystical. It resembles a fairy tale written by Th. Gautier and often reminds one of *Notre-Dame de Paris.*"[37] Despite such comparisons to Gautier and Hugo, no one noticed the extent to which Zola's medieval setting echoed Gautier's 1833 satire "Elias Wildmanstadius ou l'homme moyen-âge," in which Gautier mocked Hugo and the romantic Gothic revival. In this story, Gautier spoofs contemporaries who have become so attached to medieval interiors, pursuits, and costumes that they can no longer bear the modern age. He describes the medieval pursuits of Elias Wildmanstadius, whose fifteenth-century soul is displaced in the nineteenth century. He hides in his medieval house, carves reproductions of medieval cathedrals, and goes out only to visit his mistress, the Gothic cathedral. He is so attached to this cathedral that he dies at the very moment she is hit and severely damaged by lightning.

Zola, too, had intended *Le Rêve* to poke fun at his contemporaries' excessive attachment to medievalism. Like Elias Wildmanstadius (the romantic "medieval man") or Mérovak (the symbolist "man of the cathedrals"), Angélique has a "best friend" in the cathedral and is devoted to medieval books (*The Golden Legend*) and craftsmanship (embroidery). She is completely sheltered from the nineteenth century because of her proximity to the cathedral, and has herself become "a little stained–glass virgin."[38] She cannot bear to be separated from her beloved cathedral: once she leaves its shadow, she dies.

Through Angélique, Zola had wanted to take aim at the symbolists and the Catholics, who, he felt, exacerbated society's problems by convincing the public that life was futile and that the only possible happiness was to retreat into dreamy medieval settings and prayer. Zola had always chastised those who hid in ivory towers, those who refused to confront the outside world. Brothers of Elias Wildmanstadius and Angélique, they abdicated personal responsibility to believe in miracles and the grace of God or worse yet, they forbade independent action. Angélique's parents, for example, would rather she die than disobey Monseigneur de Hautecoeur. *Le Rêve,* which Zola considered a "pendant" of *La Faute de l'abbé Mouret,* another book that criticized excessive religious zeal, was originally intended as a satire of those people who abandoned rationalism and pragmatism (life) in favor of dreams or religion (death).[39]

Figure 2.1. Carlos Schwabe. Cover of *Le Rêve,* 1892 (*opposite*). Photomechanical. Jane Voorhees Zimmerli Art Museum. Rutgers, The State University of New Jersey. Acquired with the Herbert D. and Ruth Schimmel Museum Library Fund. Photo by Jack Abraham. 1991.0217.

À notre maître à tous
A Jean Richepin

LE VEILLEUR PUBLIC

BALLADE DU MOYEN AGE

Bonnes gens, dormez sans effroi,
Le couvre-feu sonne au beffroi,
    Le jour sommeille,
Et, sous un épais voile noir
Disparaît l'antique manoir,
    Frères, je veille!

Bonnes gens, dormez sans effroi,
Le couvre-feu sonne au beffroi,
    Tout est silence.
Le roitelet, fragile oiseau
S'est endormi sur un roseau
    Qui le balance.

Bonnes gens, dormez sans effroi,
Le couvre-feu sonne au beffroi,
    La nuit est sombre.
Le pâtre rentrant ses brebis,
Avec sa miche de pain bis
    S'en va dans l'ombre.

Bonnes gens, dormez sans effroi,
Le couvre-feu sonne au beffroi,
    Le vent est triste.
Ding, din, don!... allez vous coucher,
Din, don!... minuit sonne au clocher,
    Dieu vous assiste!

Bonnes gens, dormez sans effroi,
Le couvre-feu sonne au beffroi,
    O saints cantiques!
C'est l'heure où l'affreux Lucifer
Va précipiter en enfer
    Les hérétiques!

Bonnes gens, dormez sans effroi,
Le couvre-feu sonne au beffroi,
    Le jour sommeille.
Et, sous un épais voile noir
Disparaît l'antique manoir,
    Frères, je veille!

            JACQUES YVEL.

Dessin de HENRI PILLE.

"An Ideal Life, That of which We Dream": The Cathedral as Utopia

Zola's contradictory relationship to the cathedral in *Le Rêve* derives from this original satirical intention. Although he began his novel as a way of responding to his contemporaries' criticism by appropriating their subject matter—medieval religious architecture, hagiography, and medieval artisans—his unconscious appreciation of the cathedral and medieval art subverted the negative message, which remains only in trace form as the book's cryptic last words "All is but a dream." Ironically, in the drama based on the novel, even this reference disappears. Zola decided to omit the last scene entirely; the play ends with Angélique's miraculous healing and impending nuptials.

Zola became fascinated by medievalism during the writing of the book: he took notes about medieval architecture, stained glass, and embroidery from the *Grand dictionnaire universel du XIXe siècle;* he consulted his architect friend, Frantz Jourdain, Viollet-le-Duc's writings about Gothic architecture, and manuals about embroidery, and he plunged into *The Golden Legend.*[40] He even collected medieval furnishings, tapestries, suits of armor, and artwork, thus becoming the laughing-stock of his friends, like Huysmans, who accused Zola of being tricked into buying forgeries of medieval manuscripts.[41] In his *Journal,* Edmond de Goncourt mocked "all of the cathedralish vintage store stuff" lining Zola's studies in Médan and Paris.[42] For anyone who knew Zola as a child, however, it should have come as no surprise. In his youth, Zola had adored the Middle Ages and had even written ballads and a novel about the Crusades.[43] It was as if he had rediscovered this inner child while composing *Le Rêve.*

Descriptions of l'église Sainte-Marie exemplify Zola's ambivalent relationship to the cathedral. Although he wanted to condemn it as a symbol of the Catholic reliance on the past as he had other forms of religious architecture, he also admired the democratic harmony he felt it represented. He does give it the negative attributes of royalty and domination that he often lent to Catholic churches—it is a "sarcophagus," "a giant mass that blocks the sky," and a temple of luminary opulence—yet the positive attributes far outweigh the negatives.[44] His descriptions caress the personified cathedral. It becomes "the mother," a living, breathing structure that supports and is supported in equal measure by all of its children, the inhabitants of Beaumont-l'Eglise. Zola's vision of the cathedral creates a new and impressionistic mixture of many of the nineteenth-century ideas about it: he alternates passages that reflect Victor Hugo and Viollet-le-Duc's conception of a

Figure 2.2. Henri Pille. Illustration for "Le Veilleur public" by Jacques Yvel, from *Le Courrier français,* March 25, 1888 (*opposite*). Photomechanical. Jane Voorhees Zimmerli Art Museum. Rutgers, The State University of New Jersey. Photo by Jack Abraham. 1998.0012.004.

highly rational scientific structure with sections that echo Chateaubriand's homage to the cathedral as a testament to the genius of Christianity.

Zola's focus on the people of Beaumont-l'Eglise—the force integral to the cathedral's existence—echoes Hugo's (incorrect) emphasis on the democratic construction methods of the Middle Ages. The omniscient narrator of *Le Rêve* presents Sainte-Marie as a structure built by generations of devoted workers over a period of three hundred years. It continues to grow as new worshipers contribute to it. Angélique, like the other *primitifs*, contributes her artwork. With the Huberts, she embroiders everything it needs, just as Félicien de Hautecoeur repairs and adds to its stained glass, the priests contribute music and ceremony, the swallows build nests, and plants grow between its stones. Everyone and everything in this community voluntarily erected the cathedral, which has become the symbol of their society and the bond that unites them: "the cathedral explains everything, gave birth to everything and conserves everything."[45] It incarnates the idea of "oneness" behind the construction of medieval churches.

Echoing Hugo's passages about the technical developments of Gothic architecture, Zola also dwells on the architectural developments evident in the church—*chapelles romanes du pourtour, fenêtres à plein cintre, colonnettes, archivoltes, fenêtres ogivales, arcs brisés et des roses, contreforts* and *arcs-boutants du choeur*—and uses them to evoke the rational and scientific aspects of the cathedral's construction. In the tradition of Victor Hugo and Viollet-le-Duc, who described the cathedral as "logical and well proportioned" and "rational," Zola shows that this is no miraculous structure. It was meticulously designed to evoke a praying female figure, lifting her hands to Heaven:

> At its base [the cathedral] was kneeling, crushed by prayer, with Romanesque perimeter chapels, arched Roman windows adorned simply with slim columns under the archivolts. Then, it felt uplifted, face and hands raised to Heaven, with the ribbed arches of the nave, constructed eighty years later, high slender windows divided by mullions that carried the Gothic arches and the rose windows. Then it left the ground, delighted, perfectly straight, with the vaulting and flying buttresses of the choir, decorated two centuries later, in full flamboyant Gothic style, weighted with pinnacles, spires, and steeples.[46]

Zola points out its independent parts before showing how their sum is greater than the individual pieces. Hegel wrote that: "In its grandeur and sublime peace [the cathedral] is lifted above anything purely utilitarian into an infinity in itself."[47] Zola similarly insists that the cathedral's seemingly uncomfortable physical position in prayer is overcome by the ecstacy of its spiritual elevation. A triumph of engineering prowess, l'église Sainte-Marie also epitomizes the symbolist and Catholic ideal of a medieval cathedral devoted to faith. It is a product of both science and belief; the common denominator is the different people who came together to build it.

The three-page passage in which Angélique contemplates the cathedral from her balcony prefigures the impressionistic perspective Claude Monet would bring to his thirty studies of Rouen Cathedral four years later (Figure 2.3).[48] Though Monet is less interested in the vertical thrust of the cathedral, his goal—to capture "what there is between the motif [the cathedral] and myself"—is not unlike that of Angélique, whose view of the cathedral is affected by changes in light, weather, and time. Every morning she is amazed by the cathedral, "which she seemed to see for the first time."[49] The stones are alive with a mystical spirit that flowers during their ascension into the sky. For her, the cathedral "lives" and the three-page paean to her contemplation of the cathedral is a gorgeous set piece that evokes the ever-changing yet ever-constant view from her balcony.

The impressionistic quality of these pages builds the cathedral into a mythical, unifying being, a product of time, a reflection of time, and a vessel that captures time within it: "It was a constant wakefulness, coming from the infinity of the past, going toward the eternity of the future."[50] Zola's description of Angélique's point of view parallels the fascination with time evident in Monet's cathedral cycle, which Joachim Pissarro characterizes as "a reading of the passage of time and its mark that can be almost arithmetically measured through the progression of light against shade in the morning, or of shade against light in the afternoon."[51] Pissarro argues that Monet's choice of motifs is not insignificant, and that for Monet as for many Impressionists the cathedral's symbolism was akin to their goal: to represent the invisible, the in-between, and the nontangible. This belief was shared by contemporaries, who called the Impressionists "Gothic, in their time."[52]

For Angélique, however, the cathedral is an extremely tangible structure, more an agent of time than its product. Though she relishes the changing vista from her balcony, she sees l'église Sainte Marie, not time, as responsible for the transformations: it distributes and mixes mementoes of faith and devotion from every century and from every corner of life. For the last 500 years, life in Beaumont-l'Eglise has transpired peacefully and with goodwill because the town exists for the cathedral: "One lives there only for it and because of it." Its presence creates a kind of timeless dream state.

In fact, the cathedral of Beaumont-l'Eglise is the dream to which Zola's title refers: Angélique's fairy-tale life begins as she finds herself in its shadow and ends as she walks out of its royal portal.[53] In *Le Rêve,* Zola's lyrical and idyllic descriptions of l'église Sainte-Marie and the harmonious "mystical walled city" under its influence create a fairy-tale setting, an atmosphere he called "life not as it is, but as we dream it: all good, all honest, all happy. An ideal life, just as we wish."[54] Although he had originally planned his novel to take aim at mystical Catholic education and the false illusions it created about life, Zola's descriptions reveal his

nostalgia for such a life, a return to his childhood dreams of the Middle Ages and of communities where everyone is good, honest, and happy. Such a fantasy—like l'église Sainte-Marie—links past, present, and future.

Thus despite the antagonism he would continue to address toward churches in the Rougon-Macquart, the *Trois Villes,* and the *Quatre Evangiles* series, the Gothic cathedral was an inherently positive concept for Zola. Throughout his work he associated the word *cathedral* with dream and ideal. And because Zola portrayed Gothic architecture as a figure that represented positive outcomes—communities such as Beaumont-l'Eglise in which a dedication to values of faith, truth, justice, peace, and fraternity are inscribed within an architectural setting—it became a utopian figure in his work. A utopia, by definition, is both a good place (*eu-topia*) and a place that can be found nowhere (*ou-topia*).[55] The town of Beaumont-l'Eglise is supposed to be located two hours from Paris, yet it forms a mystical world unto itself. Unlike the thousands of inhabitants of Beaumont-la-Ville, the large city lying below Beaumont-l'Eglise, the hundreds of residents of the cathedral city are untouched by modern development and people from outside the community do not enter its walls. It is an ideal self-sufficient city—set on a mountain—that transcends time and place. Pluchart dreamed of "the immense cathedral of the future world" in *Germinal,* and he would have seen his vision realized in Beaumont-l'Eglise, a community in which poor and rich support each other and live together in perfect harmony.

"The Man of Utopias"

In the nineteenth century, the term *utopia* was synonymous with the words *ideal* and *dream*. Larousse, in his *Grand dictionnaire universel,* does not focus on utopias as impossible; rather, he insists on their feasibility: "The concept of the ideal is necessary for progress. Often what has been qualified as a utopia at one time becomes an appreciable reality at another."[56] This pragmatic belief in the power of dreaming— "the ideal is often a motive we seek to achieve"—echoes both Lamartine ("often, utopias are no more than premature truths"), whom Larousse cites, and Victor Hugo, who equated utopias to possibilities: "utopia today, flesh and bones tomorrow."[57] Despite his frequent criticism of those who dreamed of the past, Zola, himself loved to dream and believed in the utility of doing so.[58]

In his youth, Zola admired the romantics, and like Hugo, he believed that literature should contribute to society by inspiring confidence in the future. He

Figure 2.3. Claude Monet. *Rouen Cathedral: The Portal (in Sun)* (opposite). The Metropolitan Museum of Art, Theodore M. Davis Collection, Bequest of Theodore M. Davis, 1915. (30.95.250).

felt that the artist should be a "priest" or a "prophet," a visionary who could help his contemporaries devote themselves to social progress.[59] As he began to champion science, however, Zola claimed to renounce both Hugo and literature that mixed art with secular religions. Thirty years later, he returned to Hugo's idea of artistic prophecy in *Les Trois Villes,* novels that attempted to improve society by giving it an ideal.[60] His embrace of utopia in reaction to his critics is a model of the comportment praised by Hugo in his poem "La fonction du poëte." In a time of crisis ("les jours impies") when contemporaries pessimistically advised that nothing could be done to prevent society from degenerating ("quand les peuples végètent"), one must face critics by becoming the man of utopias ("l'homme des utopies"), a poet who sheds light on the future with dreams of love and harmony.[61] After Hugo's death, when writers such as Paul Bourget clamored for a new artist who would provide moral leadership for society, Zola took solace in Hugo's vision of the poet as prophet and attempted to fill his shoes.

While he meant to implicitly criticize dreamers who focused on the past in *Le Rêve,* in *Les Trois Villes,* Zola overtly planned to give his contemporaries an optimistic ideal that would provide them with the courage to confront modernity. The cathedral plays just such a role. One of the most admirable characters of the series, Father Peyramale in *Lourdes,* calls on the dream of the cathedral he is building to get through difficult times: "Ah! this constantly evoked vision gave him the courage to fight, in the middle of the silent murder in which he felt himself enveloped."[62] Zola provided an ideal like that of Pluchart or l'abbé Peyramale: a dream that would give contemporaries courage to survive.

Zola used the novel, a popular medium, to depict the problems confronting society and to transmit his positive vision of the future to his readers. He had adopted his critics' vocabulary and iconography in *Le Rêve* in order to respond to their calls for more idealism in literature, and he had capitalized on the interest in cathedrals to spread his message. In *Les Trois Villes,* he adopted a popular Catholic and symbolist figure, the priest, and a popular contemporary subject—religious pilgrimages—then reconfigured them to present his secular message about social harmony.

The priest, especially the corrupt priest, was a popular literary figure inherited from Gothic novels such as *The Monk.* He appeared throughout the century, notably in the works of Balzac, Barbey d'Aurevilly, Octave Mirbeau, and Zola, himself. In *La Faute de l'abbé Mouret* Zola created a priest torn between chastity and the pleasures of the flesh and in *La Conquête de Plassans* he exposed the political machinations of priests.[63] Zola's decision to portray a priest pulled between faith and reason in *Lourdes* created a new hero for the fin-de-siècle novel.[64] And not only did he adopt a priest as protagonist, Zola also capitalized on the nineteenth-century interest in travel by sending Pierre to Lourdes and Rome, tourist attractions par excellence.

The last quarter of the nineteenth century saw a proliferation of voyages to pilgrimage sites, especially those dedicated to the Virgin Mary.[65] From following the footsteps of medieval pilgrims to Chartres to visiting the shrines that sprang up after contemporary Marian apparitions in La Salette, Lourdes, and Paris, the French traveled to worship.[66] A good economy, the increased accessibility and price of train travel, and the development of marketing techniques for travel attracted pilgrims and tourists, who visited religious sites in increasing numbers throughout the century. But Lourdes was the most popular of all. Lured by Henri Lasserre's best-selling history of the town—*Notre-Dame de Lourdes*—and by church documents and other publicity material that advertized it as a kind of Beaumont-l'Eglise, a town unchanged since the Middle Ages, by 1900 more than half a million people a year came to visit the miraculous spring.[67] Zola's novel was the first fictional account devoted to this popular phenomenon.

Pierre Froment is a typical pilgrim. Before arriving in Lourdes he envisions the town as Henri Lasserre had described it, as unchanged since the Middle Ages.[68] He imagines the twelfth- and thirteenth-century cathedral as the symbol of the magical "heroic times of the Church" when faith and public devotion united mankind. Pierre sees the cathedral as a shelter, a place that belongs to the people and symbolizes their faith, generosity, and goodwill toward one another:

> [Pierre] recalled old cathedrals shivering with the belief of the masses; he saw once again the antique liturgical objects; imagery, silver and gold plate, saints of stone and wood, whose force and beauty of expression was admirable. It was because, in those far off times, workers believed, gave their flesh, gave their soul, in the overwhelming naivete of their emotion [. . .][69]

He understands the cathedral as a refuge, a harmonious spot where one abandoned oneself to faith in God: "When the people knelt under the same breath of credulity, in the terror of ignorance, and entrusted themselves, for their own happiness, to the hands of God the all-Powerful [. . .] was the church not their home, the refuge where consolation awaited them day and night?"[70] Pierre's vision provides him with a religious and social ideal that echoes the utopia of *Le Rêve*. His imaginary cathedral is a mother and a protector—another église Sainte-Marie—that serves as a mythical gathering spot for a harmonious society. Pierre Froment seeks this ideal—as did many of Catholics of the time—because he is convinced that it will restore and nourish his faith in Catholicism.[71] As he journeys to Lourdes, Rome, and Paris, however, his dream is progressively transformed. When he compares his imagination of medieval pilgrimage sites to modern, he begins to realize that Catholicism no longer worships the values he thought it did.

"Ceci tuera cela": The Dueling Churches of *Les Trois Villes*

In *Les Trois Villes,* told primarily from the perspective of Pierre Froment, Zola relies heavily on description to suggest narrative tensions of which his protagonist remains unaware. Zola filters events through Pierre's eyes, yet the protagonist does not always understand the significance of what he sees. His idealized vision of the Gothic cathedral is progressively modified by his contact with real architectural structures: Notre-Dame de Lourdes, Saint Peter's of Rome, and the Sacré-Coeur basilica. Descriptions of churches take on an allegorical function in these novels: they incarnate the forces that struggle to gain control over fin-de-siècle society.

In spite of the scientific objectivity advocated in "Le Roman Expérimental," Zola carefully planned his descriptions to advance plot and to incarnate visually the ideas he wanted to emphasize: "Our descriptions no longer have a purely picturesque role, they are there to present all of the drama, the characters and the surroundings that act on them." Zola's specificity about the emphasis surroundings—houses, churches, parks—play on characters is important because he indicates that they are not mere accessories; they "act upon" the characters as would other characters.[72] The cathedral in *Le Rêve*, for example, is not simply part of the decor. It is largely responsible for Angélique's mystical development and for defining and regulating the lives of its inhabitants. Zola took great pains to construct l'église Sainte-Marie: "As for my cathedral, it is built for the needs of my story, following the model of our French cathedrals [. . .] All of this is extremely studied, quite voluntary, and no one will ever know the trouble I have had."[73] The cathedral cannot be separated from *Le Rêve* because it is one of the central forces acting on Angélique and the townspeople.

Zola builds these houses of worship into powerful forces that control cities. Like Beaumont-l'Eglise, in which every street was a vein leading to l'église Sainte-Marie, every event in *Les Trois Villes* leads back to a church, which observes and controls the actions occurring beneath it. While the reader senses the malevolent presence of the churches through Zola's figurative language, Pierre remains largely oblivious until the end of each novel. Like the statues and images on a cathedral, Zola's descriptions model for Pierre the good and bad forces that will lead him to find his way in the world.

We can see this process at work in *Lourdes*. Zola took abundant notes (242 pages) about his trip—interviews with doctors and invalids, descriptions of the pilgrimage train, the layout of the city, its people, and historical sketches about Bernadette Soubirous's visions of the Virgin—yet they tended to focus on his impressions.[74] In the basilica of Lourdes, for example, he remarks the profusion of ex-votos and banners, which remind him of his billiard room at Médan. He is impressed by the masses of donated objects; he admires the way they reflect the light; yet he describes the effect as "not too religious."[75] In the novel, however, Zola transforms what he saw as a rather cluttered and well-lit church into an ostentatious, flaming structure that gloats over the ruin of another church:

> Pierre [. . .] saw the Basilica rise up, radiant in its triumph. This was not the fulfillment of Father Peyramale's dreams—officiating, blessing the kneeling

crowds while the organs rumbled with joy. The Basilica over there invoked itself, ringing with a flurry of bells, proclaiming the superhuman joy of a miracle, ablaze with flames, with its banners, its lamps, its silver and gold hearts, its clergymen clothed in gold, its monstrance a golden star. It burned in the setting sun, it touched the sky with its spire, surrounded by the billions of reverberating prayers from which the walls trembled. Here, was the church dead before being born, the church forbidden by a summons from the bishop, fallen into powder, open to the four winds [. . .] And nothing was more desperately anguishing than this desired ruin, across from its triumphant rival, the Basilica shining with gold.[76]

Zola's description of the basilica, in which the word gold—*or*—is repeated four times and whose golden image is intensified by words such as *brasillante, flammes,* and *astre,* sets this church on fire. This image differs significantly from that of his notes, which portray it as little more than a cluttered and gaudy church. The tensions between the glorious basilica—flaming with silver and gold—and the dead church—the ruin—parallel the narrative tensions that Zola wanted to establish between the greed of the monks who run the modern basilica and Pierre's vision of a simple pilgrimage site in which kneeling worshipers pray together.

This passage comes late in the novel, after Pierre has learned the history of Lourdes. Through discussions with his father's old friend, Docteur Chassaigne, Pierre learns the story of the political struggles, persecution, and greed that led to the construction of the contemporary pilgrimage site. Although the parish priest of Lourdes—Father Peyramale—had felt that the town should honor Bernadette's visions of the Virgin by building a cathedral in the tradition of the Middle Ages, a group of monks—les frères de la Grotte—opposed him. They wanted to make more money by building a bigger church in a more accessible part of town. Father Peyramale's church was almost completed when the frères de la Grotte's political persecution—in the form of denunciations to the Bishop—caused the stress that finally killed the increasingly sick priest. Zola accuses them of having murdered the older priest.[77] The flaming, glorious basilica triumphing over the victimized church thus parallels the sordid story underlying Lourdes's foundation as a spiritual site. His notebooks spell this out clearly: "Struggle between the upper city and the lower city [. . .] put above all Bernadette, with the old Lourdes and the new, all of this abominable humanity, the struggle of Peyramale and the priests, the church in ruins."[78]

The anguish with which Pierre sees the conflict between the two churches reflects Lourdes's triumph over his own ideal of a harmonious Catholicism. Father Peyramale's dream was identical to Pierre's. They both envisioned the city as a medieval pilgrimage site, structured by the cathedral, a place to welcome kneeling worshipers: "[Father Peyramale] dreamed of a magnificent church, a cathedral of giant proportions, able to contain a huge crowd."[79] While examining the ruins, Pierre imagines Father Peyramale's church in a three-page description that caresses the simple beauty of the cathedral's architectural forms. The symmetry of the roof, its archivolts, columns, steeple, and rose windows contribute to its overall effect of grandeur and simplicity.[80] Unlike the gaudy basilica, whose meaning has been corrupted by commercialism, the ruined cathedral reflects the purity of its spirit. Pierre envisions Father Peyramale closing his eyes to dream of the finished church on the first day of mass: he sees and hears the masses of kneeling worshipers, surrounded by the sound of the organ, gorgeous stained glass, and beautiful and intricate artwork made by pilgrims from around the world.[81] The priest welcomes visitors to this edifice where they will be surrounded by the simplicity and beauty of artwork made by hand and given from the heart. This vision strikingly resembles Pierre's ideal Middle Ages.

The moldy ruins— "this assassination of a monument"—of the splendid dream seem like a cemetery to Pierre, markers of the death of faith, which has been killed by modern Catholic greed. These stones are the last vestige of a good religion, buried by the frères de la Grotte who run the city: "And the city belongs to them, and they hold their shop here; here they sell God, wholesale and retail." The inhabitants of Lourdes no longer believe in God; their overriding concern is to exploit the flood of pilgrims who come for miracles: "The entire country rotted, the triumph of the Grotto had brought such a rage for lucre, such a burning fever to possess and to delight oneself, that, under the driving rain of millions, an extraordinary perversion worsened every day, changed the Bethlehem of Bernadette into Gomorrah and Sodom [. . .]"[82] The death of Father Peyramale's cathedral, which was supposed to be built by and for the people, constitutes a major setback for Pierre's attitude toward modern Catholicism. It serves as an example of the duplicity of Lourdes and its false publicity; Pierre understands that modern pilgrimages will not help him recover his faith.

Although the basilica of Lourdes has triumphed over the cathedral, hope for the future lies in the ruins. The rusted locomotive, which sits under a shelter in the ruined church, foreshadows the time when the positive human values incarnated in the cathedral— "the great heart"—will return to "wake the Sleeping Beauty Church from its heavy slumber of a ruin."[83] Although it seems paradoxical to see the future in a rusted machine, Pierre echoes a nineteenth-century Republican *topos:* technology will triumph over Catholicism and progress will reform humanity.[84] At the end of his trip Pierre realizes that the ostentatious, superstitious Catholicism of Lourdes gives people consolation, but is incapable of curing mankind's spiritual suffering. Pierre suddenly understands that the only religion capable of curing humanity will be a secular religion, based on reason. It will give people hope by stressing work and life: "a new religion, a new hope, a new paradise."[85] Pierre's dream of social harmony remains unchanged, but he has modified his goals for achieving it. In time the basilica, too, will be destroyed, and the locomotive, the machine of work, will bring back the human values incarnated in the mythical sleeping cathedral.

Often, as is the case in *Lourdes,* the triumph of one space over another in Zola's work reflects the victory of one character or ideological belief over another. This kind of spatial tension is summarized by the slogan "This will kill that," the concept Hugo's Claude Frollo applied to the victory of the printing press over the cathedral in *Notre-Dame de Paris.* Zola recycled this phrase in his 1872 *Le Ventre de Paris,* the only work of the Rougon-Macquart series to give a prominent role to an existing house of worship, Saint-Eustache. Claude Lantier, a young painter, predicts that modern structures such as Les Halles marketplace will kill old structures such as Saint-Eustache: "This will kill that, iron will kill stone, and the time is near [. . .] Don't you see, it's an entire manifesto: modern art, realism, naturalism, whatever you want to call it, which has grown up opposite old art."[86] In reviving Hugo's concept of the evolution of artistic forms, Zola pronounced naturalism the successor of romanticism while establishing Saint-Eustache as the solid fictional antagonist against which he could oppose his modern agenda: new technology and new ideas such as those evident in Les Halles and its iron construction would replace antiquated Catholic structures and their superstition. "Ceci tuera cela": the new will kill the old; iron will kill stone; the locomotive will return to kill the basilica of Lourdes; the cathedral of the future will kill the Church.

In *Les Trois Villes,* descriptions of Notre-Dame de Lourdes, Saint Peter's, and the Sacré-Coeur summarize the narrative tensions and hint at their outcome. Where he represented the basilica of Lourdes as flaming with gold, an icon of the modern French Church's commercial exploitation of miracles, in *Rome* Zola turned Saint Peter's of Rome into a similarly bejeweled crown, a symbol of the Vatican's sterile, intractable dedication to tradition. The "dominating roundness" of its dome subjects the city to its power: "that dome [. . .] reigning over the city as a giant king that nothing could shake."[87] Yet in spite of its monolithic exterior, the basilica's interior reveals its weakness. It is dying for lack of a soul: "There was the splendid skeleton of a monumental colossus whose life was slipping away. To fill it, to animate it with its true soul, would take all the magnificence of religious ceremony [. . .] sacred luxury in a decor and a staging of formal opera."[88] The church advertizes eternal power, but it must put on displays of empty ritual in order to match its solid image.

The emptiness and lack of worshipers in Saint Peter's strike Pierre. He longs to leave its sterile luxury to return to the simplicity of French cathedrals and the faith they harbor:

> And he, in this deserted opera house lit up with such a blaze of gold and purple, he who was arriving with the shiver of our Gothic cathedrals, dark crowds sobbing among a forest of pillars! He, who was carrying the sorrowful memory of emaciated medieval architecture and statuary—all soul—in the middle of this ceremonial majesty, this enormous and empty pomp and circumstance that was all body![89]

Zola's juxtaposition of Saint Peter's powerful soul with the empty but imposing body of the Roman church foreshadows the defeat of the Vatican that concludes the novel.

The battle between the regal corporeality of Saint Peter's and the popular spirituality of the Gothic church also provides a concrete image that encapsulates the narrative conflict. Although his enthusiasm for the blind faith of the past was dampened in *Lourdes,* in *Rome* Pierre has great hopes for what he calls a socialist or democratic Catholicism that will revive the soul of the Church. After his experiences in Lourdes, he has written a book called *La Rome nouvelle,* a kind of Lamennaisian work in which he appeals to the Pope to adapt Catholicism to the modern world by focusing on democracy and the plight of the poor. The narrator describes the book in the first chapter of *Rome:* it is divided into three parts, corresponding to Pierre's three visions of Rome—past, present, and future. Pierre's thesis states that every religious change results from economic tensions as the poor revolt against the rich, thereby destroying the old religion in favor of a new one. Christianity, he writes, was essentially a democracy— "a democracy, a socialism, a struggle against Roman society."[90] Since Christ, however, Pierre argues that Roman Catholicism has grown into the tyrant the primitive Christians wanted to overthrow. New rebellions are growing among the poor, who are ignored by modern Catholicism. In order to repair these inequalities, Pierre suggests that the Church renew itself by embracing socialism and democracy, by going back to its primitive evangelical roots.

Pierre's book has been condemned as seditious by the Index, the congregation that censors books for the Vatican, so Pierre has come to Rome to convince Pope Leo XIII (1878–1903) of the importance and feasibility of his projects. He has great confidence in this Pope, whose *Rerum novarum* (1891) was the first encyclical treating the economic conditions of the working poor. Pierre imagines him as a new messiah who will descend from his throne to lead the masses along the path to fraternity, thus beginning the new Catholic order that Pierre describes in the third part of *La Rome nouvelle.*

In his book, Pierre describes a world that echoes his earlier dream of a primitive, happy, harmonious society sheltered by cathedrals, but, once again, he displaces it into the future. According to his predictions, secular and religious societies will return to the wonder of a forgotten Golden Age of Christianity:

> [. . .] rejuvenated Catholicism, bringing to dying nations health and peace, the forgotten golden age of primitive Christianity [. . .] civil and religious society would overlap so perfectly that they would be one; and it would be the age of triumph and happiness predicted by all of the prophets, no more struggles possible, no more antagonism between body and soul, a marvelous equilibrium that would kill evil, that would put the kingdom of Heaven on earth. The new Rome, center of the world, giving the world the new religion.[91]

The themes that emerge from Pierre's vision of a reformed Catholic world—the perfect blending of secular and religious factions of society, a lack of arguments, and the resolution of troubles between body and soul—provide a synthesis to the major troubles ravaging Zola's time. This utopia, like Pierre's dream of the cathedral, is based on faith, harmony, and happiness.

In *Rome,* however, Pierre's hopes are for nought. Although he attempts to gain an audience with a number of people who can plead his case, the Vatican cares only about dominating politics, making money, and regaining the papal states. Pierre witnesses murders and intrigue as rival factions attempt to gain control of power. Even the friends he meets in Rome, star-crossed lovers, die as a result of their families' powerful role in Roman society. When he finally sees the Pope, Pierre realizes that he is just "another Caesar" in his determination to reign.[92] His reluctance to change squelches Pierre's hope of achieving social harmony through the Church. There will be no "new Rome" in Rome, because it has returned to the tyranny of the Roman Empire as it was in the days of primitive Christianity. In his bitterness, Pierre believes that only revolution can triumph over it now as it did in the early years of Christianity.[93]

Furious at his abortive trip to Rome, Pierre has a nocturnal vision of a future in which Saint Peter's is destroyed: "And he imagined that the time had come, that truth had just blown up the dome of Saint Peter's."[94] Like Father Peyramale's cathedral in Lourdes, killed by the basilica, in Pierre's vision all that remains of Saint Peter's are fragments lying in the grass. But where the cathedral in Lourdes was killed by its own religion, Catholicism, Saint Peter's will be vanquished by the truth, an aspect of the Christian doctrine it neglected to uphold. As his anger calms, Pierre's reason takes over. He has great faith in humanity's ability to form communities that work for the good of mankind. Eventually, he knows he will achieve the goals of his *Rome nouvelle,* his utopian "cathedral of the future world"— "Ah! this unique homeland, the earth pacified and happy, in how many centuries and what a dream!"—but he will not do it through Catholicism.[95] In Zola's novel, modern Catholicism has killed the religious principles on which it was based. Pierre's confidence has shifted to human values: truth will return to triumph over Catholicism.

The importance readers attached to Zola's portrayal of space can be gauged by his publisher's decision to advertise *Paris* with a Steinlen poster of the Sacré-Coeur (Figure 2.4). The basilica lies at the center of the poster, high above Paris, while workers mobilize in the foreground. To the left, an allegorical female figure representing Truth, Liberty, or perhaps Paris itself, gesticulates at the basilica from a distance. Zola placed the church at the center of his novel, which is set in Montmartre. Every event takes place under its watchful eye. The domed Sacré-Coeur emerges from the pages of *Paris* as an evil fleur-de-lis, the modern incarnation of the French monarchy and its oppression. The elements on which Zola focuses— its size, its obstinacy, and its royalty—transform the basilica into the symbol of

Figure 2.4. Théophile-Alexandre Steinlen. *Paris*, 1898. Lithograph. Jane Voorhees Zimmerli Art Museum. Rutgers, The State University of New Jersey. Norma B. Bartman Purchase Fund. Photo by Jack Abraham. 85.110.016.

every negative force in the city.[96] In the novel, Pierre sees the basilica at daybreak, as it emerges from shadows; it gloats in its victory over the sleeping city it dominates, much as the basilica of Lourdes had triumphed over the ruined cathedral in *Lourdes:* "It was no longer a lunar apparition, the dream of domination, set against the nocturnal Paris. The sun bathed it in a splendor, it was golden and proud, and victorious, blazing with immortal glory."[97] Like Notre-Dame de Lourdes and Saint Peter's, the Sacré-Coeur conquers the city with the ostentation of its physical presence. In accordance with Victor Hugo's theories about form and function, these domed structures are testaments to the oppressive theocracy that constructed them. They demand to be overthrown.

The Sacré-Coeur encapsulates Pierre's frustrating encounters with the Parisian clergy. His experiences in Lourdes and Rome have disillusioned Pierre about Catholicism's ability to practice faith and hope, two of the principle Christian virtues. In *Paris,* however, he realizes that the Church no longer values charity, the third virtue, either. Pierre says mass at the Sacré-Coeur, and works with people in extreme misery, helping clothe and feed them. Pierre's friend, the kindly and destitute Father Rose, gives everything to them, thereby embarrassing the Church leaders: like a medieval saint he parts with all of his material possessions including his clothes. Pierre attempts to solicit money from bourgeois parishioners to support the needy, but is frustrated by the false charity of the Church leaders and their congregations, who are too occupied by political conquest and by building the Sacré-Coeur basilica to care for the impoverished. As in Rome, he finds that the basic Christian virtues no longer seem to motivate Catholicism: "The Gospel has aborted for nearly two thousand years now. Jesus atoned for nothing, humanity's suffering has remained just as great, just as unjust."[98] Pierre finally renounces Catholicism and leaves the Church to dedicate himself to his family and scientific work.

His struggles between religion and science in *Paris* take place against the backdrop of the anarchist bombings that plagued the city in 1892–1894. Because they have been kept in poverty by the rich upper classes, the workers in Zola's novel have become desperate and believe that they can achieve social reform through violence. The Sacré-Coeur becomes the symbol of this conflict. Pierre's brother, Guillaume—a chemist who has discovered a new kind of powerful explosive—is so fed up with society's inequalities that he has decided to blow up the Sacré-Coeur during a pilgrimage. In a suspenseful scene in a cavern under the church, Zola depicts the confrontation between brothers as Guillaume discovers that Pierre has followed him. Zola alternates between the brothers' arguments, the physical struggle over the explosives, and descriptions of religious ceremonies taking place in the church above. Although Guillaume has hit him in the head with a brick, Pierre is able to prevent his brother from lighting the bomb's fuse. Guillaume's horror at spilling his brother's blood puts an end to his violent plan and converts him to Pierre's newfound belief in the power of science to reform humanity peacefully.

Guillaume thus changes his mind, and uses his explosive to build a motor dedicated to improving mankind. The bloodshed under the Sacré-Coeur is the sacrifice that will bring redemption to the family and to humanity: it is the sacred act that brings the brothers together and sanctifies the new religion of science that Pierre has begun envisioning.

The Novel as Cathedral

Les Trois Villes chronicles Pierre's spiritual education; the reader follows him from one symbolic capital of nineteenth-century Catholicism to another, as he loses his ideals and discovers new beliefs. In addition to this primary plot, the novel contains a profusion of captivating secondary plots. But as one reviewer pointed out, they are poorly constructed and more or less interchangeable. The love stories, political intrigues, and mysteries—the stuff of most nineteenth-century novels—are only there "to keep the reader's curiosity in suspense" and to sell books. "The real subject of Paris is the 'dechristianization' of Father Pierre Froment."[99] Indeed, Pierre does little but debate historical, political, or theological issues. Unlike the Rougon-Macquart novels, in which plot tended to center on human impulses—characters driven by lust, greed, ambition, or guilt—*Les Trois Villes* focuses on process: the reader follows Pierre as he observes society from the outside, collecting and interpreting information about it. As he travels from one holy site to another, as a pilgrim might have traveled from one cathedral to another in the Middle Ages, he completes his education about the world. Each location and each group of people provide models—*exempla*—that destroy his belief in Catholicism, while leading him to formulate a new religion. In fact, the plot of the three novels is less about the "dechristianization" of Pierre than about his "rechristianization." With *Les Trois Villes*, Zola creates a new kind of novel in which descriptions are best interpreted as figures, like the statuary and stained glass of a cathedral. *Les Trois Villes* requires a discerning reader who can put aside concerns about realism in order to explore Pierre's visions.

The preponderance of descriptive passages (like those evoking churches and cathedrals), long didactic segments about contemporary politics or religion, coupled with the multiplicity of subplots, caused great discomfort for most of Zola's readers, who did not enjoy the books and who struggled to interpret them. They remarked on the disparity between Pierre's investigation of the minute details of contemporary sociology and the powerful imagery of his descriptions. Albert Giraud, a critic for *La Jeune Belgique,* lambasted *Rome* for containing three books in one: "The romance novel could be by Mr. George Ohnet, the mystery novel by Eugène Sue, and the study of Roman politics seems to be the response of M. Homais to Mr. Melchior de Vogüé."[100] Zola's use of his novel to spread his message about repairing society puzzled Giraud and other readers. Did Zola mean to favor the fictional aspects of his novel—the love story and the political intrigue—or was the book really a poorly composed journalistic inquiry into the problems of fin-de-siècle France? The combination of fiction and ideology turned these books—each of which surpassed 600 pages—into novels that, despite their focus on documentation, cannot be read successfully as one would a traditional plot-driven novel.

The difficulty with which one reads *Les Trois Villes* today (as then), stems largely from the didactic impulse—evident in Pierre's proselytizing—and also in the lengthy and highly charged descriptions of people and places. Zola wanted to improve society; his reformist and evangelistic tendency is pronounced both in his titles—*Les Trois Villes* and *Les Quatre Evangiles*—and in interviews and correspondence in which he insists on the social importance of the novelist, who must be a prophet, "building hypotheses about the future."[101] Given such insistence on transmitting a message about improving society, Clive Thomson has suggested that the *Trois Villes* are "romans à thèse." David Baguley has gone even further, proposing that *Les Trois Villes* are allegories. Allegories, he argues, are akin to "romans à thèse," yet they differ in their reliance on multiple layers of signification.[102]

Zola's tendency to create allegory is manifest in *Les Trois Villes*. Although each novel contains a profusion of characters, social and professional milieus, subplots, and ideology, Zola subordinates this information to Pierre's point of view. And Pierre tends to see social conflict in terms of symbolic figures. He envisions Notre-Dame de Lourdes, Saint Peter's, and the Sacré-Coeur as mythological monsters— "L'Ennemi!"—that fight against the good spaces of his dreams: the abandoned church of Abbé Peyramale; the idealized Gothic cathedral; and Paris, the city of light. Pierre replaces the scientific, sociological, or theological discourse he has heard in his travels with figures that represent their conflicts. In *Les Trois Villes*, the battles for the future of mankind do not occur among people who argue about science and religion. They are waged through Pierre's nightmarish visions of combat in which the positive space of his dreams triumphs over the evil spaces challenging it. Zola's focus on Pierre's Manichean vision of the world creates a system in which each step of Pierre's spiritual quest is accompanied by allegorical figures that incarnate the struggles he witnesses.

Zola carefully planned such conflicts. We have seen how he structured his descriptions of churches to provide a visual summary of the narrative tensions between religion and science; he did the same thing for characters, developing them according to their relationship to Pierre's beliefs. In *Lourdes*, good characters—Father Peyramale, for one—combat the evil frères de la Grotte. In *Rome*, virtuous families ("les blancs") support the Italian government instead of becoming embroiled in the murder and intrigue of those who support the Vatican ("les noirs"). Each character and event in Rome can be read in terms of Pierre's book and its thesis: "The mother and the daughter give me Roman society. With the husband I can have the other city, the Quirinal. This will oppose the two worlds."[103] In

Paris, Zola pits the workers' belief in democracy against the Catholic bourgeoisie's interest in preserving the status quo. Every element in the series provides a moral lesson for Zola's readers: the characters, spaces, and activities in *Les Trois Villes* are either for or against Pierre's values. Although its length, profusion of characters and subplots, and mass of documentation gives the impression of a "botched composition," Pierre is the central figure whose beliefs in the future structure and elucidate the world around him. The books were constructed for the purposes of illustrating and explaining the central values behind Zola's dream of social harmony.

The insistence on portraying good and bad behavior resembles the didactic impulse latent in the symbolism of the Gothic cathedral. In fact, as David Baguley suggests, the problematic structure of *Les Trois Villes* holds together when interpreted on an allegorical level: the pilgrimage motif, the symbols Pierre interprets, the *psychomachia* between science and faith, and Zola's use of biblical imagery and names link these novels to the structure and themes of a work such as Bunyan's *Pilgrim's Progress.*[104] While Baguley proposes *Pilgrim's Progress* as a model, Zola was probably much more familiar with French models of medieval allegory. He knew *The Golden Legend;* he owned an illustrated fifteenth-century breviary; and he studied Gothic cathedrals.

From Hugo, he knew that the cathedral was a stone book: "Each stone of this venerable monument is a not only a page of the history of the country, but also of the history of science and art."[105] Zola believed in the educational role of the cathedral, instrument of moral instruction. This is particularly clear in *Le Rêve,* where l'église Sainte-Marie is a mother, friend, teacher, and illustrated Bible, Angélique's source of knowledge of the world and of human behavior. On the first page of the novel, as Angélique takes shelter from the snow under a statue of Saint Agnes, she sees the story of the saint told in the cathedral's sculptures: "And, in the tympanum, above the lintel, in high relief and with a naive faith, we find the entire legend of the child virgin engaged to Jesus."[106] Later, she discovers similar images in a 1549 edition of *The Golden Legend.* Curious to understand the full extent of the figures, she learns to understand the Gothic script and medieval abbreviations of the book, which teach her about the vices and virtues exemplified by the characters she has seen. She uses this newfound knowledge to decipher the stories figured in the cathedral. As a result, she modifies her bad natural disposition by emulating the virtuous behavior of the saints whose lives she admires.

Zola understood the cathedral as a book and appreciated its ability to instruct by example. As a young writer, he had argued that the novel should strive to improve peoples' behavior: "The novel does not have painting as its only purpose; it must also correct." He added that it was more important to give people examples of ideal behavior than to criticize them: "I believe that it is not in brutally revealing his evil to a man that one heals him, but, on the contrary, in making him see the happiness he would taste if he had followed the right path."[107] Medieval theologians transmitted their didactic goals to groups of sculptors and artists in order to influence the masses that would come to the cathedral. Zola, too, painted Pierre's positive dreams—the harmonious life of medieval Christians gathered around the cathedral, the peaceful future world of a "Rome nouvelle," or the community contemplating a golden future—as a way of improving society. He wanted his readers to imitate the virtuous human values of his new religion and to recoil from vice.

Angélique sees sculptural representations of stories in the cathedral before understanding their underlying moral values and Zola must have hoped that the readers of *Les Trois Villes* would learn to interpret the virtues and vices represented in his books. Zola portrays Notre-Dame de Lourdes, Saint Peter's of Rome, and the Sacré-Coeur of Paris as triumphant, bejeweled crowns that oppress their respective cities, but it is not until Pierre explores the cities themselves and questions dozens of people from all social classes and professions that the reader understands the full import of Zola's opulent, tyrannical representation of churches. Pierre's commentary about the events and people he encounters in Lourdes, Rome, and Paris explains the tensions between religion and science that figure implicitly in descriptions of religious architecture. In Lourdes, greed triumphs over faith; in Rome politics destroy Pierre's hope of social reform; and in Paris self-interest undermines charitable contributions.

In the end, Zola's "tormented, disturbing, and deformed"[108] *Trois Villes* series can be more effectively read in allegorical terms than as a plot-driven novel. Early nineteenth-century thinkers had similarly categorized the Gothic cathedral as "sickly," "spindly," or "lame" because of the seeming inconsistencies and fantasies of its structure. In *Les Trois Villes* Zola's descriptions create set pieces that seem realistic, but that really function as *exempla,* the equivalent to the cathedral's sculpture and stained-glass representations of good and bad behavior. We follow Pierre, whom Zola called a saint, much as Angélique follows the stories of the saints displayed in the tympanum of the cathedral of Beaumont-l'Eglise.[109] He is a Christ-like figure who has shed his blood for his new religion, after completing his pilgrimages to Lourdes, Rome, and Paris. We see him struggle with both virtue and vice as he attempts to find the faith that will allow him to build his own church. Each character he meets as he explores modern Catholicism takes his or her place in Zola's cathedral–novel. Martyred saints—Father Peyramale in *Lourdes,* the primitive Christians in *Rome,* and l'abbé Rose and the anarchists in *Paris*—occupy one wall; while Saint-Simon, Fourier, and Comte—the prophets of Pierre's new religion—are on another. Vices and virtues, from the evil frères de la Grotte in *Lourdes* and the Pope in *Rome* to abbé Rose of *Paris* also line the portals of Zola's edifice. A cathedral's sculpture often represents historical and biblical figures such as Aristotle or King David and *Les Trois Villes* has its equivalent: the Caesars and Christ himself. Zola includes descriptions of Nature, portraits of people from all walks of life and all professions, and stories of Pierre's life, much as a Gothic cathedral contains the astrological symbols, the seven Grammatical arts, and representations of Christ's life. Firmly anchored on the royal portal, announcing the new religion to all who will listen, is Pierre Froment.

Zola's Human Scriptures

It is only in *Paris,* at the very end of nearly 2,000 pages, that Pierre finally realizes that his dream of faith, truth, justice, fraternity, and peace cannot exist within the framework of modern Catholicism. He finds a modern example of his ideal religion—the faith he formerly imagined as taking place in the shadow of medieval cathedrals—by watching the simple secular life of his brother's family: "this life of unremitting work, of peaceful tenderness, in the modest little house where the strictest economy regulated expenses and satisfied needs."[110] Guillaume lives happily with his three sons (a mechanic, an engineer, and an artist), his mother-in-law, and Marie, the daughter of one of Guillaume's inventor friends. Although he had glimpsed work as a way of activating the human values latent in the "Sleeping Beauty Church" in *Lourdes,* it is only after his failures in Lourdes and Rome that Pierre realizes that manual labor will allow him to reconcile both religion and science. This discovery heals his soul by resolving his conflicts between intelligence and passion: "And what peace to have reconciled them, to have satisfied them together, to feel complete, normal, and powerful."[111] The end of the novel portrays a character, who, finally at terms with his own psychological struggle, is capable of providing an ideal for mankind.

Zola borrowed the popular fin-de-siècle image of the cathedral—a reflection of Chateaubriand's harmonious primitive Christians gathered in the forest—yet progressively emptied it of Catholic associations and refilled it with the "religion of science," a faith that blends the doctrines of Catholicism with those from the secular nineteenth-century "religions" of Saint-Simon, Fourier, Comte, and Proudhon.[112] Pierre formulates the principles of his belief by choosing values common to all religions: the defense of the poor, the equitable sharing of resources, the need for happiness.[113] This does not seem strange to Pierre, because his understanding of religion is rational; he believes that all of these different faiths, including Catholicism, share the same goal: "Like all religions, it is at heart only one explanation of the world, a superior social and political code destined to make peace and all possible happiness reign on earth. From that moment on, this code, which embraces the universality of things, becomes human, mortal, like things human."[114] Although he has been accused of being the most "antireligious" writer since Hugo, Zola admired religion, and like Michelet or Vico he felt that it was a central aspect of society, an eternal sentiment that ordered society.[115] In the great nineteenth-century tradition, Zola thus advocated a secular religion dedicated to human values. By the end of *Paris,* Pierre has discovered that all humanity—from Catholics to anarchists to social philosophers—share the same dream. Though it would seem contradictory, there was no fundamental difference for Zola between the most basic of Christian values and the goals of "the immense cathedral of the future world," the ideal community to be attained by secular workers. Both were dedicated to bettering humanity.[116]

Like Saint Peter, his namesake, the rock on which Jesus founded his Church, Pierre is the cornerstone of Zola's "cathedral of the future." A prophet (or saint), he foretells a time in which science will have created a Golden Age. And Pierre does not simply dream of the future; he is a writer, one of the few in Zola's works, who paints the world to come with his exuberant language. He resembles Pascal Rougon, the "benedictine of science" featured in the last novel of the Rougon-Macquart series, who calls his faith in science his "Credo."[117] But in the tradition of prophecy, Pierre also tells the future without revealing the practical details necessary to its accomplishment. He chants the magic words of his faith—peace, knowledge, religion, desire, and justice—without giving further instruction.[118] The enthusiasm conveyed by exclamation points, verbs in the future tense, and the peaceful vision of the Earthly paradise that will take over the world is almost enough to inspire confidence in the truth of such a vision:

> A religion of science is the marked, certain, inevitable outcome of humanity's long march toward consciousness. The latter will arrive as if in a natural port, peace finally placed in certainty when it will have passed through all ignorance and fear [. . .] We always forget that Catholicism took four centuries to establish itself, to germinate in a long underground battle before growing and reigning in the sun. Let us thus give centuries to this religion of science, whose silent growth announces itself everywhere, and we will see the admirable ideas of Fourier constituted in a new gospel—desire will have become the lever that lifts the world, work accepted by all, honored, regulated as the very mechanism of natural and social life, the passionate energies of man excited, contented, used—finally—for human happiness! [. . .] The universal cry of justice [. . .] is only a cry for this happiness to which we aspire. The time will come when this kingdom of God will be on earth and when the other false paradise will be closed, even if the feeble-minded must suffer, for a moment, the death of their illusion, because it is a courageous necessity to operate cruelly on the blind in order to drag them from their misery, from the long and awful night of their ignorance![119]

The religion of science will evolve slowly as an enlightened populace replaces the Catholic heaven with a harmonious heaven on Earth. This positive vision summarizes nearly all of the positive social theories in Zola's works, notably the prophetic scene of human growth that closes *Germinal.* His novels portray society's sickness, yet they also propose an alternative.

Pierre's new religion, however, is sadly lacking in detail. He knows that it will be accompanied by justice and truth and that it will reactivate what he calls the primary virtues of Christianity—faith, hope, and charity. Yet he leaves the particulars to the four generations it will take to establish the "new Jerusalem," this "dream of a single people." Here, as elsewhere, Zola's attempts to propose a social ideal through literature fall into the realm of utopia. But after all, a novelist is not a social scientist. Should we really expect Zola to provide a functional model of social change? Did he ever intend his "religion of science" as a social manifesto?

Zola believed in the novelist as a prophet and felt that painting a positive vision of the future—like l'abbé Peyramale's vision of the cathedral that gets him through hard times—could help contemporaries. I would argue that although Zola believed that he was contributing to society by writing optimistic novels that gave society a "new vision," he did not necessarily believe that the social philosophies he espoused were feasible. He was more concerned with trying to inspire his contemporaries with an "ideal," a way to break out of their "degeneration," than with writing a practical manifesto for social change.

In fact, his notes to *Les Trois Villes* reveal that Zola wanted to portray the future as a "new Jerusalem"— "the hosannah, the United States of Europe, the dream of a single people [. . .] the ideal city, the powerful architecture"—a social utopia that echoes Pluchart's cathedral of the future.[120] Zola's use of the idealized architectural image to evoke the future is a technique common to many writers of utopian fiction. Using familiar images—a city, a cathedral—appeals to readers by encouraging them to respond intellectually to a vision of the future while reacting emotionally to memories from the past.[121] Zola uses a well-known sacred ideal to achieve his secular goals: his dream of building a new Jerusalem taps into an age-old tradition of evoking social and religious harmony. Walter Benjamin has suggested that relying on names or images from the past serves as a way for society to develop positive myths about science. Attaching old myths of social harmony to the new gave power to modern discoveries; such idealized "wish images" could inspire people to achieve the scientific goals promised by the dream.[122]

Zola's plan to reactivate his contemporaries' interest in a future driven by science does just this. *Les Trois Villes* series closes with a scene of pastoral bliss. The family, including Pierre and Marie's newborn son, Jean, gathers around the life-giving explosive-driven motor Guillaume and his sons have developed. From the window of the workshop, the secular cathedral where they worship technology, they look down on Paris. Suddenly, the familiar panorama vanishes; it is wiped out by a flood of wheatlike golden sunlight: "Wheat, wheat everywhere, an infinity of wheat whose golden swell rolled from one end of the horizon to the other. And the sun thus bathed all of Paris with an even radiance, and it really was the harvest after the sowing season [. . .] as if there were no longer anything but one earth, reconciled and fraternal."[123] Wheat, the symbol of prosperity latent in Pierre Froment's name, and the analogy John uses for Christ's death and resurrection, predicts the rich harvest of the new religion. Science finally triumphs over the hulk-ing Sacré-Coeur as it frees up the blocked horizon to reveal the fields of yellow wheat that signal a new era, the Golden Age in which work will bring the social harmony Pierre has so desired.[124]

Once Pierre has theorized his religion of the future, he replaces its old ar-chitectural symbol—the cathedral—with a new organic one—fields of golden wheat. The fertile reference wins out as Pierre chooses between the two forces la-tent in his name—Pierre (stone) and Froment (wheat) and nurtures a family. This new symbol, with its insistence on fertility, will come to replace the old ideal of the cathedral, while adopting its positive symbolism (shared faith, democratic labor, and social harmony). It is no coincidence that the last words of the novel bequeath the future to the infant Jean, the new generation who will harvest the wheat.[125] Originally, Zola had intended for him to be the hero of all four *Evangiles*—like Jean Macquart of *La Débâcle* he would be a soldier, but where Jean Macquart was devoted to death (war), Jean Froment was to work for life (disarmament)—but Zola expanded his work to include other "evangelists"—Mathieu, Marc, and Luc. Jean, like his brothers, will help convert the old world to the secular religion of the future. Zola's choice of the name Jean is doubly important given the emphasis he places on creating the "new Jerusalem," since Jean is the witness and the prophet of the Book of Revelations. The scene that ends *Les Trois Villes*, as Jean and his fam-ily look down from the top of Montmartre on the golden harvest of Paris below, echoes Saint John's vision: he, too, is shown the New Jerusalem from the top of a cliff, where he sees the city and its tree of life bathed in a golden filter of brilliant light. Jean Froment, the child who foresees the future and whose name promises him its rich harvests, is linked both to prophet and to Christ child.[126] In fact, the entire Froment family whose symbol is a giant tree, can be read as a secular Tree of Jesse, a stained-glass window representing the genealogy of Christ.[127]

But while these marvelous biblically inspired tableaux ostensibly represent the results of the "religion of science," nothing in the text suggests scientific or tech-nological breakthroughs. The golden age Pierre predicts is, in fact, notable for its lack of science: it is a simple world where fertile people work the land in harmony. In *Les Quatre Evangiles*, where the religion of science is practiced, each novel ends as a family or tightly knit community stands outdoors, in nature, looking out over the horizon toward the future.[128] Science is upstaged, in these scenes, whose ca-maraderie and simplicity evokes the medieval country scenes from *Les Très Riches Heures de Jean, Duc de Berry*, in which villagers sow and reap their wheat while a Gothic church looms in the distance.[129] Zola uses these utopian visions as what Benjamin calls "wish images," to encourage the embrace of science as the path to a better future. The enthusiasm with which Zola describes these scenes, however, also exemplifies his tendency to create messages in his fiction that he did not con-sciously condone.

Messidor and the Golden Cathedral

The confusion between Zola's stated objectives and his fiction is perhaps most striking in *Messidor,* a lyrical drama performed in 1897, in which the destruction of science—represented by the annihilation of a beautiful new machine—makes way for a pastoral scene of wealth represented by golden fields of wheat. Although he did not intend to glorify the violent overthrow of industry for an agricultural utopia, this is what his audience understood.[130] *Messidor,* written at the same time as the *Trois Villes,* epitomizes much of the contradiction between what Zola wanted to do in his novels and what his audience understood. Because there was a great deal of publicity surrounding the play (notably four columns on the front page of *Le Figaro* dedicated to "*Messidor* expliqué par les auteurs"), it provides us with valuable insight into both Zola's goals and audience reactions.[131] Perhaps the most problematic figure of the play is a golden cathedral that clarifies the contradictory symbolic position the cathedral held in his other works. The importance of this figure for the play reveals Zola's true belief in the cathedral as a dangerous vestige of the past, but also as an admirable and legendary figure with the power to lead men to social, religious, and aesthetic harmony.

The play itself takes place in l'Ariège, not far from Lourdes, and although it is not supposed to be set in a time of legend, it is full of folk tales. The most powerful of these is the myth of the golden cathedral. As the curtains rose at the 1897 performance, spectators were dazzled by the set, which represented a natural golden cathedral formed out of a cave. Zola's description of the decor in the libretto is extremely specific: it is the most flamboyant of Gothic cathedrals, with many arches, "flowering" chapels, and a "lacework of stone." Although purely a work of nature, it is still a "nave of dreams" and everything within it is made of gold and full of a bright "supernatural" golden light. At the back of the apse is a giant, yet simple Byzantine statue of the Virgin Mary holding a baby Jesus on her knees. Through his hands run two streams of powdered gold.

"La Légende de l'or," a ballet, served as a prelude to the play. As Zola described it, the Queen (representing the human desire for power and domination) and the Female Lover (representing the human desire for material and carnal possession), vied for the attentions of Gold. Their legions battled each other in a desperate attempt to possess the Gold: "it is the battle, the frenzy for Gold." It is only when Gold tells them that he is not for them, but for charity, goodness, and beauty that the two camps reconcile in a "religious danse of the cult and force of love [. . .] the apotheosis of Gold [. . .] a hosanna in the middle of the dances."[132] The dance's allegory provides a succinct summary of the moral of the play: social dissonance is caused by excessive love of power and money; it can be resolved by charity, goodness, and love. From the beginning, the play fell under the auspices of legend; the powerful myth of the corrupting and beneficial power of gold.[133]

After this spectacular prologue, the spectators found themselves in a much more mundane and realistic country setting, with characters dressed in muddy boots; they were thrust back into contemporary life. Véronique, the mother, explains the myth of gold right away: the country is in a time of terrible trouble caused by drought and poverty, but in the past everyone in the village was rich because the river flowed with gold, which was free for all to enjoy. The gold, she believes, comes from a golden cathedral (the one seen in the prologue), which is hidden deep in the hills. In the cathedral reigns a baby Jesus who turns sand to gold. If ever a human finds this sacred spot, however, the gold will vanish. As inferred by the prologue, the play's plot centers around issues of jealousy, greed, and social injustice. The gold no longer flows freely because Gervais, a former friend, has created a machine that collects it.

The characters in *Messidor* are transparent (one critique remarked that "All is symbol") and Zola freely admitted this in *Le Figaro:* "Symbols, here, are of such clarity that children will understand them." Véronique, with her vision of the golden cathedral, represents, for Zola, the "antiquated faith" that is waiting to be replaced by the "new faith," while her son, Guillaume, who prefigures the scientist Guillaume of *Paris* in his struggle between anarchy and social harmony, incarnates the "triumph" of work and fecundity. Their cousin, Mathias, who comes back to the community after a long absence, is an anarchist— "the destroyer"— who convinces the townsfolk to rise in revolt and to destroy the gold-collecting machine. Gervais, the rich industrialist, epitomizes unjust capitalist practices, and his daughter, Hélène, will "people" the future world with Guillaume. Continuing his explanation of the opera's symbolism, Zola labels a shepherd who comes down from the hills a prophetic figure.[134] The play is a kind of *psychomachia,* in which each of the various character-values clash.

Zola's symbolic meaning seems transparent until the culminating point of the play in which the machine—the ostensible cause of the social conflict—is destroyed. Although Zola insisted that he had intended nature—in the form of a giant storm and avalanche—to crush the factory, he creates a great deal of ambiguity as to the responsible party. Two other interpretations are equally valid: first, just as the storm arrives, the anarchists congregate at the machine to destroy it; second, Véronique enters, saying that she has found the golden cathedral and her discovery will trigger the destruction of the gold. Following the allegorical system Zola had established earlier in the play, it was only natural that the audience would have interpreted the storm as yet another symbol. When a critic proposed that the sight of the golden cathedral precipitated the demise of the machine, Zola protested: "How can you not have seen that, in the symbol of *Messidor,* the only believer, Véronique, is there to tell about the death of the old legend?" He insists that only Véronique saw it, that it is not a real story, but that she interprets it through her superstition. He confirms that the avalanche destroyed the machine.[135] Zola vociferously dismissed the cathedral as a legend ("a room of dreams," "a hallucination of [Véronique's] faith"), yet as Jean-Max Guieu has pointed out, representing it on stage convinced spectators of its validity. They actually saw it, so how could it be legendary?[136] This is a prime example of the ways in which Zola's enthusiasm for representation—a dazzling set or a glorious description in a novel—often undercut his overtly stated goals.[137]

The end of the play, which parallels the conclusions of *Paris* and *Les Quatre Evangiles,* also leaves the reader confused. The avalanche redistributes wealth as it has caused the river to run underground, thus bringing a golden harvest of wheat and returning the country to the time of the golden cathedral, before the gold was tapped by a single man.[138] This ending repeats, nearly verbatim, the end of *Paris,* which was written at the same time (1897). As in *Paris,* the fields of golden wheat have replaced both the golden cathedral and the factory. Once again, Zola takes one value system and calques it on the other. The new fields of wheat, though in another form, reactivate the positive values he had originally placed in the uncorrupted golden cathedral of the prologue. If man can avoid putting himself and his desires (generally the seven deadly sins) before others, gold can be a positive force that brings all groups of society together to do "the religious danse of the cult and force of love [. . .]." Zola's opera portrays gold as a destructive value when minted, and a charitable and enriching vision when used organically, to help mankind.

This equation could be applied to Catholicism: bad when used for power and money; good when applied to humans. As if to insist on Catholicism's potential for social harmony, Zola concluded the opera by paralleling a Catholic ceremony—the procession of Rogations—with a secular celebration of work. The final scene depicts the entire community marching through the fields, repeating the Litany of the Saints in Latin as priests bless the fields. Alternated with the lyrics—*Ut fructus terrae dare et conservare digneris, te rogamus, audi nos*—the town residents celebrate the secular "holiday of work." In addition, Zola gives the Church the last word—*Et clamor meus ad te veniat* ("and let my cry come unto Thee")—a prayer of supplication. The insistence on Catholic tradition, in a play in which religion has been virtually absent, and by an author who generally condemns such "antique traditions," adds a confusing element to the play and paradoxically seems to approve the Catholicism it had dismissed as legend.

In reality, Zola does praise Catholicism, but only a specific type: the "primitive Christianity" of the Middle Ages. Rogations is one of the most simple and rural of the Catholic feast days and it is also one of the oldest; its tradition dates from the fifth and sixth centuries. Its ritual—blessing the land—probably evolved from Roman or pagan traditions. By incorporating this scene into the conclusion of his play, Zola once again draws a parallel between "pure" or "primitive" early medieval Catholic practices and the positive practices of the future. This unconscious tendency seems to be confirmed by his description of the scene in *"Messidor* expliqué par les auteurs."* He makes no reference to the highly Catholic nature of the conclusion. Instead, he focuses on the future: "All sing the victory of work and love, the hosanna to life, to the future harvest of fraternity and peace."[139]

How then should one interpret the golden cathedral? Is it, as Zola says, that we should dismiss it as Véronique's "antique faith"? He overtly rejects the cathedral as a representative of the old, superstitious system, but if he truly believes what he says then why does he give it such a large role, lavishing detail on his stage directions? Why does he invest it with positive values—the baby Jesus turning sand to gold in order to improve the plight of man—if he truly dismisses the cathedral? And why would he conclude the play by returning to a positive Catholic setting that mirrors the benevolent scene that opens the play?

First of all, the golden cathedral reflects Zola's tendency to say one thing while describing another. As in *Le Rêve,* he wanted to criticize the superstition he felt the cathedral represented, yet he was so attracted to the architectural and artistic grandeur of Gothic architecture that he could not resist devoting long descriptive passages to it. Such enthusiastic admiration of the cathedral undercuts his criticism because he explicitly shows that the cathedral (and the Church for that matter) is good in and of itself; it is human greed that corrupts its social harmony. Second, although Zola intended the cathedral in *Messidor* as a legend (as he did l'église Sainte-Marie in *Le Rêve*), the sheer physical presence of the church transforms it into a real structure. The cathedral is so visible and so powerful a force that one cannot imagine it as legend, especially as it is drawn into the realistic representation of the rest of the production. For it to be a legend everything would have to have been set in another time. Critics noticed this friction between realism and symbolism in his critique of *Messidor,* and insisted that it was necessary to set such allegorical subjects in a time of "history or legend, distant in time or space."[140]

The clash between realism and allegory is one of the major problems readers experienced with the *Les Trois Villes.* While *Le Rêve* was allegedly set in a contemporary time, it was really a kind of fairy tale in which characters acted as if they were from the Middle Ages. There was thus little conflict between legend and reality. In *Les Trois Villes,* however, the realism is ever constant because of the specific setting: Lourdes, Rome, Paris. Such geographical and thematic specificity conflicts with Zola's allegorical descriptions. David Baguley has argued that allegory—multiple readings of an image or idea—is inherently incompatible with realist narrative (which insists that what one sees is what one gets). Much of the reader's discomfort in *Les Trois Villes* comes as Zola puts accounts of history, politics, and religion into the service of Pierre's theories. Because political and religious characters (Pope Leo XIII), churches in Lourdes, Rome, and Paris, and recent historical events (Italian independence, anarchist bombings, Panama Affair scandal) were well known to the reader, Pierre had to gloss, describe, and manipulate constantly in order to make them conform to his allegorical vision of good and evil. His persistent intervention and commentary clash with real events, which speak for themselves.

Baguley suggests that the protagonist of allegorical texts, who returns constantly and obsessively to his message, causes "the discomfort of the reader." He cites Northrop Frye, who argues that "the commenting critic is often prejudiced against allegory without knowing the real reason, which is that continuous allegory prescribes the direction of his commentary, and so restricts its freedom."[141] At odds with a character who constantly interprets signs for us, we balk at *Les Trois Villes* without explicitly recognizing the elements of the story that cause us discomfort. Unlike Zola's earlier naturalist works, where milieu forms characters, in *Les Trois Villes* a single character, Pierre, forms milieu and characters in accordance with his apocalyptic visions. These tensions between allegory and naturalism are precisely the elements that make reading *Les Trois Villes* so unfulfilling.

Indeed, Pierre's constant interpretation of signs ends by subverting even the allegorical elements. *Les Trois Villes* are what Frye would call a "naive allegory," in which images are simply "disguised ideas," and, as he says, the text is "so eager to make its points that it has no real literary or hypothetical center." The insistence Zola places, both in preparatory notes and in Pierre's commentary, on reading images and characters as direct transpositions of the ideas he is making, brings the text closer to a history of ideas than to a work of fiction. As naive allegory the message overcomes the books' literary core and calls into question its generic status. This is why the Rougon-Macquart series is so much more interesting: the novels have relatively simple plots, a manageable cast of characters, and a wealth of description. Readers derive their own conclusions from the books.

Luckily for Zola, however, he was already a celebrity; the novelty of his subject matter was enough to turn these books into best-sellers. *Les Trois Villes,* which were serialized then printed in book form, were a huge popular success, thanks largely to the immediacy of their subject matter and to aggressive marketing. The publicity surrounding Zola and his trips to Lourdes and Rome spawned gossip that he had embraced Catholicism,[142] while each novel created huge public debate about contemporary religion.[143] Though the public was confused by these books, they felt that Zola had given society an ideal. Even Maurice Barrès, who was not prone to complimenting Zola, praised *Lourdes* as "beautiful" because of its positive affirmation of work, family, and social harmony.[144] Huysmans, too, grudgingly praised *Lourdes* for its innovation.

> Since the collapse of naturalism, there has been, I must admit, confusion—and truly, so mediocre, such stupid ideas, that it may be that the *Lourdes* of Zola may very well be the only book that has come out in a long time [. . .] It is written with a coarse art of illumination, but it is still far superior to the little grey turds painted by Bourget and Barrès. It is sad to say, but nevertheless the truth.[145]

In a time when description was increasingly subordinated to a straightforward exploration of psychology and ideology in the works of writers like Bourget and Barrès, Zola's continued focus on literary tableaux and myth gives power to his works.

In calling it a "coarse art of illumination," Huysmans linked Zola's work to illuminated manuscripts and to the religious art of the medieval "primitives" he and the symbolist painters so admired. He hints at the allegory that underlies Zola's late novels.

Zola's Legacy

Despite the problems with these novels, Zola's formal and thematic experimentation did ultimately invigorate the novel. His decision to portray a priest pulled between faith and science was a new literary type that would inspire Catholic writers Mauriac and Bernanos. Zola's focus on pilgrimages was similarly innovative: *Lourdes* was the first French novel to treat the nineteenth-century passion for miracles, and it inspired a number of imitators as well as a huge influx of pilgrim-tourists who carried his novel as a guidebook.[146] His descriptions of churches drew people to Lourdes, where they compared l'abbé Peyramale's "sleeping beauty church" to the basilica of Lourdes.[147] His depiction of the ways in which an idealistic single character perceives contemporary history also deeply influenced novelists Roger Martin du Gard and Jules Romains, whose multivolume post–World War I novel series *Les Thibault* and *Les Hommes de bonne volonté*, respectively, combined a realist exploration of contemporary society with their characters' secularized religious visions for the future. During a time that universally proclaimed the death of the novel, Zola's hybrid mixture of realism, psychology, symbolism, sociology, idealism, travel guide, and sketchbook puzzled his readers and fascinated them.

Zola's works also fueled two very different kinds of interest in the Gothic cathedral: a mystical legendary cathedral of dreams and a secular ideal of the cathedral as a model for grand scientific and social accomplishments. Although Zola's theoretical writings insist on the importance of getting rid of the old to make way for the new, his fiction reveals his profound attraction to cathedrals, to which he responded emotionally. His heart, nourished by an amalgam of ideas from earlier thinkers—Chateaubriand, Hugo, Viollet-le-Duc, Michelet—could not abandon them as he built his own concept of the cathedral. His descriptions thus caress the cathedral and turn it into a protective communal shelter, a brilliant artistic and engineering marvel, and an elaborately significant stone book. Jean Lorrain identified Zola as one of the first to inspire the "mystical" revival of the 1890s—with *Le Rêve*—and attributed the profusion of sketches and homages in magazines to Zola's enthusiastic portrayal of the l'église Sainte-Marie.[148] "Le Veilleur Publique," a "medieval ballad" by Jacques Yveil with artwork by Henri Pille (Figure 2.3) is the perfect illustration of Zola's influence. Published during the serialization of *Le Rêve* (1888), both artwork and poem emphasize the stable, protecting eternal nature of the cathedral; they echo Zola's praise of l'église Sainte-Marie as a hen and mother, sheltering her city "from the cold by her wings of stone."

Zola inspired an appreciation of the mystical, timeless qualities of Gothic architecture, but his primary goal was to turn it into a "wish image," a figure from the past that could be applied to modern accomplishments to make them seem more feasible or more palatable. Mouret's "cathedral of modern commerce," Pluchart's "cathedral of the future world," or Pierre Froment's "new Jerusalem" conform to this tendency, which would later be used to refer to modern structures. The expression "the cathedral of commerce," first applied to the gallery of machines at the 1885 World's Fair, went on to become a common epithet, used especially for the new "cathedrals," American skyscrapers. The 1913 Woolworth Building was promptly christened "The Cathedral of Commerce," and French visitors to New York—Paul Morand, for example—compared New York's buildings to spires, "aiming at the sky an enthusiasm both mystical and economic."[149] In the 1939 *Quand les cathédrales étaient blanches,* even Le Corbusier proposed skyscrapers as an futurist alternative to campus architecture—a *ville radieuse*—to supplement the backward-looking Gothic structures favored by American universities.

The most concrete example of a "cathedral of the future" in Zola's work occurs in *Travail,* where a factory has replaced the church as house of worship. Built by Pierre Froment's son Luc, a Christ-like figure who shares his father's love of social harmony, it incarnates the values Pluchart placed in his "cathedral of the future world."[150] Like l'église Sainte-Marie, the mother cathedral of *Le Rêve,* the aptly named Crêcherie (little nursery) also cultivates its children in a special climate, modeled on "enormous and delicate" Gothic forms: "The wide picture windows let streams of air and sun penetrate the light covered iron and brick halls of La Crêcherie, which were an original wonder [. . .] this air and sun that bathed the great light rooms, the cheerfulness of work [lay] less heavy on shoulders.[151] Through his friend Jordan's scientific advances in steelwork and electricity, all of the villagers have improved their quality of life, and, over three generations, have grown, both literally and figuratively, into one big family that worships each other's company. As Pierre Froment's dream of social harmony comes true, Zola empties the cathedral—his former dream—of its ideals, only to apply them to another structure, the democratic factory of *Travail.*

Zola's admiration of the cathedral and his embrace of it as a model for future development uncannily echoes the attitude of Viollet-le-Duc, who, as Françoise Choay puts it, was "nostalgic not for the past but for the future."[152] Viollet-le-Duc, who conceived of thirteenth-century architecture as the ultimate representation of rational French spirit and as proof of the medieval bourgeoisie's rebellion against the nobles, strongly advocated the imitation of Gothic architecture as the best way to renew French architectural tradition. His theories were put into use by the founders of Art Nouveau architecture throughout Europe, notably Hector Guimard, Victor Horta, Henry Van der Velde, and Gaudí, who were influenced by Gothic forms.[153] Choay attributes many of Viollet-le-Duc's liberties with historical accuracy in his restorations to his attitude: he was so "obsessed" by the creation of a "type" that may never have existed, that he neglected the preservation of older or unique features of the structures.[154] Such an attitude also explains his great admiration for new structures, such as Baltard's 1851 enclosed marketplace, Les Halles, which took inspiration from Gothic architecture.[155]

Zola, too, was fascinated by modern architecture inspired by Gothic style, as is evident in his 1871 novel *Le Ventre de Paris,* set in Baltard's marketplace,[156] or in *Au Bonheur des Dames,* in which the modern department store becomes "the cathedral of modern commerce." He describes it as "vast as a church" with its grand entryway, "high and deep like a church portal."[157] Whether he realized it or not, Zola modeled the ideal spaces and structures in his novels on the traits the nineteenth century praised in medieval religious architecture: they are airy, clean, simple, well-lit and immense. Solid and light, functional yet elegant, they are structures that combine new scientific techniques with art, and imitate nature with new materials.[158] Although they are modern, the structures Zola admires and re-creates in his work correspond to the nineteenth-century *topos* for Gothic cathedrals: they are "enormous and delicate."

Zola was less interested in describing or preserving existing cathedrals than in promoting them as a "type," an ideal of social and aesthetic perfection. By the 1890s, the cathedral was nearly absent as a physical presence in his work; he had replaced cathedrals by *the* cathedral, a myth of religious, scientific, and artistic harmony that guides his protagonists in their quest to find its modern counterpart. The insistence Zola placed on the moral or spiritual values of religious architecture distinguish him sharply, however, from thinkers like Viollet-le-Duc. Where the architect saw Gothic architecture as primarily rational and democratic and only grudgingly admitted its religious inspiration, the novelist admired its fusion of science, religion, and art.

Zola would certainly have admired Notre-Dame du Travail, a church designed by Jules Astruc between 1899 and 1901. The Parisian church was inspired by the works of Baltard and Eiffel and built from modern materials, notably recycled segments from the structures admired by Zola at previous World's Fairs. Its design was planned to suggest a factory embellished by art, while reminding the worshiper that the Church, like the factory, worked incessantly (albeit on the spirit).[159] Indeed, this church produces an effect eerily akin to that of a Gothic cathedral. With its profusion of iron and glass, it is the living incarnation of Zola's La Crêcherie. The combination of beautiful new architecture modeled on Gothic forms, Catholic dedication to workers and their craft, and the spiritual nexus the church was to provide for the brotherhood of workers, corresponded, in many ways, to Zola's vision.

At a time when Art Nouveau architects were building completely new structures inspired by Gothic architecture, Zola was writing about an "immense cathedral of the future world" based on his idealized interpretation of Gothic architecture. He used this figure as a way of encouraging contemporaries; the cathedral was a familiar cultural figure that provoked them to respond emotionally to his intellectual vision of a future France. Zola's prophecies about truth, justice, fraternity, and social harmony spilled over from fiction into reality during the heavily publicized serialization of *Paris*. On January 13, 1898, when only half of *Paris* had appeared in print,[160] Zola published his famous letter, "J'accuse," to Felix Faure, the President of the Republic. In keeping with Pierre's dedication to the human values of truth, justice, and fraternity, Zola lambasts the President, who had previously done so much for "truth and liberty."[161] Zola's ten-page letter rings in defense of truth, justice, and happiness, the sacred values of his "cathedral of the future world." His letter, in combination with *Paris,* whose happy ending for humanity appeared in print a few weeks later, was instrumental in pushing society into action: the two works inspired violent debates about the Dreyfus Affair.[162]

Zola compiled beliefs about the social harmony of the Gothic cathedral as he did Pierre Froment's religion of science: he made an amalgam from the intersecting ideas of previous thinkers. But it is the blending of so many conflicting ideas—political, religious, aesthetic—into a common social ideal that makes Zola's vision of the cathedral so unique. It is also the technique that makes *Les Trois Villes* unusual hybrid novels. Zola responded to the ideas of his time in these books; he experimented with them by using a character who tries to find points of compromise among them; he listened to readers; and he created a new version of these ideals to influence them. Zola did not recommend a return to the past, nor did he advise his contemporaries to design new cathedrals modeled on those of the twelfth and thirteenth centuries. In the end, he was "nostalgic for the future," for a kind of social and artistic ideal that did not yet exist, but that he hoped to help build.

THREE

"The Soul of Arches":
Huysmans and the Medieval Church

[Des Esseintes] may have been drawn toward the priesthood because the Church alone had collected art, the lost form of the centuries [. . .] the majority of the precious objects catalogued in the Musée de Cluny, having miraculously escaped the vile brutality of the sans-culottes, are from the old abbeys of France. Just as the Church preserved philosophy, history and literature from barbarism in the Middle Ages, so it has saved the plastic arts, protected until now those wonderful models of fabric and jewelry that manufacturers of holy objects spoil as much as they can even though they are unable to alter their initial, exquisite form. It was not thus surprising that he had sought out these antique bibelots, that he had, like many other collectors, taken these relics away from the antique stores and the secondhand country shops.

—Huysmans, *A rebours* (1884)

Zola and Huysmans were fundamentally unhappy with their time. Jean Jaurès, in an 1895 article for *La Petite République Française,* commented on the sense of dissatisfaction that permeated fin-de-siècle life: "Some throw themselves into the socialist fray to finish with the ignominious world that no longer knows how to atone for the pain of the exploited with the joy of the exploiter. Others, like Huysmans, disdainful and wounded, take mental and emotional refuge in cloisters, in the deep fervent peace of the mystical Middle Ages."[1] Jaurès sums up the public perception of Zola's and Huysmans's differing reactions to the 1890s. While Zola seemed to reform society through his political activity, Huysmans appeared to withdraw: he converted to Catholicism and began writing books about the symbolism, mysticism, and hagiography of the Middle Ages. By using the phrase "mystical Middle Ages," Jaurès capitalizes on a term made popular by the otherworldliness of Huysmans's *Là-Bas,* and applied by contemporaries to visions, apparitions, and dreams. Jean Lorrain, for example, distinguished mysticism from religion in an article for *Le Courrier français:* "[Mysticism] is fabulous poetry, the exaltation of imaginations that take offense at the harshness and rationalism of dogma."[2] This popular definition, which concentrates on conflicts between reality and fantasy, differed both from Huysmans's use of the word mysticism—an attempt to "articulate the inexpressible"—and from that of the Middle Ages—a way of speaking about using and understanding religious terms.[3] Although contemporaries perceived Huysmans as an escapist who hid from the problems of his time by fleeing into a neomedieval dreamworld of saints, cloisters, and cathedrals, part of this misconception developed from their incomprehension of his relationship to mysticism. His characters did not take solace in the darkened interiors of medieval houses of worship on a whim; like Zola, Huysmans used an idealized image of the cathedral in his novels in order to bring moral equilibrium to a society he perceived as corrupted by materialism and individualism. Where Zola claimed the cathedral for a secular religion of the future, Huysmans used it promote Catholicism. This chapter questions the ways in which Huysmans capitalized upon his contemporaries' fondness for museums, medieval art, and music to encourage them to treasure the cathedral and the religion it harbored.

Des Esseintes's attraction to the Church as creator and preserver of dispersed medieval art echoes contemporary attitudes toward the cathedral, which was compared to and defined in contrast to the museum. Janell Watson, Rosalind Williams, and Rémy Saisselin describe the extent to which the bibelot (knickknack, curio, or other collectible) fascinated the bourgeoisie. Collecting conferred a prestige that set one apart from the lower classes, and by the end of the nineteenth century artists and bourgeois alike felt compelled to express their superior aesthetic sensibility by acquiring and organizing objects. Goncourt, Zola, Montesquiou, Claude Monet, and Anatole France were all collectors, and literary and artistic movements of the 1880s from Joseph Péladan's Rose+Croix salons to a symbolist interest in the Pre-Raphaelites produced a popular vogue for creating what Rosalind Williams calls "dream worlds," private realms of carefully amassed and arranged objects. Edmond de Goncourt believed that collecting gave people an immediate pleasure, a nearly human tenderness for things that made them forget the problems of the outside world.[4] He could have been describing Des Esseintes, who likes to "snuggle up, far from the world [. . .] hide [him]self away in a retreat [. . .] muffle [. . .] the continuing racket of inflexible life" by cloistering himself in his house, which he fills with medieval artwork, literature, and furnishings.[5]

Des Esseintes's desire to "repossess" antique objects from the unappreciative stores where he finds them and his anger at the fragmentation and maltreatment of the "lost" religious objects now housed in museums, seem to link him to museum curators, who sought to assemble, organize, and preserve vestiges of the past. The Musée de Cluny, which he mentions, was originally the private collection of Alexandre du Sommerard, who arranged his medieval objects in "thematic" rooms, a technique continued by the state when it took over the collection in 1843. His artifacts were then combined with those of Alexandre Lenoir, who had salvaged many pieces during the vandalism that followed the French Revolution.[6] "Being enveloped by the good old chivalric times"—as one visitor described the effect of du Sommerard's collection—was a sensation prized by the nineteenth century; it was behind the institutional vogue for restoring period buildings and castles, like the Bibliothèque Nationale, Versailles, or Chantilly.[7]

Des Esseintes appears to preserve objects and to create such a nostalgic atmosphere through the arrangement and display of his purchases. He builds a pulpit, an altar, and a monk's cell to showcase his bibelots. But, in fact, he is not interested in authenticity or public display; he appreciates churches and monasteries only because they have saved the "antique bibelots" long enough for him to find them. Instead of helping maintain the cultural heritage he seems to admire, Des Esseintes appropriates it; he contributes to the process of removing medieval art and manuscripts from their religious and communal context by purchasing them to satisfy his whims. What is more, he revels in parodying and perverting religious spaces by creating secular equivalents, from the pulpit that he constructs to preach sermons on dandyism, to the altar that displays specially commissioned editions of Baudelaire's prose poems, to the comfortable monk's cell that becomes his bedroom. He consistently subverts religious artifacts by appropriating them for private use, while replacing religious values with commercial. This behavior reflects what Janell Watson calls "the movement of the museum into the salon." "The museum as interior becomes a private shrine of the cult of Art, rationalized by the doctrines of the cult of Science."[8]

Cathedrals are defined in relationship to collecting not only because many bibelots were once found in churches, but also because most cathedrals were still used for worship in the late nineteenth century; their art still functioned within the context for which it was created.[9] These "collections" of art were therefore deemed more authentic than those in a museum because their sense had not been lost. While bibelots on the market—everything from statues to stained glass to liturgical objects—were considered scattered vestiges of a "lost" past, the same objects found in a functioning cathedral were not considered bibelots, because the cathedral and its religious services defined them within a unified system. As Charles Morice put it in 1914, "Museums are cemeteries [. . .] where works, diverted from their initial destination, lose the best of their sense and their splendor."[10] Aloïs Riegl distinguishes between "historical value" (interest in objects as mementos of a past age) and "use value" (objects valued for their function). Once removed from the church, religious art loses its "use value" and becomes a bibelot, appreciated for its "historical value." Bibelots can only gain meaning through artificial arrangement, while religious objects are determined by the relationship to their function, which has changed little since the creation of the Catholic liturgy.

Des Esseintes, like many of his collector contemporaries, was drawn to religious art because of the authenticity conferred by its "use value," yet he denied religion because he did not want to abdicate reason for faith.[11] Fear of acknowledging the religion of the cathedral is common in Huysmans's early works; his characters are attracted to Catholicism, yet they rationalize their fascination by attributing it to the aesthetic sensations produced in them by bibelots, detached from their religious context. Gothic churches thus appear in the background of Huysmans's early fiction as works of art that impress characters by their size and the intricacy of their sculpture. In "Sac au dos," Eugène stops to admire the cathedrals of Rouen and Evreux as he passes through with the military, while in *En rade* Jacques Marles is fascinated by the decaying church of Lourps.[12] It was only in the Durtal cycle, as Huysmans responded to the social and literary arguments that condemned naturalism and called for a "spiritual" alternative, that he began placing religious architecture at the center of his novels: *Là-Bas* takes place in and around the church of Saint-Sulpice in Paris; in *En Route* Durtal frequents many Parisian churches and smaller chapels; *La Cathédrale* evolves around Notre-Dame de Chartres; and *L'Oblat* takes place in a Benedictine monastery and in the churches of Dijon.

Huysmans argued that most of his contemporaries were like Des Esseintes; they admired cathedrals for the individual pieces of art contained within them—potential bibelots—but dismissed their spiritual dimension. Leading proponents of the cathedral—Hugo, Montalembert, and Viollet-le-Duc—had saved cathedrals from the vandalism of their contemporaries by focusing on the artistic and historical value of the Gothic style, but they tended to practice "monumental materialism"; they worshiped the cathedral's body, not its soul. His contemporaries thus respected the structures themselves, while divesting cathedrals of their religious decoration, in order to sate their fury for bibelots. They had forgotten that the music, stained glass, sculpture, illuminated breviaries, altars, paintings, and ceremonies worked in tandem to produce the church's spiritual dimension.

As tensions between Republicans and Catholics grew, culminating in a series of anticlerical laws that definitively separated Church and State and ended state support of religious ceremonies, Huysmans increasingly worried about the "use value" of French cathedrals, the continued performance of religious rites that made them more than just museums. By eliminating religious services and divesting churches of their art, contemporaries would break up these meaningful "collections," thus reducing them to bibelots, devoid of the Catholic faith that gave them transcendent meaning, and transforming churches into empty shells, secular buildings like any other. Where Hugo used *Notre-Dame de Paris* to call for an end to the post-Revolutionary physical vandalism of cathedrals, thus convincing his contemporaries to preserve the cathedral as a national monument, Huysmans drew attention to the "spiritual vandalism" now destroying them. He was as concerned about the cathedral's body as its "soul," the spirituality that gave sense to medieval religious architecture and the art it harbored.[13]

But why would Huysmans, whose early works (*Les Soeurs Vatard, En Ménage,* and *A vau-l'eau*) so closely traced the links between milieu and bourgeois behavior that he was ridiculed as a "sous-Zola" and chastised for his base materialism, and whose *A rebours* (1884) was proclaimed "the breviary of the decadence," have concerned himself with the soul of religious architecture?[14] His own work repeatedly dealt with prostitutes, the working class, and social misery; his novels were hardly of high moral caliber.

First of all, the visual arts provide the most important and persistent focus of his writing. As the title of Fernande Zayed's *Huysmans: peintre de son époque* suggests, painting was of crucial importance to Huysmans, and one of the central themes he used to describe his literary production.[15] He liked to remark that everyone in his family had painted, but he had "substituted a pen for brushes;" he treasured his ability to paint with words.[16] Huysmans's descriptions always set him apart, even in his naturalist novels, as Zola remarked in an article entitled "Céard et Huysmans", "there is little analysis in his books, one finds almost nothing but paintings."[17] Art is the common denominator of all of Huysmans's literary production. Although scholars tend to categorize his work according to his affiliation with literary movements—naturalist (1876–1882), decadent (1884–1891), and religious (1895–1903)—he was an iconoclast who refused generic labels.[18] The books generally excluded from criticism of Huysmans's work reflect the hybrid nature of his literary production; they are part art history and part literature.[19] Huysmans published collections of essays, prose poems, and "croquis," which treat a variety of artistic, historical, and scientific subjects often concentrated on the Middle Ages and the nineteenth century: the lives of historical characters such as Jan Luyken, Adrien Brauwer, and François Villon; critiques of the work of modern writers and painters; and modern technological inventions such as the Eiffel Tower or the omnibus.[20] Huysmans's hybrid interests merged in the cathedral, where sculpture, stained glass, and tapestries depicted history and biblical stories.

Second, in 1892 Huysmans converted to Catholicism. Although many of his contemporaries doubted the legitimacy of his faith (scholars continue to deny that the cynical Huysmans could truly have believed), it is clear from his correspondence and contemporary accounts of his behavior that he was serious about his new vocation and that he exercised an enormous influence on others.[21] What does it mean to convert? Frédéric Gugelot has established that, for the late nineteenth century, the word "conversion" signified radical change or transformation, but could also refer to the renewed interest of a lapsed believer: "It is defined not only by a simple change of religion or confession, but also by the vigor of the religious commitment." For most of Huysmans's fellow converts, the embrace of Catholicism was initiated by a moment of grace, a sudden flash that encouraged them to adopt new values, new attitudes, and a new understanding of the world.[22]

Although Huysmans's style and aesthetic preoccupations remained constant throughout his career, the postconversion novels reflected his new priorities; they carry a didactic weight that is not evident in earlier works. As Huysmans changed his habits, point of view, and preferences, he increasingly dedicated his novels to publicizing the art and liturgy of the Catholic Church. He used the novel's fictional frame to advertise the importance of the cathedral and the Catholicism it summarized. In a time that was characterized by increased loneliness and a feeling of moral fragmentation (individuals were like the dispersed bibelots adrift in the Paris market), the Church proposed a system in which each person (like each piece of religious art) participates in and gains meaning from a united whole. "The majesty of art brings back into simple unity everything thus divided up and partitioned."[23] Huysmans portrayed the cathedral as a summary of the entire Church: "a harmony, a synthesis, it encompassed everything; it was a Bible, a catechism, a moralizing class, a history class and it replaced text by image for the uneducated."[24] Instead of continuing to criticize his contemporaries for their ignorance, as he had done in *A rebours,* he began to use his novels to teach them about the traditions of communal prayer and social unity that were being forgotten by an increasingly secular, individualistic, and materialistic France. Huysmans did not encourage pessimism or flight into dreams, but optimistically felt that he could make headway in transforming contemporary values by publicizing medieval art, which encouraged social and spiritual harmony. Like, Zola, in *Les Trois Villes,* Huysmans proffered the cathedral as an ideal. His dream, however, incarnated a different set of values and a clearly defined plan for social improvement, based on existing religious traditions of the French nation.

In contrast to those who have portrayed Huysmans as an author who surpasses the romantics in his escapism,[25] I argue that Huysmans's appreciation of the Middle Ages and its architecture began as a personal nostalgia for the past, but later developed into a positive social message for his contemporaries. A number of scholars have remarked the importance of the Middle Ages in Huysmans's work, including Michel Viegnes, who describes them as a primordial time for Huysmans, a "legendary" origin after which all else deteriorated, a foundational myth to which France should return, "spiritually or symbolically."[26] This is true to a certain extent, but with a few provisos. First, unlike contemporaries who glorified the entire Middle Ages as a time of harmony, Huysmans focused his praise on the medieval Church, its art and ceremonies. Second, his dream is not lost. It still exists, tucked away in real Gothic churches: Saint-Séverin, Saint-Julien-des-Pauvres, Notre-Dame de Chartres. Both the Durtal cycle and Huysmans's correspondence focus on his astonishment at finding his medieval ideal flourishing in the nineteenth century, preserved in Gothic churches and monasteries.

The differences between Huysmans's love of the medieval art, documents, and traditions preserved in the nineteenth century and the romantic or symbolist nostalgia for a lost Middle Ages is crucial to an understanding of Huysmans's goals in his late works. Zola's Pierre Froment dreams fondly of the Middle Ages as a "golden age" of prayer and social harmony. Huysmans, however, knew that medieval people were not superior in nature to contemporaries.[27] He was interested in bringing attention to the history of medieval Catholic traditions and art in order to show his contemporaries that Catholicism was not a dead religion, but a system of belief that responded perfectly to the spiritual needs of the modern world.

Huysmans was committed to action, not to escape: he wanted to convince his contemporaries to preserve and heal the spirit of France—Catholicism—still present in her cathedrals.

The Cathedral and the Pilgrim

In *Là-Bas,* the first novel of the Durtal cycle, the narrator describes a medieval Dutch painting that hangs on the wall of Durtal's apartment. The painting portrays a hermit, crouched under a hut of branches, who, in a series of scenes, travels by boat and foot from a village to the Orient. The unknown saint's quest comes to an end as he climbs a hill toward an unfinished cathedral. As Ruth Antosh has noted, Huysmans probably intended this painting to prefigure Durtal's spiritual quest, which also ends with a cathedral. In his description of Durtal's apartment, the narrator mentions that this painting hangs over the fireplace in the space generally filled by a mirror. In fact, Huysmans owned this painting and knew the identity of the saint. It was Jerome, the translator of the Bible, a scholar who gave up worldly literature to study religious texts. Huysmans's decision to leave the holy man of the painting nameless thus invites a link with Durtal, who has no given name, no family, and is also a hermit who abandons secular literature for that of the Church.[28] Durtal and the saint make a physical journey that parallels their spiritual quest.

The relationship between Huysmans and his pilgrim character is complex: Huysmans, too, converted to Catholicism after writing a work about satanism. Through contacts with priests and through research into the alchemy, medicine, and hagiography of the Middle Ages, both men were drawn to the mysticism and symbolism of the Church. Both were enamored of the history and aesthetics of Catholicism, and both managed to tear themselves painfully from carnal desires in order to convert. After long struggles, they both become Benedictine oblates, thereby officially attaching themselves to religious communities. Both were forced back to Paris after their congregations fled to Belgium. Because of these similarities, the Durtal cycle is often interpreted as a thinly veiled autobiography.[29] But as Michel Viegnes has suggested, Huysmans uses Durtal to play a game of "hide and show": Durtal allows him to rewrite his life more positively than an autobiography.[30] Huysmans did, in fact, borrow from his own experience to portray Durtal's struggles to convert, but Durtal is not a true reflection of Huysmans.

Durtal, the hermit and pilgrim was free from social attachments, while Huysmans could never distance himself from them. For thirty years (until his retirement in 1898), Huysmans worked as a government employee, notably at the Ministry of the Interior (he was named *Chevalier* then *Officier de l'ordre de la légion d'honneur* for his achievements in administration); he ran his mother's book bindery once she died; he went on trips and corresponded regularly with his friends; and he took care of his sick mistress, Anna Meunier, his stepsisters, and his friends, Bloy, Verlaine, and Villiers de l'Isle-Adam. He was the executor of the estates of both Villiers and his friend Edmond de Goncourt, and became the first president of L'Académie Goncourt. Remy de Gourmont summed up Huysmans's tendency to complain bitterly about his job, his family, and social obligations while upholding them all to the best of his abilities when he said: "Until the end he remained vicious in words and kind in deeds."[31] It is ironic that Huysmans, who, for years, routinely dealt with problems caused by the Panama Canal scandal, the anarchist attacks of 1892–94, and the Dreyfus Affair while at work,[32] should be thought an escapist, while Zola, who spent half the year writing in Médan or Aix-en-Provence—in what he called "my hole"—should be praised as a social activist.[33]

Huysmans wrote at work and during vacations; Durtal lives from his writing and has no other obligations. Huysmans went to churches accompanied by his friends George Landry and Gustave Boucher; Durtal is always alone in *En Route,* a solitary observer of church art and ceremony. While Huysmans shared a house with a married couple, the Leclaires, during his time as a Benedictine oblate at Ligugé, in *L'Oblat* Durtal lives with no one but his housekeeper. Durtal is a purified, simplified version of Huysmans, with no responsibilities. Although the outline of their conversion is similar, Durtal is not Huysmans, but an idealized alter ego from which all complications except the spiritual have been removed.

In many ways, Durtal was the instigator of his author's quest. Huysmans conceived of *En Route* as a way of capitalizing on the novelty of satanism and mysticism. He saw it as a "white book"—the sequel and opposite ("à rebours") of *Là-Bas.*[34] It began as "Là-Haut," a study of Christian mysticism and the writings of Teresa of Avila and Mary of Agreda. But as Huysmans frequented churches to gather information about Durtal's studies, he himself converted to Catholicism.[35] Reading *Là-Haut,* which was rediscovered in 1965, gives one the impression that Huysmans was practicing in fiction what he would go on to do in reality, as if his future crystallized as he wrote his novels.[36] There is a constant interplay between Huysmans's documentation for the Durtal cycle and his self-transformation as he wrote about Durtal.

The murky give-and-take between autobiography and fiction in the Durtal cycle can be clarified in light of the numerous late-nineteenth–century French conversions to Catholicism. Huysmans's novels are less autobiography, per se, than "conversion narrative," a genre that derives from the great Christian tradition of Augustine's *Confessions.* In his study of the 160 conversions of intellectuals that took place in France from 1885 to 1935, Frédéric Gugelot proves that the sheer volume of spiritual chronicles published at this time allows us to set this genre apart from other kinds of personal narrative. Accounts of conversion took many different forms (journals, essays, stories, novels) and differed in length, but like the Durtal cycle, all focus on the spiritual evolution of the principle character. Written at a distance from the actual event (hindsight was crucial for the analysis of the steps leading to conversion), the author's primary allegiance was to psychology.

Such accounts, written by intellectuals as varied as Léon Bloy, Adolphe Retté, François Coppée, Henri Ghéon, Paul Claudel, and Francis Jammes, sought to understand a unique conversion experience and to present it to others. Conversion was thus not only a private act between a believer and God, but also a public act of social and religious engagement for the Church. A confession narrative could edify unbelievers by demonstrating to them the rocky but rewarding path from loneliness and isolation to spiritual fulfillment. This journey is one step in the two-part dynamic of religious practice that Michel de Certeau breaks into "the act" and "the place." The "act" involves accepting faith and attempting to embrace the difficult and unending journey it entails, while the "place" is the destination, the longed for infinite experience. Because it is impossible to be assured of arriving at the final term of this journey—that is to say the exchanges and sharing that take place in a religious community— "community practice" is, for all intents and purposes, the "*real* place of religious life." "There is no longer any room for individualism."[37] The conversion narrative, which illustrates the ways in which an individual embraces faith and attempts to leave egotistical practices for spiritual completion at the heart of a community, provides a message that appealed to a society anxious about fragmentation and isolation. By proposing model itineraries and by naming welcoming communities, this genre was an extremely successful way of bringing people to the Church.[38] The Durtal novels should be considered within this Catholic context; the entire series takes shape and meaning in light of Durtal's spiritual journey.

Durtal is a simple figure; Huysmans's brilliance was to turn his own conversion narrative into a fictional product in which his everyman character provides a model for contemporaries. In his well-known review of *A rebours,* Barbey d'Aurevilly had remarked on the symbolic nature of Des Esseintes, whose spiritual torment served as an allegory of the soul of materialistic modern society: "In writing the biography of his hero, [Huysmans] not only presents the peculiar confession of a depraved and solitary character, but, simultaneously writes a case study of a society putrefied by materialism."[39] Durtal's bourgeois background makes him an even better reflection of modern society's spiritual illness than the flamboyant Des Esseintes. They both long to escape from the modern world and the *ennui* it inspires, but where Des Esseintes is the last of a degenerate race, Durtal is destined to evolve. His name implies both aridity and the possibility of change, as Huysmans told a friend: "In the languages of the North, [Durtal] signifies 'Valley of aridity' or 'Valley of the door.'"[40] Durtal wanders the wasteland of modern society seeking spiritual refreshment. Not unlike Zola's Pierre Froment, he is a figure of compromise who wants to believe. He visits all the churches of Paris, stays in a Trappist monastery, goes to Notre-Dame de la Salette, studies Notre-Dame de

Chartres, visits the monastic community of Solesmes, and finally becomes an oblate attached to a Benedictine community.

How does the cathedral become a recurring motif and an emblem that helps his character along his journey? Durtal's spiritual adviser, l'abbé Gévresin, often tells Durtal that change in environment is necessary to gauging spiritual progress. In the Durtal cycle (as in *Les Trois Villes* and *A la recherche du temps perdu*), descriptions of cathedrals at stages of his journey reflect the character's spiritual evolution. They reveal his psychological state by externalizing his point of view. In *Là-Bas,* Durtal admires churches as does Des Esseintes; he considers them medieval museums that have preserved intriguing art from the past. As he learns more about the Church and its traditions in *En Route* and *La Cathédrale,* however, he begins to see cathedrals in a spiritual dimension. He is horrified by those who (like Des Esseintes), buy altarpieces, tapestries, and lamps that used to belong in churches. Durtal begins to feel that a church's soul is dependent on the continuation of music, ornamentation, and ceremony. Yet at the end of *La Cathédrale* and in *L'Oblat,* he realizes that the art's material pales in comparison with its role in disseminating a spiritual message. In the Durtal cycle, descriptions of the cathedral accompany Durtal's shifting attitude toward public and private space, aesthetic and commercial production, didacticism and intuition.[41]

Second, as Huysmans developed the Durtal cycle as a conversion narrative, he adopted the cathedral as a model that reflected the form and content of his novels. Like Victor Hugo, he represented the cathedral as the foremost example of medieval art— "the most magnificent expression of art that the Middle Ages left us"— while describing literature as the pinnacle of modern art: "the most complicated, the most interlocking, the most haughty of all the arts."[42] Huysmans saw the cathedral as way for the Church to teach the uninitiated about the Christian community; similarly, he saw the novel as a way of educating his contemporaries about the communal values an increasingly secular and materialistic society had neglected. The cathedral's ability to link a seemingly infinite variety of art forms, theological messages, and social functions by subordinating them to a central value— Catholicism—also provided Huysmans with a model for his novels, in which description, dialogue, didactic messages, and plot were subordinated to Durtal's evolving consciousness.

The Cathedral as Museum

At the beginning of *Là-Bas,* Durtal incarnates the spiritual exhaustion of the fin de siècle. He is a former naturalist who has stopped writing novels because he is tired of elaborating fiction to surround his research and he can no longer bear the pettiness of literary squabbles. He is barely able to leave his Paris apartment because he so despises other people. In order to occupy himself, he has begun writing a study of Gilles de Rais, the marshal who assisted Joan of Arc before becoming a mass murderer, the diabolical model for Bluebeard.[43] Durtal is fascinated by Gilles de Rais's sudden shifts between Catholicism and satanism. But above all, he enjoys his project because it allows him to escape from the real world: "He had plunged into the terrifying and delicious late Middle Ages [. . .] he began to live in cool contempt for his surroundings and created for himself an existence far from the hubbub of literature, mentally cloistering himself, when all was said, in the castle of Tiffauges."[44] His research shuts him off from his problems and serves as therapy for the depression that ruins his health.

Like his contemporaries, Durtal has great admiration for bibelots. In fact, Durtal is fascinated by Gilles de Rais's conspicuous consumption. In an interesting act of self-referentiality, Huysmans describes Gilles de Rais— "the Des Esseintes of the fifteenth century"—as a writer, an artist, a musician, and a collector who isolated himself in the castle of Tiffauges in order to indulge his exotic tastes:

> The luxury of his chapel and collegiate church was practically demented. A complete metropolis of clergy—deans, vicars, treasurers, canons, clerks, deacons, school boys, and choir boys—was in residence at Tiffauges; an inventory remains of surplices, stoles, and amices, and fur choir hats lined with vair. Sacerdotal ornaments abound; here, one finds altar coverings of vermilion cloth, curtains of emerald silk, a cope of crimson and violet with gold trimmed borders, another of rose damask, satin dalmatics for the deacons, canopies embroidered, engraved with Cyprus gold; there, dishes, chalices and ciboria hammered and encrusted with uncut jewels, set with gems, reliquaries, including a silver head of Saint Honoré, a mass of incandescent treasures that an artist, installed in the castle, cuts to order.[45]

Durtal's rapture with Gilles de Rais's material possessions is striking in the three pages of this passage, which is less a description than an illustrated catalog of bibelots that he has elaborated for his friend, Des Hermies. Durtal is fascinated by Gilles de Rais as collector. The chapel explodes with color and light: from the red, green, purple, and blue fabrics to the reflections emanating from the gold, silver, and gem-encrusted artwork. Durtal revels in the opulence of the chapel without commenting on it. He makes no judgments about the ceremonies that might have been performed in such a radiant chapel, nor does he consider Gilles de Rais's beliefs or actions. He relishes the simple pleasure of rolling the names off his tongue. His enthusiastic enumerations of events in Gilles de Rais's life continue in this vein: he describes medieval documents pertaining to the Hundred Years War, alchemy and satanism, hagiography and hygiene, dress and interior design, and legal records with similar litanies of objects.[46] His appreciation of the Middle Ages and medieval religious architecture derives from the pleasure he takes in appropriating information and coveting rare objects from the past.

Durtal's fascination for collecting the dispersed documents recounting Gilles de Rais's life and reassembling them in his own work strikingly resembles the process by which Des Esseintes constructs his private cloister or chapel in *A rebours.* Durtal chooses only those documents that most interest him, thus turning his own writing into a thematic space in which he re-creates Gilles de Rais as a reflection of his own perverse imagination. He delights in the inanimate excesses of Gilles de Rais's collecting habits, yet he also lingers over the grisly details of the satanic rites— "litanies of lust"—practiced by the Marshal. Gilles de Rais raped his altar boys and dismembered over 800 children in what could be called his chapel *à rebours,* the bloody chamber in which he practiced his diabolical activities:

> Once their senses are phosporized, dazed by the powerful venison juices, kindled by inflammatory beverages laced with spices, Gilles and his friends retire into a distant chamber of the castle. The little boys locked up in the cellar are brought there. They are undressed, they are gagged; the marshal fondles them and forces them, then he gashes them with a dagger, taking great pleasure in dismembering them, piece by piece. At other times he splits their chest and he drinks the breath of their lungs; sometimes he opens up their belly, sniffs it, enlarges the wound with his hands and sits inside. Then, while he macerates in the mud softened by warm entrails, he turns himself around to look over his shoulder, so as to watch the supreme convulsions, the last spasms.[47]

Huysmans listed precious articles to evoke Durtal's materialistic fascination with Gilles de Rais's sumptuous chapel. But here the profusion of body parts— "chest," "lungs," "belly," "hands," "entrails"—coupled with the violence of the rapidly succeeding verbs— "fondle," "force," "gash," "dismember," "split"—creates a dizzying effect of mass butchery. The immediacy of the present tense places Durtal at the scene of the crime and exposes his vicarious enjoyment of the sacrilegious activities that take place in the bloody chamber. Unlike the chapel, which Huysmans described using archaic names and adjectives of color linked by a profusion of commas and semicolons, here the power of the spectacle derives primarily from the barrage of simple clauses in which verbs violate nouns.

How are we to interpret Durtal's perverse pleasure in recreating the decadent chapel and torture chamber of Gilles de Rais? Does Huysmans, too, delight in such grisly enumeration? Or is Durtal, like Des Esseintes, intended as a tongue-in-cheek mockery of contemporary excess?[48] The most likely answer, as for *A rebours,* is both. With Gilles de Rais, "the Des Esseintes of the fifteenth century," Huysmans pushes the caricatured collector of *A rebours* one step further in his continued psychological study of the lengths to which a desperately bored person will go in search of excitement. Such parallels between medieval and modern are constant throughout the novel, especially as Durtal discovers satanism in modern

Paris. He participates in a similar—though slightly less bloody—scene near the end of the novel, when he attends a black mass with Hyacinthe Chantelouve, a married woman with whom he has an affair. What seems, at first glance, a normal low mass held in a chapel, becomes, by the end, a ceremony that completely violates the Eucharistic adoration with words, gestures, and bodily fluids. The mass culminates in a wild and obscene orgy in which the priest—a practicing Catholic priest—debauches choir boys, women, and men in equal numbers while they desecrate statues, the host, and people around them.[49]

As an antidote to such dissipation, Huysmans creates an alternate group that meets at the top of Saint Sulpice church in the lodgings of Carhaix, the bell ringer. Durtal discusses his adventures and tells his friends that he is not surprised that fin-de-siècle society is in such disarray when even spiritual counselors desecrate their vows by becoming degenerate agents of corruption. He insists that the nineteenth century is no worse than the Middle Ages; his time simply lacks moral direction. Gilles de Rais was able to repent and was forgiven by the victims' families, who prayed for him— "the soul of the Middle Ages shone in all its candid splendor"—but his modern ancestors continue to degenerate.[50] Carhaix believes that Catholicism will improve contemporaries, but Durtal and Des Hermies are less confident. Because they feel that belief in the supernatural has vanished, they fear that the children of the future will continue to worship their individual interests and consumerism, thus sinking further into the morass: "They will stuff their guts and flush souls through their loins."[51] The book closes with these words.

The sheer invective Durtal and his friends spew at nearly every sphere of society—politics, religion, science, literature, art—often make this work uncomfortable to read. In fact, Huysmans had intended to disturb his public by pointing out their superficiality and materialism.[52] The last thing he expected, however, was a resounding commercial success. Not only did the novel inflame the literary battles of the Huret interviews, but it was also banned in train stations, became a best-seller, and was labeled "the breviary of satanism," thus turning it into a vogue.[53] Two years later, Huysmans was still flabbergasted by the impact of the novel: "The strange thing about all of this—is that in spite of Panama [. . .] people talk about nothing but enchantment, black magic [. . .] I really shook things up."[54] Though Huysmans's violence was meant to disturb his contemporaries by showing them the dark side of modern France, his emphasis on communal spirituality introduces a solution. The book is not a unilateral condemnation of contemporary values, but suggests (albeit rather grudgingly) good morals as the basis for social renewal. Durtal is too attached to reason and materialism to abandon himself to faith, yet he senses that he must do so in order to end his spleen.

Durtal, a figure who so clearly encapsulates contemporary fascination for the unusual and the rare, provides Huysmans with a way of commenting on society's unhealthy obsession with materialism. He opens the door to what he calls "spiritual naturalism." *Là-Bas* begins with an extended commentary on this concept, which he illustrates by studying the ways in which the *Karlsruhe Crucifixion* of Mattheus Grünewald carefully represents material elements (naturalism) while commenting on the way they represent religious exaltation (spiritual). Huysmans's literary tableaux—from dazzling chapel to bloody chamber to Gothic courtroom—reflect this technique as the art itself reveals Durtal's spiritual state. By the end of the novel he has changed. We find the inveterate loner and shut-in of the first pages at the top of Saint-Sulpice, philosophizing with a group of friends about how to save society. In this warm, cozy space, high above Paris, Durtal learns to appreciate the company of others.

"The Soul of Arches": Sanctuary

In *En Route* (1894), Durtal has fallen in love with the atmosphere of churches; he spends his free time visiting the houses of worship of Paris. Above all, he has come to appreciate medieval architecture—Gothic and Romanesque—in which darkness and old artwork give him the sense of intimacy he had felt in Carhaix's quarters: "Ah! the charitable churches of the Middle Ages, the humid and smoky chapels, filled with ancient songs, exquisite paintings, and that smell of extinguished candles, and that aroma of burning incense!" In Gothic and Romanesque churches like Saint-Séverin, Durtal feels spirituality enter him through all of his senses, an impression that puts him in touch with his repressed emotions:

> In Paris, there remained only a few specimens of that art of old, only a few sanctuaries whose stones truly oozed faith; among them Saint-Séverin seemed to Durtal the most exquisite and the most safe. He felt at home only there, and he told himself: here, the soul of arches exists. The fervent prayers, the desperate sobs of the Middle Ages have forever soaked these tanned pillars and walls; this vine of pain where saints harvested bunches of grapes hot with tears, has preserved, from this admirable time, emanations that sustain, exhalations that still seek the shame of sin, the confession of tears![55]

He construes the atmosphere produced by smoke, humidity, music, paintings, and incense— "the soul of arches"—as a physical manifestation of the prayers that have been said in the cathedral since it was built. The walls, columns, and vaulting of Saint-Séverin ooze faith and form "a petrified cradle of very old trees, all in flower, but leafless" that nurses Durtal's wounded soul.[56] He feels as though he could pray in this church because it retains the supplications of all who preceded him. It provides him with a sanctuary and shelters him from the physical desires that tempt him in the outside world.

But how has Durtal, who reveled in Gilles de Rais's slaughter of young boys, come to find himself in a Parisian house of worship, admiring its spirituality and wishing that he could pray? One day, after the sudden deaths of Carhaix and Des Hermies, his companions from *Là-Bas,* he wandered into a church "out of curiosity, to kill time." The atmosphere and music turned his soul inside out, and suddenly he believed in God.[57] Despite his best efforts to rationalize this sudden transformation in his spirit, he cannot. He knows only that he has arrived at the Church through religious art, whose atmosphere draws him to its spirituality and distracts him from his material desires (above all, an irresistible attraction for a particularly talented prostitute).[58]

Readers were shocked by the sudden change in Durtal's character.[59] His chastened admiration of the agonizing souls he senses in Saint-Séverin is a far cry from his perverse enjoyment of the misery of Gilles de Rais's victims. But if experiencing grace is truly the unexplainable life-transforming force he describes, then Durtal's sudden humility should not be so surprising. The novel's opening passage is a four-page masterpiece in which Durtal evokes the *De profondis,* the psalm of penitence, in terms reminiscent of Baudelaire's "Correspondances." The lyrics, music, and atmosphere of the church combine to lament humanity's plight: "Bouquets of voices spun under the arches, fused with the greenish sounds of harmonicas, the sharp timbres of breaking crystal."[60] Durtal's soul is pierced by the poignant tension of such music.

He understands that in the Middle Ages the painting and sculpture of the Primitives, mystical poems and prose, Romanesque and Gothic architecture, and plain chant were all produced for the same reason: to worship God. It is both the historical nature of this phenomenon and the emotional response generated by the intersection of so many different arts that help convince Durtal of the validity of his newfound belief.

> Ah! the true proof of Catholicism was this art that it had founded, this art that no one had yet surpassed! In painting and sculpture it was the Primitives; the mystics in poetry and prose; in music, plain chant; in architecture, Romanesque and Gothic. And all of this held together, blazed in a single bouquet, on the same altar; all of this culminated in a tuft of unique thoughts: revere, adore, serve the Distributor, in showing him, reverberated like a faithful mirror in the soul of his creature, the still immaculate loan of his gifts.[61]

In the tradition of Wagner, who believed in a *Gesamtkunstwerk,* a total work in which arts functioning together produce an effect that none of them alone could achieve, in *En Route* Durtal conceives of Catholicism as a spray of flowers in which the combined effect is more vibrant than that of any single stem. It is the profusion of different genres, different styles, different media—all in praise of the same object—that convince him that he is going in the right direction: "Then, once steered onto this track, he had covered it, left architecture and music, had wandered in the mystical territory of the other arts and his long visits to the Louvre, his forays into breviaries, into the books of Ruysbroeck, Angela of Foligno, Saint Teresa, Saint Catherine of Genoa, Madeleine de Pazzi, had strengthened his beliefs."[62] In *En Route* Durtal begins to understand the common force—the Catholic faith—that unites disparate works of medieval art. He begins linking medieval art in museums to Gothic churches such as Saint-Séverin in order to understand these works in their original context. Accordingly, he dreams of constructing the perfect Parisian house of worship, where he can combine the aesthetic elements that most touch him: "Ah! if Saint-Séverin could be soaked in the blazing atmosphere of Notre-Dame-des-Victoires and if its thin musical program could be added to the powerful repertory of Saint-Sulpice, that would be all I need!"[63]

Huysmans brings Durtal to the Church, in *En Route,* yet his character is still unable to go beyond a subjective appreciation of it. He has surpassed his exclusively materialistic fascination with Gilles de Rais's decadent chapel and sacrilegious chamber, but his possessive response to the visceral aspects of religious architecture—he wants to create his own private chapel—still reflects Des Esseintes's embrace of his artificial monk's cell, transferred to a real church. Durtal considers religious art sacred, but cannot yet abandon his aesthetic preferences.[64] He is thus disgusted by most modern churches, which he sees as "inert" and "deaf to prayers":

> How could one meditate in these naves where souls left nothing of themselves, or where, when they were about to open up, they had to pull themselves back together, fold themselves up, disgusted by the indiscretion of photographic lighting, offended even by the abandonment of these altars where no saint had celebrated mass?[65]

He criticizes the sacrilegious ugliness of the exterior of the Madeleine, which bears no crosses and whose interior resembles "the great lounge of a Continental or a Louvre."[66]

For Durtal form corrupts function.[67] He believes in the importance of using art to express emotion and beliefs. He dislikes these churches not because they are modern, but because of the utilitarian nature of their form. Instead of being carefully created in honor of the church, they look like any other modern building:

> By the baseness of their forms [these churches] could serve the most profane customs, because above all they did not bring [. . .] this gift of art that [God] himself had loaned to man and that permitted him to be reflected in the abridged restitution of his work, to take pleasure in front of the blossoming of this flora whose seeds he had sowed in souls that he had picked with care, in souls that he had, after those of the saints, truly elected.[68]

For Durtal, Gothic and Romanesque are the only forms appropriate to spiritual goals because their buttresses, crosses, and portals were created explicitly to symbolize religious postures: the stretch toward Heaven and bowed prayer. Other forms, especially columns and loggias are essentially utilitarian because they appear in pagan temples, theaters, train stations, or hotels.

Through the monologue that constitutes the first four chapters of *En Route,* Huysmans paints Durtal's spiritual torment, but he also uses Durtal to glorify medieval churches and their services as a remedy for such agony. In contrast to the modern world and its utilitarian edifices, Durtal argues that the Gothic cathedral provides a space dedicated exclusively to prayer. Medieval music, devoted to the same goal of praising God, exerts a similar attraction: he enjoys the atmosphere of both the Madeleine and Saint-Sulpice as long as the ceremony distracts him from their appearance. He loves Saint-Sulpice by night, when its music takes over the church, just as he feels that the Madeleine's lounge-like nature is purified by its funeral services: "Like an otherwordly antiseptic, like an extra-human herbal remedy, the liturgy purifies, disinfects the sacrilegious ugliness of this spot."[69]

En Route can be read like *Là-Bas,* as an intriguing novel that explores a little-known aspect of contemporary life (satanism or conversion). While such a reading is certainly valid, it also reduces Huysmans's book to a single dimension, which underestimates the attractive force of his lyrical descriptions of church interiors. These were the elements most prized by critics and one of the reasons why, until the 1940s, *En Route* was included on a list of the twelve major novels of the nineteenth century.[70] The exquisite passages in which Durtal's soul intertwines with the music, art, and prayers of real Parisian churches draw the reader irresistibly to them. Even if one has no religious inclination, the sincerity of Durtal's appreciation is so great that one longs to see what could have prompted such a "wringing of the soul."

Huysmans's literary tableaux did stimulate his readers' imagination. The churches he had praised in the novel became hubs of social activity, tourist stops on the *En Route* itinerary. After the publication of the novel, he repented having put real structures in his works because he could no longer enjoy the solitude and anonymity he had previously enjoyed: "Alas! With my book, I've ruined my experience of the sweet and solitary chapel." In another letter he complains about the throngs that line "his" churches and his displeasure at being "chased like a rabbit" and "scrutinized during services"; he is accosted by reporters everywhere he goes.[71] Huysmans became a celebrity as a result of *En Route.* Between 1895 and 1898 the book sold over 20,000 copies and attracted fan mail from all over the world.[72] He had become a "confessor" for his readers, and his correspondence, which he described as "endless," was so abundant that he wrote a new preface to *En Route* to stop the flow of letters.[73] Some of his readers later became so persistent that they stalked him.[74]

Though certainly more subtle than the posters that flourished in France after the relaxed press laws of 1881, Huysmans's book exerted a similar attraction. Rosalind Williams has argued that store owners courted consumers at this time by creating window displays, posters, and fairs designed to appeal to the imagination, which in turn brought consumers to merchandise.[75] A case in point is the Bon Marché department store, which billed itself as a "sight of Paris" while hosting concerts and other diversions to attract clients.[76] Huysmans similarly tempted his readers by appealing to their interest in art and music, and by offering them a way of distinguishing themselves from simple concert goers. His descriptions of church interiors inculcated in readers the (imagined) need to visit these churches and to experience their amazing atmosphere.

Despite his disappointment at having to give up the solitude he had formerly enjoyed in "his" churches, Huysmans was extremely happy to have brought so many people to the Church; this was, in fact, his original intention.[77] Conversions were public scandals, and Huysmans may very well have expected an uproar over his, given his distinctly bad reputation.[78] He had planned *En Route* to draw unbelievers, especially intellectuals, to Catholicism; he hoped his praise of cathedrals and their art would help readers appreciate a religion that they might not otherwise have embraced.[79] *En Route* appeals to the same readers that admired *A rebours,* and once again Huysmans played on their fondness for the rare, the unusual. He drew them in by glorifying religious art and its traditions.

After his praise of Gothic cathedrals and the ceremonies practiced in them, *En Route* introduces readers to classics of mystical literature. Durtal contacts l'abbé Gévresin, a learned priest he has previously met in a bookstore. Durtal thought that spiritual life would be easy once he accepted faith, but he finds life harder than ever. Abbé Gévresin thus consoles him by reminding him that spiritual fulfillment is not an easy path and by putting his trouble in the context of the fifth mansion described by Teresa of Avila in *Interior Castles.* He urges Durtal to take solace in the writings of the saints, who have been victorious over their bodies and souls. Together they discuss Durtal's soul and its relationship to the writings of mystics Ruysbroeck, Saint Teresa, and Angèle de Foligno, among others. In these passages, they discuss mysticism as a way to "articulate the inexpressible" and to "make visible, audible, almost touchable, this God who remains mute and hidden for all."

In essence, *En Route* comments on the standard reading list for new converts of the time. It is almost as if Huysmans had planned this section as an advertisement for interested readers, who can use the books to cope with their own struggles with conversion.[80] L'abbé Gévresin's teachings also provide a transition to the second part of *En Route,* which continues Durtal's shifting conception of houses of worship as he takes a trip to a monastery; his love of medieval art begins to give way to an appreciation of the spirituality underlying it.

Huysmans dedicates the second part of the novel to showing the importance of monks—the contemplative orders of the Catholic Church—by revealing that the mystical practices of his readings still exist. Durtal leaves Paris for a Trappist monastery where monks carry on a simple routine barely changed since the days of Saint Benedict. Brother Siméon, the pig-keeper of the monastery, is a "true saint, as they existed in the eleventh century [. . .]."[81] Durtal's experience in the monastery, in which he is able to pray and, finally, to confess, is a major development in his quest. He comes to realize that the material trappings of Catholicism, although beautiful, cannot compete with the rapture of faith. Although the form of religious architecture can put one in the mood to pray, true worshipers are not restricted by milieu. In the monastery Durtal is only a short step from *La Cathédrale,* in which he is finally able to subordinate material concerns to faith.

En Route was the first of the Durtal novels to exploit the concerns of contemporaries (unhappiness with the material world, fascination with art and the supernatural) in order to provide them with a course of action. But *En Route* is often summarily dismissed as a "Catholic" novel, without further explanation. In fact, Durtal is a terrible Catholic who hates the contemporary Church and is largely unable to pray. Despite his conversion he remains an outsider, more a figure of a contemporary observer than a "good Catholic." Because of this, most priests of the time refused to acknowledge Huysmans's conversion and persisted in seeing him as a dilettante.[82] Durtal was, in fact, a highly suspect Catholic who, because he incarnated so many of his contemporaries' concerns, appealed to a non-religious mainstream audience. Through his character, Huysmans was able to turn conversion into a kind of fad—thanks to his novel, even monasteries came into vogue!—a new way of functioning within the world.[83] François Mauriac would name him as one of the major forces (with Claudel) that persuaded a generation of young artists to convert to Catholicism: "One had to be 20 in 1905 to measure the impact of books like *En Route* and *La Cathédrale.*"[84] *En Route*—a novel—was hundreds of times more influential for his contemporaries than a sermon, a lecture, or a newspaper article about Catholicism.

La Cathédrale: Notre-Dame de Chartres

La Cathédrale publicizes the aesthetic beauty of Notre-Dame de Chartres, explains its spiritual and historical importance for modern France, and proposes a translation of the cryptic messages spelled out in its sculpture and stained glass. It provided contemporaries with a manual or guidebook to the cathedral. The spiritual distance traveled by Durtal between *Là-Bas* and *La Cathédrale* can be measured by comparing his fascination for Gilles de Rais's chapels to his admiration for Notre-Dame de Chartres. In *La Cathédrale,* he is so impressed by the cathedral that he tunes out the guide who comments on it. He cannot bear to analyze the cathedral without first reveling in the effect it has on him:

> Enveloped in the mystery of its shadow clouded by the rain's mist, it rose ever more clearly as it soared in the sky-white of its naves, exhaling like a soul purifying itself in a bright ascension as it climbs up the path of the mys-

tical life. The ribbed columns fly in slim sheaves, in slender sprays so fragile that they seemed as if they might bend at the slightest breath; yet it was only at vertiginous heights that these stems bent over, launched themselves from one side of the cathedral to the other, above the emptiness, grafting themselves, mixing their sap and blossoming, at last, like a basket in the once gilt pendants of the keystones. This basilica was the supreme effort of matter striving to lighten itself, rejecting, as if ballast, the diminished weight of its walls and replacing them with a less heavy and less lucid substance, substituting the diaphanous skin of its windows for the opacity of its stones. It grew more spiritual, becoming all soul, all prayer, as it sprang toward the Lord to join him; light and slender, nearly imponderable, it was the most magnificent expression of beauty escaping earthly debris, beauty become seraphic.[85]

Durtal is struck by the ways in which the cathedral's spirit—represented by its form—overcomes the heaviness of its stone body as it raises itself to God. Huysmans brings out his vision of the cathedral as a female figure—*la* cathédrale—attempting to escape her materiality, by using dark-colored adjectives and nouns indicating heaviness to refer to the base— "ombre," "la fumée des pluies," "lest," and "poids"—and light-colored attributes— "claire," "blanc," "lucide," and "diaphane"—to evoke the term of the journey. This technique creates an impression of ascension. Unlike *Là-Bas* and *En Route,* in which Huysmans focused on objects—jewels, tapestry, and incense—and the effect they produced on Durtal, in *La Cathédrale,* Huysmans makes every effort to avoid naming tangible items. As Durtal's eyes move from bottom to top, he sees the cathedral as a transparent, ethereal object, floating in the air and impossible to tie down. The use of progressive verb forms—the imperfect and the present participle—accompanied by verbs "monter," "gravir," "s'élever," and "s'exhausser," which indicate rising, evokes the cathedral's quest to escape its "body." Its stretch toward verticality, toward fluidity, causes its form to reflect its soul: beautiful, diaphanous, and airborne.

This was, in fact, the effect l'abbé Suger wanted to produce when he first imagined towering, light-filled Gothic structures. Basing his beliefs on theories elucidated in Dionysius the Areopagite's *Of the Celestial Hierarchy—Of the Ecclesiastical Hierarchy,* Suger planned the cathedral as an illustration of the dispersion of God's light as it falls down on the universe and progressively into shadow. Each being reflects some light back up to God, but must constantly work toward increasing radiance. The cathedral thus figures this "procession toward the light"; its bottom is heavy and dark, while it grows increasingly light and immaterial as it comes closer to God.[86] Durtal's vision of the cathedral as a mythical image stretching toward Heaven shows that he understands the cathedral as an analogy for the human soul. It reminds him both of the slender Virgins of medieval painter Roger van der Weyden and of the medieval accounts he has read about the soul's attempts to escape materiality: "It was the same mystical conception of a spindly body—all length—and an ardent soul, which, unable to shed itself completely of that body, attempted to purify it, reduce it, render it nearly fluid." Although she is not quite able to escape her physical presence, the personified cathedral, like the Virgins of Fra Angelico and Van der Weyden's paintings, leaves her "earthly debris" to travel in mystical spheres.

Huysmans's representation of Notre-Dame de Chartres as a pale Virgin from medieval paintings highlights the difference between his version of the cathedral and that of Hugo and Zola. They all personified the cathedral as a woman, but for Hugo the cathedral was a hulking mass, a partner and mother for Quasimodo, whose highly sensual relationship with the bells was less than spiritual. And for Zola the cathedral was above all a protective mother whose solid body harbored the huddled masses. In *Le Rêve,* Angélique is in awe of l'église Sainte-Marie's stretch to the Heavens, but Zola returns constantly to the solidity and immutability of the cathedral, which protects everything in the town. Huysmans avoids materiality at all cost by representing Notre-Dame de Chartres as a slight girlish Virgin with little relationship to the surrounding town. "She is a thin, blue-eyed blond" with whom he has fallen in love.[87] Huysmans's ethereal, androgynous description of the cathedral demonstrates his admiration of its beauty and delicate artwork, but also betrays his repulsion for bodies, and especially female flesh.[88] Both Hugo and Zola are interested primarily in the "body" of the cathedral, while Huysmans seeks to understand its "soul."

Above all, for Huysmans, Notre-Dame de Chartres incarnates the Virgin Mary. At the end of *La Cathédrale,* Durtal decides that since no church documents agree about Mary's appearance, it is likely that she is reflected in the contours of the cathedral.[89] The laughter of the Virgin shines from the blue eyes of the stained-glass windows; the fluid white stones of her body are covered by "a brilliant robe of flames, striped with striations," and her golden hair radiates from the windows like a nimbus.[90] The cathedral merges with the Virgin Mary, melds with her and illuminates her virtues.[91] Durtal is in love with the ultimately inaccessible woman, the woman whose body is stone. He comes a step closer to spirituality in *La Cathédrale,* yet his focus is still egotistical; he incestuously adulates the Virgin Mary, our Mother, in accordance with his own aesthetic preferences.

The Cathedral of Communal Prayer

Durtal's attraction to Notre-Dame de Chartres exposes his lingering appropriation of it as "his," yet *La Cathédrale* is a book in which Huysmans places even greater emphasis on community and social involvement. In Chapter 1, we saw a description in which Huysmans glorified the cathedral as a project that implicated all levels of medieval society; this passage was from *La Cathédrale.* As he begins to pray in Notre-Dame de Chartres, Durtal will discover yet another facet of the collective nature of the cathedral: the magic of communal prayer. At the end the novel, Durtal will realize that his spleen is not caused by the outside world as he thought, but by his unrelenting and egotistical focus on himself.

In *La Cathédrale,* Durtal has moved to Chartres with l'abbé Gévresin and his housekeeper, Madame Bavoil. As in the other Durtal novels, the reader is privy to Durtal's thoughts, overhears his dinner discussions with friends, and accompanies Durtal on the guided tours of the cathedral given to him by l'abbé Plomb, a vicar. As Durtal explores Notre-Dame de Chartres, he is impressed by its sculpture and stained glass, but even more so by its "soul," which he discovers in the crypt, Notre-Dame de Sous-Terre. It oozes faith as did Saint-Séverin: "This cave abounded in memories. The soulful vapors, the exhalations of accrued desires and regrets had created, even more, perhaps, than the smoke of the candles [. . .] the saintly soot of the arches."[92] Durtal feels as though the Virgin resides in this crypt where thousands of prayers have left their mark. He affirms that it is the best place to pray.[93]

Finally, Durtal is interested in the community instead of claiming churches (like Saint-Séverin) for himself. Durtal explains his theory of the "soul" of a church for his friends. It is not a material aspect of the church, but rather an ambience that has been kept alive by worshipers since the Middle Ages:

> I am not speaking of the soul of the monument from the moment when man, with divine help, created it; we are unaware of that soul though precious documents do tell us about Chartres; but of the soul that other churches have saved, the soul they have now and that we help keep alive with our more or less constant presence, with our more or less frequent communions, with our more or less fervent prayers.[94]

As Durtal's repeated use of "we" and "our" suggests, the soul of a church comes from communal worship over years of intense prayer. Such psychic energy creates an ambience that promotes reflection. Durtal sees cathedrals as vessels that have protected the prayers inside them for hundreds of years, "the eternal image of Peter's boat that Jesus guided through the storm," and "Noah's ark, the ark without which there is no safety."[95] Cathedrals are the ultimate symbol of synthesis, preservation, and durability; they are great spiritual arks of religious art and faith that have sustained Catholicism through the years. Durtal and his friends continue this tradition of communal support by adding their prayers to those kept in Notre-Dame de Chartres.

Durtal finally understands why he so admires the cathedral; it is not just because of its beauty or because of its collection of religious art. The difference between a cathedral and a museum lies largely in its "soul" the "use value" that puts all of the disparate elements of it into context. Huysmans's description of the "soul" recuperates a medieval understanding of the cathedral as a representation of the Christian community. A fifteenth-century illustration for Vincent de Beauvais's "Le miroir historique" provides a particularly apt representation of this concept (Figure 3.1).[96] Prophets and martyrs from the past join hands in the present to help kings and judges build a cathedral. Every member of the church—past, present, and future—must participate in maintaining the cathedral—through physical work and through prayer—for it to persevere. Durtal finally understands that this is what he has been seeking all along; he has longed for a system in which individuals are protected and reinvigorated by their continued function as part of a larger community. Durtal has discovered what De Certeau calls "community practice," the only viable way to experience the religious journey. Notre-Dame de Chartres becomes the ultimate symbol of social and spiritual harmony. It continues the sense of community he so admired in the crowd that prayed for Gilles de Rais: people join together in prayer instead of following their egotistical desires.

Suddenly, Durtal realizes that this precious heart of Catholicism is endangered, not only because of increasing individualism and secularization, but also because such communal spirit has only been preserved in the few churches where services have never stopped. Increasingly secular congregations have abandoned Notre-Dame of Paris, of Amiens, and of Laon, and turned them into secular monuments, devoid of religious spirit and the worshipers to maintain it:

> Take Notre-Dame de Paris; it was patched up and restored from top to bottom; its sculptures are mended when they are not entirely modern; in spite of Hugo's eulogies it remains second rate; but it has its nave, its marvelous transept; it even possesses an ancient statue of the Virgin [. . .] Well, they tried to reanimate a cult of Notre-Dame in its nave, to establish a pilgrimage movement, yet all is dead! That cathedral no longer has a soul; it is an inert corpse of stone; try to listen to mass there, to approach the altar, and you will feel an icy cloak fall on you. Is it a result of its neglect, of its dull services, of the muttered sauce they whip up there, of its rushed evening closure, of its late morning awakening, long after dawn? Or is it a result of the authorized visits of indecent tourists, the London boors that I have seen, speaking loudly, talking at the top of their voices, and staying seated—in complete disregard of the most simple courtesy—right in front of the altar while the sacrament was being blessed in front of them! I do not know, but I can certify that the Virgin no longer lives there day and night as at Chartres.[97]

Amiens and Laon, too, he goes on to add, are empty, dead, and soulless. Durtal argues that without the continued presence of worshipers' prayers, cathedrals' souls burn out. Once extinguished, they cannot be reanimated. Other cathedrals— Reims, Rouen, Dijon, Tours, le Mans—are not yet "dead" but are in their death throes. He is disturbed that cathedrals, the center of French communal life since the Middle Ages, are losing influence because of dwindling congregations and ap-

Figure 3.1. *Building the Church.* Vincent de Beauvais, "Le Miroir historial." Bibliothèque nationale de France ms fr. 50.

athetic parishioners. He and his friends agree that the soul of churches parallels that of modern France: it is dying.

Why does Huysmans portray such a bleak picture of cathedrals in these novels, especially if his contemporaries value them as giant museums with good concerts? Huysmans was not simply interested in the cathedral as a nostalgic image of the Middle Ages. He was equally concerned by the cathedral's function in the nineteenth century. For him, the "soul of arches" forms a crucial link between past and present. It constitutes the spiritual history of France and transcends the petty social, political, and economic worries of his contemporaries. His correspondence describes his goal of "reanimating" and "building" the cathedral within a fictional frame: "I have already built three chapters of it; I hope that all will go well, as difficult as it is to resuscitate and to erect medieval cathedrals in their setting and in the atmosphere that we are creating for them today."[98] He literally wanted to reanimate the cathedral (*re* + *animare*), to bring it back to life.[99] He knew his works could reach a wide audience, and he hoped that they might attract more people to existing cathedrals, where contemporaries would learn about the Catholic faith: "Perhaps this volume will make Notre-Dame de Chartres and her house in Chartres better loved," he wrote in a letter to the abbess of Solesmes, while telling l'abbé Ferret that he hoped to reach non-Catholics, "those for whom conversions are possible."[100]

In *La Cathédrale,* Huysmans did for cathedrals what Hugo had in *Notre-Dame de Paris*. He adopted a building that contemporaries had begun to take for granted, and he personified it in a novel. By endowing the cathedral with life, he was able to endear it to readers before alerting them to its impending demise. He gives readers a chance to defend the cathedrals that are not yet "dead." Nearly every page is filled with praise of the art, history, or meaning of this precious resource, "the cathedral" of the title. The book was his greatest success yet: it sold 20,000 copies in less than a month and was followed by a press scandal (erroneously) saying that Huysmans had become a monk. There was so much publicity that the clergy of Chartres asked Huysmans not to attend midnight mass for fear of scandals.[101] The extent to which Huysmans reactivated the cathedral as an important entity for the French can be gauged by the outpouring of affection for Notre-Dame de Chartres that followed the novel's publication. Gugelot lauds Huysmans for "making the cathedral fashionable," for turning it into "the symbol of cathedrals," while inspiring student and scout expeditions. Mauriac credits Huysmans with "the resurrection of the pilgrimage to Chartres."[102] By 1912, the French had even founded a Société des amis des cathédrales.[103]

Symbolism: "The Psychology of Cathedrals"

In *La Cathédrale,* Huysmans uses a similar technique to that employed in *En Route:* his beautiful description of religious art leads readers into the novel before he lectures them about mysticism or theology. In *La Cathédrale,* he focuses above all on medieval symbolism, a topic that would have fascinated his readers because of the popularity of the symbolist movement in literature, art, and music. In *La Cathédrale,* Huysmans uses Durtal and his discoveries to explain medieval symbolism for his readers, much as he had used Durtal's praise of medieval religious art and architecture in *En Route* to discuss medieval mysticism. *La Cathédrale* helps the reader understand the mysterious hidden messages of the cathedral.

Durtal calls symbolism "the psychology of the cathedral, the study of the soul of sanctuaries, so completely disregarded since the Middle Ages by those professors of monumental physiology called archeologists and architects."[104] Because advocates of the cathedral—notably Victor Hugo and Viollet-le-Duc—had praised the cathedral's exterior, its "body," people had begun to forget that it was not simply a beautiful object. It also contained messages that could be studied through symbolism. He realizes that his contemporaries understand Gothic architecture as an impressive monument, and not much more. Durtal himself knows very little about symbolism on his arrival in Chartres; it is l'abbé Plomb who indoctrinates him into this science. He begins by giving Durtal a general sense of the cathedral's important relationship to Catholicism and its beliefs:

> Everything is in this edifice [. . .] the Scriptures, theology, the history of the human race summarized in outline form; thanks to the science of symbolism a mass of stones could be turned into a macrocosm. Yes, I shall repeat it, everything fits in this vessel, even our material and moral life, our virtues and our vices. The architect takes us from the birth of Adam and guides us through the end of time. Notre-Dame de Chartres is the most colossal repertory that exists of heaven and earth, of God and man. All of its figures are words; all of its groups are sentences; the difficulty lies in reading them.[105]

The cathedral is thus both a summary and a reflection of the universe. In what seems a paradox, l'abbé Plomb presents the cathedral to Durtal as both a microcosm—a vessel, a repertory, and a book that contain the Scriptures, theology, and humanity—and as a macrocosm. How can the two be compatible? For l'abbé Plomb, the key lies in a knowledge of symbols. He defines symbol in the broad sense, according to Littré, as "a figure or an image used as a sign of something else," but he narrows it to the Catholic notion expressed by Hugues de Saint-Victor: "a symbol is the allegorical representation of a Christian principle, in a tangible form."[106] The cathedral only becomes a macrocosm when one deciphers its symbols: the multiplicity of cross-references do not reduce each character to a single meaning, but gloss on it, thus raising it to another level, that of a macrocosm, the universe.

L'abbé Plomb explains that symbols have always existed in Christian thought, notably in images such as the Tree of Good and Evil in the Book of Genesis and the parables taught by Christ. They are of divine source, but allow humans to understand abstract concepts in material terms. The Middle Ages, he continues, wanted to emulate Christ's tradition of using parables to evoke God and his messages:

> [The people of the Middle Ages] made use of a practical means of making themselves understood. They wrote a book that was accessible for the most simple people by replacing text by image, instructing, in this manner, the uneducated. This was, in fact, the idea circulated by the Synod of Arras in 1025: "That which the illiterate cannot comprehend in writing must be taught them through depiction." In short, the Middle Ages translated, in sculpted or painted lines, the Bible, theology, saints' lives, apocryphal gospels, legends, and put them within reach of all, and summarized them in signs that remained like a permanent marrow, like a concentrated extract of these lessons.[107]

Durtal is enthralled by l'abbé Plomb's lesson and compares the medieval concept of symbolism to teaching catechism to "grown-up children." L'abbé Plomb's analogy of the cathedral as a primer for the ignorant consciously avoids treating the complex theological messages also represented in it. Comparing a cathedral to a book is itself an allegory that allows Durtal to grasp concepts still beyond his understanding. L'abbé Plomb gives Durtal the critical apparatus necessary to gain introductory knowledge of the cathedral (as does Huysmans for the readers of his book).

A common problem for the modern reader lies in taking Huysmans's analogies literally. Statements such as "all of its figures are words; all of its groups are sentences" can be taken as an invitation to read the cathedral as one would the Bible. And, in fact, this is how Durtal initially approaches the church. L'abbé Plomb warns him, however, that these are distilled substances—marrow and concentrated extract—and not direct translations. Jean-Luc Steinmetz has pointed out the impossibility of reading art as sentences. Although Huysmans equated figures to words and groups to phrases, the symbolic images in the cathedral escape the confines of language and cannot be read as a book: each symbol is not tied to a specific referent, but reflects "a global significance."[108] De Certeau also evokes the futility of transcribing images, especially in his analysis of *The Garden of Delights* of Hieronymus Bosch, another medieval work with a similarly allegorical intent: "This painting plays on our need to decipher. It enlists in its service a Western drive to *read.* The meticulous proliferation of its figures calls irresistibly for indefinite narrativizing [. . .] The Garden cannot be reduced to univocity. It offers a multiplicity of possible itineraries [. . .]."[109] The cathedral, too, draws one to gloss on and to decipher the meaning hidden in its images, while it refuses to bend to a single interpretation. Huysmans's analysis introduces the reader to only a few of the many interpretative itineraries.

After l'abbé Plomb's lesson, Durtal spends the rest of the novel "narrativizing," discovering references to biblical stories from those of the *Old Testament* kings who prefigured Christ to that of the local saints. Huysmans uses his character's discoveries to introduce his readers to the cathedral; it is not coincidental that a number of critics referred to the novel as a "Baedeker."[110] François Coppée mentioned that everyone he knew had a copy and remarked that the book was written "with the meticulous precision of a guidebook."[111] Philosopher Jacques Maritain remembers having spent three days with his wife at Notre-Dame de Chartres, "spelling it like a Bible" and admiring the cathedral as "a mistress of theology, of saintly history and exegesis."[112]

Huysmans transformed understanding of the cathedral by introducing readers to its symbolism and by allowing them to begin adding meaning where Durtal leaves off. Huysmans's effect on his contemporaries was, once again, calculated to profit from contemporary interests—art, symbolism, and travel. The period saw a veritable proliferation of guidebooks, but there was no existing guide to medieval symbolism.[113] Huysmans took enormous pains to create one, so much so that he published a twenty-five page index to accompany La Cathédrale. His letters to Arij Prins evoke the breadth of his documentation, which relied heavily on unedited archival material:

> I am plunged into an overwhelming work, with my book which, unfortunately, is becoming erudite, but there is no other option. I am redoing all of medieval symbolism, something that no longer exists—it's insane!—two monks at Solesmes have been mobilized to examine old manuscripts for me—and I have engaged a provisional secretary whom I send to the Bibliothèque Nationale to take notes for me [. . .][114]

Such letters reveal the scholarly intent of Huysmans's project. He wanted to bring to light all of medieval symbolism in order to make his novel a comprehensive guide of the cathedral and its teaching. Accordingly, as a book of erudition, it devotes sections to each aspect of medieval symbolism. La Cathédrale treats topics ranging from the symbolic importance of a cathedral's individual parts, including bell towers, steeples, roof, walls, windows, and stained glass,[115] to numbers, liturgical clothing, and objects used in church ceremony,[116] and to colors, precious stones, plants, animals, and perfumes.[117]

Before Henry Adams and before Emile Mâle—both of whom read him—Huysmans produced a book about the cathedral and its symbolism for the general public.[118] And although he was a novelist, the public accepted his work as that of a specialist and scholar.[119] Extracts of La Cathédrale were published in L'Echo de Paris in October 1897 and the book version was sold in February 1898 to triumphant public success.

The "guidebook-like" aspects of La Cathédrale are even more striking when compared to Emile Mâle's doctoral thesis, L'Art religieux du XIIIe siècle en France, which was published later that year. Despite the fact that Huysmans was writing a novel and Mâle a dissertation, La Cathédrale and L'Art religieux du XIIIe siècle are quite similar, especially in their central premise about medieval symbolism. Both argue that the cathedral is an intrinsically legible text when one understands how to decipher it. A comparison of *La Cathédrale*'s index with Mâle's bibliography reveals that both men consulted many of the same authors (notably Didron, Quicherat, and Viollet-le-Duc), but that Huysmans consulted more medieval manuscripts than did Mâle, who relied heavily on previous works of nineteenth-century art historians. While their content and main points are comparable, their approach differs significantly. Instead of interpreting and subordinating his sources to one another, as did Mâle, Huysmans tended to give them all equal weight. His profusion of documents creates the impression of a never-ending gloss on the cathedral. He does not reduce each symbol to a single meaning, but opens each one to an abundance of multiple interpretations. Where Mâle was interested primarily in explaining the function of symbolism in religious architecture, Huysmans wanted to revive the atmosphere, the context of religious thought in which cathedrals were built. *La Cathédrale* thus creates a rich mixture of discussion and interpretation.

Huysmans's tendency to build the cathedral into a generator of significations reflects Durtal's ultimate understanding of medieval symbolism. He has come to admire the cathedral as a total work of art, in which painting, stained glass, sculpture, music, sacred objects, worshipers, and ceremony create an atmosphere of communal spirituality that conforms to l'abbé Suger's dream of "oneness." But as Durtal continues to learn his "catechism," he also discovers another level of signification. He already understands the cathedral as "the most magnificent work of art the Middle Ages left us" and as "an immense dictionary about medieval science, God, the Virgin, and the saints."[120] But now he realizes that all of these individual symbols combine to project a spiritual view of the universe, a model that helps worshipers along their path to salvation:

> The Middle Ages [. . .] knew that everything on earth is a sign, a figure, that the visible is only worth what it extracts from the invisible; the Middle Ages [. . .], which were not gullible, as we are, to appearances, closely studied this science and made it the caretaker and the servant of mysticism. Convinced that the only goal important for man to pursue, that the only necessary end, down here, was to reach for, to enter into direct communication with Heaven and to arrive there before death, by pouring oneself, by melting as much as possible into God, it led souls, submitted them to a temperate schedule of cloisters, stripped them of their earthly preoccupations, of their carnal designs, and oriented them constantly toward the same thoughts of humility and penitence, toward the same ideas of justice and love, and, to hold them, to protect them from themselves, the Middle Ages enclosed them with a fence, surrounding them forever with God, in all aspects, in all forms.[121]

Durtal cherishes this concept of the spiritual world, especially when he links it to the individualism and materialism of his time. He longs to throw himself into just such a protected community, where he would think of nothing but images and forms that remind him of God. The cathedral was one such manifestation of this protective barrier; it was not simply a beautiful and awe-inspiring work of art, but also a house of worship where one could surround onself with a reflection of the Gospels; its system of representation was a constant reminder of God and the afterlife. André Vauchez affirms the central role of the cathedral in the Middle Ages as an "illustration of the medieval Christian conception of time: time not merely as flux but as preparation, within each individual as well as in the world, for the coming reign of God." Accordingly, he argues, the cathedral's statuary and labyrinths served as examples of the difficult path to salvation, and encouraged the worshiper to imitate them in order to arrive at the new Jerusalem. The cathedral epitomizes "all aspects of religious experience, at once local and universal, historical and eschatological."[122] Such a vision soothes Durtal, who can imagine himself accompanied by the cathedral's figures as he continues up his tortuous path. He finally understands that he is not alone. Seeing the cathedral and the rest of the visible world as a reflection of the invisible world to which he strives will help him overcome his attachment to the material realm and to approach God.

At the end of *La Cathédrale,* Durtal embarks for the Benedictine community of Solesmes, where he plans to live and work, in order to cloister himself with symbols that will "orient him toward humility and penitence." He hopes that all of his travels and studies will help him finish his education about the traditions of the medieval Church:

> By attaching [these new experiences] to my own studies of religious painting stolen from sanctuaries and now reunited in museums; by adding my remarks on the various cathedrals that I will have explored, I will thus have covered the entire cycle of mysticism, extracted the essence of the Middle Ages, I will have reunited in a kind of bouquet these separated stems, scattered for so many centuries, and have observed in more detail one of them, symbolism, about which so many aspects were nearly lost through neglect.[123]

By reconstituting and reassembling fields that have become dispersed or forgotten, Durtal hopes to better understand symbolism, "the essence of the Middle Ages" that has helped him find his own place in the universe. He returns to his original fascination for collecting, but his work will focus not on creating his own private chapel, but on reuniting a bouquet of knowledge for everyone to enjoy.

In a time that Huysmans saw as devoted to self-fulfilling art produced by money-grubbing modern architects, the idea of communities of people who devoted their faith and skills to a nonmaterial ideal fascinated him.[124] Medieval religious architecture is the ultimate model for artistic production in the Durtal cycle. It is a material edifice that does not serve as an end in itself, but that attempts to accede to a higher order. The cathedral, "the architecture that alone symbolized all of Catholicism," is the key to Durtal's progressive journey from collector to regenerator of spirituality. It persuaded him that a "mass of stones" could open a macrocosm. With his discovery of symbolism, Durtal's spiritual conversion is complete. Although he still wrestles with his aesthetic dislikes and material impulses, he construes religious art in terms of the spirituality it conveys, just as he finally understands that he needs to make the best of this life in waiting for the next. Like the unknown saint in his Dutch painting, Durtal's spiritual quest ends as he climbs the hill to the cathedral.

"The Church's Best Form of Propaganda": Huysmans as Publicist

One expects the Durtal cycle to end here, with a spiritual consummation in Solesmes, the jewel of medieval abbeys. Five years later, however, Huysmans resurrected his character in an epilogue, *L'Oblat,* which was set against the years 1900–1901, a time during which monasteries feared a bill requiring every congregation to apply for legal authorization from the government or be dissolved. When the Law of Associations was, in fact, passed in 1901, many monks—like those with whom Durtal was staying—chose to flee to Belgium rather than have their application refused by the French government. Published in 1903, after the passage of this law, the novel serves as a call to arms for the persecuted Catholic Church.

Huysmans's defense of the Church was in the air of the times. As increasingly severe measures were taken against Catholics (both Huysmans and Claudel, who worked for the government, were pressured to keep their Catholic views quiet), artists attempted to contribute their talents to helping the Church.[125] Huysmans had already used *En Route* and *La Cathédrale* as what we might call "advertizing," in order to attract secular readers to religious architecture and church services. But in *L'Oblat,* the message was directed primarily to Catholic artists. He champions art as "the church's best form of propaganda":

> One has to be extremely ignorant [. . .] to deny the power of art. It was the most reliable assistant of mysticism and liturgy in the Middle Ages; it was the beloved eldest son of the Church, its go-between, the one in charge of expressing its thoughts, of exposing them in books, on cathedral porches, on retables, during mass. It was he [art, the eldest son] who commented on the Scriptures and inflamed the crowds; who threw them, laughing in joyous prayer, at the feet of mangers, or who shook them with sobs in front of tearful scenes of the Calvary [. . .] But alas! All of this is so far away. What a terrible state of abandon and anemia the Church has been in since it has lost interest in art and art has withdrawn from it. It has lost its best form of propaganda, it most faithful method of defense. It would thus seem that now that

it is under attack and has failed everywhere, it should beg the Lord to send it artists whose works would certainly achieve more conversions, would bring it more champions than those useless old stories that priests, stuck in their ways, discharge over the resigned heads of believers from the height of their pulpits![126]

This, expressed in a novel, is certainly one of the greatest paeans to art as savior. Huysmans recommends using art to attract and encourage the prayers that are so crucial to the Christian community. He argues that the Church needs to cultivate more artists, the high priests who will bring new converts to the flock. But while sending out a rallying cry for renewing the Church's relationship to the people through art, Huysmans also reveals the extent to which he broke with mainstream Catholicism. His underlying message about replacing priests with artists was not appreciated by members of the clergy. In fact, the entire novel harshly criticizes modern Catholicism, which he holds responsible for the political situation. Because priests were stuck in the status quo and in their allegiances of power with the bourgeoisie, they neglected religion, the soul of the Church. This was an extremely widespread opinion of artist converts to Catholicism, who, like Huysmans, argued that the modern Church should focus exclusively on religion.[127]

At the beginning of *L'Oblat,* we learn that Durtal's Solesmes project has failed because of the monastery's excessive materialism: it was too beautiful and its schedules too regimented. Durtal resettles in the fictive Le Val-des-Saints, not far from Dijon, where he lives attached to another Benedictine community, the monastery of Notre-Dame de l'Atre.[128] He decides to become an oblate, a participant attached to the monastery through official vows and devotion to upholding the beliefs of the Benedictine order, yet living apart from the monks. Much of the book is dedicated to extolling the virtues of this situation, which is perfect for those who do not have the physical stamina to become monks or who (like artists) still have social obligations that necessitate leaving from time to time.

Durtal has just become an oblate when rumors of the government's impending decision to break up congregations reaches the monastery. He is heartbroken by the impending departure, especially since he cannot join them. Without his monastery he dejectedly decides to return to Paris. But Durtal has evolved. Unlike Des Esseintes, who ended *A rebours* with a plaintive prayer to live anywhere away from the modern world—"anywhere out of the world"—Durtal has overcome his loathing for the modern world. Although he resents having to move back to Paris at the end of *L'Oblat,* he subordinates his own material desires to those of God. Like Des Esseintes, he prays, but to live anywhere close to God: "anywhere [. . .] far from ourselves and close to you."

As Durtal worries about the future of Catholicism once the monks have left France, he does not give up on life, but dreams of founding a brotherhood of artists who will renew the Catholic Church by using art to attract new worshipers.

Throughout the novel, his research into the role of the oblate in the Catholic Church teaches him that many of them—Claus Sluter, for one—were working artists. Unlike monks, whose schedules were often too occupied by services to create, oblates traditionally had the time to undertake major works of art.[129] In the modern world, Durtal thinks, an artistic association—with no politically stated religious affiliation—could work and pray without difficulty, unlike a monastery, whose religious vows would subject it to the Law of Associations. In this fashion, communities of oblates could sustain and regenerate the Church until the return of the monks. He is convinced that oblates are the people to bring new converts to Catholicism in its hour of need. Huysmans, himself, attempted repeatedly to found this type of religious community, but all his efforts resulted in failure.[130]

But why does Huysmans so continually insist on the importance of bringing new recruits to Catholicism? In fact, he was less interested in politics than in spirituality; he was compelled to maintain "the soul of arches," the community worship that gives cathedrals life. For him, the Church is the community; its death, by dispersal or attrition marks the end of spiritual life. As Michel de Certeau puts it "He who thinks that he can be separated from his brothers without being separated from God is no longer religious." The Christian community that built and maintains the cathedral protects and gives meaning to the souls of its individual members by putting them in contact with God. Without it they are nothing. Like Huysmans, De Certeau concludes his essay about religious belief by affirming the importance of remaining a part of the collective: "let me never be separated from you."[131]

In addition to this core motivation, Huysmans was also influenced by a radical notion about the importance of prayers. He believed that everything we see is a tangible manifestation of an event occurring on another—invisible—plane. This theory is most clearly exposed in *Sainte Lydwine de Schiedam* (written before *L'Oblat*), in which Jesus Christ lifts the suffering Lydwine into the air to see a panorama of her time. Europe has become a giant chessboard where saints— "God's pawns"—are ranged in battle with the forces of evil. Disaster strikes each time Satan gains the upper hand. As long as there are enough people who have abandoned themselves to God, however, equilibrium and peace will reign. Although this Manichean belief in a battle between good and evil may seem simplistic and naive by today's standards, Griffiths and Gugelot have shown just how widely accepted an explanation it was in Catholic circles for the seeming "degeneration" of the fin de siècle. Believing that an imbalance of evil leads everyone to eternal damnation gives one a strong moral imperative to restore the balance of power. How better to do so than to create a legion of good forces for the Church?

Huysmans failed in his attempts to establish a monastic community of artists, yet his goal of attracting artists bore fruit. His vibrant descriptions of the cathedral and the medieval art it contained intrigued them and drew them closer. Catholic novelist François Mauriac credited Huysmans with coming to the aid of the Church just at the right time:

The liquidation that followed the Dreyfus Affair was atrocious. The winners settled their accounts. The separation of Church and State, the condemnation of modernism gave a young Catholic the impression of belonging to a declining and vanquished minority. What change today! [. . .] The French Church has progressed [. . .] since my adolescence, and in spite of dechristianization, it has been marvelously renewed.

Mauriac's enthusiasm shows the extent to which Huysmans's novels provided contemporaries with hope and a positive model for surviving such a time. Mauriac credits Huysmans with a number of feats: he brought a new influx of artists and intellectuals to Catholicism; he was almost singlehandedly responsible for the restoration of plain-chant to churches other than monasteries; and he was a pioneer in the turn-of-the-century renewal of the cult of the Virgin. In a eulogy to Huysmans, fifty years after his death, Mauriac focused on the number of people—"what a crowd in black and white"—who were convinced to convert by Huysmans.[132] Gugelot, too, returns over and over, in his study of the conversion of intellectuals from 1885 to 1935, to the idea of Huysmans as a "precursor."

The Novel as Cathedral

Huysmans used the novel, which he considered the most influential form of literature, to bring new believers to the Catholic Church.[133] The books were successful as recruitment devices for the Catholic Church, yet they continue to confuse many readers. "Are the novels of Huysmans even novels?" is a common query.[134] The question is legitimate, especially since scholarly information plays such a central role that the novels literally rival the works of art historians. Given their indexes and glosses on Church art and doctrine, these works are like no other novels. Critics have traditionally focused on the excessive documentation and fragmentation of the Durtal cycle, in which description and research overwhelm plot. This was Léon Blum's concern: "[. . .] imagine the mixed fragments of a treaty of ecclesiastical history, of a museum catalog, all interspersed with religious articles and motley descriptions [. . .] Mr. Huysmans does not subject himself to the most simple, most typical techniques of a novelist."[135] Durtal's quest to resolve his spiritual dilemma by traveling from church to church overwhelms the traditional action-based plot of the novel. His conversations with other characters, his own personal research, and long descriptive passages create a new kind of structure dominated by meditations on science, religion, and art.[136] Huysmans's project has long puzzled critics and the mixed reception of the Durtal novels was not unlike that which greeted Zola's *Trois Villes*. Both series are largely ignored today because of their hybrid nature.

But the fact remains that these books are novels, if for no other reason than that Huysmans said so, and that his critics interpreted them as such. Perhaps an even more crucial question is *why* they are novels. Why did Huysmans want these texts to be novels when he could much more easily have written an essay about symbolism, a guidebook of Chartres, a letter to the editor about the injustice of anticlerical laws, or a prose poem about the beauty of Chartres in the morning? First of all, Huysmans *had* published a great number of essays, historical studies, and prose poems. These works had met with only marginal popular success. Given his post-conversion goal of publicizing the Church through art, he needed a way to be sure that his message would be read. Because he firmly believed that the novel was "the only path to success today,"[137] and because he was a recognized novelist with a reliable number of readers, he took a chance at using the novel to spread his message about the importance of religious art.

Huysmans's correspondence makes his priorities clear. He told Henri Hennezel, a friend who was writing a book similar to *L'Oblat*, that in order to succeed in teaching the public about Catholic traditions one must tempt readers into reading specialized information by presenting it through fiction:

> The devices you can use—conversations, soliloquies, or personal chapters—are not very varied, but after all they serve their purpose. Obviously, as we've said before, a novel planned on those lines is a mongrel and a hybrid, but there's nothing else to be done. Otherwise your book is certain to be a flop, because no one will read a brochure on the Liturgy, the clergy least of all. And after all, you are doing useful work in masking the taste of technique with a succulent sauce.[138]

For Huysmans, the novel was a form that allowed him to transmit information to his readers, while giving them a bit of entertainment. He understood all along that he would have to push the limits of the genre, but he was willing to take his chances in order to initiate his contemporaries into the medieval practices of the Catholic Church.

Second, Huysmans saw the novel as the form best positioned to resuscitate the moralizing function of medieval art in the modern world. In *La Cathédrale*, he drew a parallel between the cathedral and the modern novel, both of which appealed to the public by portraying the ideas of their time in a pleasant form. Both are true to the conception of symbolism he attributes to Saint Augustine in *La Cathédrale:* "A thing announced through allegory is certainly more expressive, more agreeable, more imposing than when one expounds it using technical terms."[139] Durtal tells himself that the modern novel depicts the effects of psychological struggles between good and evil behavior just as medieval churches represented the virtues and vices in its sculptures in order to encourage good conduct and discourage the bad. He planned to use his novels as the medieval church used the cathedral: as a catechism for adults.

Throughout his work Huysmans criticized the modern Church for its temporal concerns—money and politics—and criticized the laxity of its education. In

La Cathédrale, Huysmans argued that priests did humanity a disservice by shying away from portraying battles between vice and virtue. He is particularly surprised by the Church's prudish fear of modern art—"unheard of ignorance," "instinctive hatred of art," "apprehension of ideas," "terror of terms"—because it makes priests avoid a basic educational premise—teaching by example. He fully approves of the medieval Church's attempt to teach the Scriptures through pictures.[140] Huysmans argues that even the groups of statues figured on the cathedrals of Saint-Benoît-sur-Loire, Reims, Mans, and Bourges, in which naked people cavort in sinful postures, are representations of the Scriptures destined to educate the public.[141] He suggests that the modern Church should embrace its medieval roots instead of recoiling from the representation of vice.

Both the modern novel and the cathedral can inspire horror for evil. In this Huysmans agrees with Barbey d'Aurevilly, whose preface to *Les Diaboliques* insists that one must show the full extent of vice through literature and art in order to understand its horrible consequences. Durtal does not mention his studies of Gilles de Rais, but his brutally naturalist descriptions of this murderer's evisceration and profanation of the bodies of small boys inspires repulsion in even the most hardened reader.[142] In a time when contemporaries had become increasingly disgusted with the Church's involvement with politics, Huysmans felt that reaffirming its links to a didactic medieval tradition would valorize it in the eyes of a society curious about both medieval art and stable systems of faith. He knew that the modern novel, like a Gothic cathedral, could provide an accessible medium for contemporaries to learn about virtue and vice.

Though Huysmans understood that he was pushing the limits of the genre by including so much dialogue, description, and lecturing, his novels do adhere to an internal logic. In an astute analysis of *A rebours,* Janell Watson has noted that among the set descriptive pieces, it is Des Esseintes who holds the novel together; his subjectivity serves as "a selection and organizing system. This is why the novel does not seem fragmentary or unstructured, despite its many enumerative passages and its lack of action."[143] The structure of the Durtal cycle is similar: a single protagonist's psychological needs provide structure for what Watson calls the *enumeratio*—the collection of various descriptions, meditations, digressions—that make up the novel. But given the structural similarities between *A rebours* and the Durtal cycle, why does the latter seem so much less cohesive?

I believe that the Durtal novels reuse the "catalog form" of *A rebours* in the sense that Watson describes it, but that the issue of religion poses an ancillary problem for the Durtal cycle. In his review of *La Cathédrale,* Paul Valéry identifies mystical representation as the central difficulty for the reader. He begins by asserting that only a mystic can read another and thus begs incompetence; his understanding of the linguistic problems latent in Huysmans's novels is clear. Valéry remarks that mysticism is "a sort of pure, individual science" with a "new, personal dictionary." It borrows from conventional language while creating new and often contradictory meanings for familiar words; although one may seem to recognize the words used, one has to know the points of difference in order truly to understand. If not, one remains an outsider.[144]

Most modern readers remain outsiders to the Durtal cycle. We find the novels fragmented and disjointed because we take them at face value: we interpret them simply as the story of Durtal's travel and study of religious art. Without considering the vocabulary and the practices associated with conversion (especially the practice of confession and spiritual self-examination), it is easy to criticize the Durtal cycle as overly fragmented. In an increasingly secular society, as Michel de Certeau has noted, we tend to consider religious manifestations as "products" of the Church and not as "allegories": "Religious content hides the conditions of its production. It is the signified of something other than what it says. It is an allegory to decipher."[145] It is no coincidence that the one reader who pointed out the allegorical nature of *A rebours* was a Catholic novelist, Barbey d'Aurevilly. Deciphering the Durtal cycle depends on reading it within the frame of reference of the Church.

Huysmans admitted that his fiction was the "silver coating that hides medicine," and identified Durtal as no more than "a simple pawn in this game."[146] Huysmans has often been accused of writing a thinly veiled autobiography in the Durtal cycle, but in fact, the character is far too simplistic; his only real distinguishing characteristic is that he smokes nearly constantly. Like playing pieces or statues, Huysmans's characters—pawns—are essential to his didactic project (game); without them the novels would have been pure art history. His characters are stone figures moving between good and evil on the chessboard of the world as Huysmans represented it in *Sainte Lydwine de Schiedam*. Through parables, the Durtal cycle provides the rules of the game of survival in a world ruled by materialism and individualism. Durtal's progressive discovery of the cathedral's spiritual aspects is supposed to relate to the reader's life. Paul Valéry was, perhaps, the ideal nonreligious reader of Huysmans; he identified Durtal's spiritual awakening as the crux of the series: "The succession of these three works is not simple. It brings about in us something that matures, that changes fervor and browns, a sensitive being, bringing man and the settings he navigates into a written world."[147]

Durtal's spiritual journey, which leads along a rocky road from the atheism and Satanism of *Là-Bas* to the struggles between body and soul in *En Route* to the Catholicism of *La Cathédrale* and *L'Oblat*, provided a model evolution for fin-de-siècle readers discouraged by the futility of the modern world. Durtal's perseverance in his struggles between materialism and spirituality, satanism and Catholicism makes him an imperfect and human protagonist, torn between good and evil. François Mauriac credited Huysmans for his depiction of these forces, especially in a time that had become unable to distinguish between the two:

> Huysmans did even more than understand evil. We often repeat Léon Bloy in saying that "There is only one misfortune, that of not being saints." I

would be tempted to say: "There is an even worse misfortune, that of not knowing what evil is, that of belonging to a generation that has lost the ability to recognize it."[148]

Durtal is not a saint. He is a flawed pilgrim who does his best to resolve his interior battles between good and evil. Ultimately, his faith in God allows him to find peace with himself. In a time when many people were famished for moral direction, Durtal's conversion provided them with the positive message he had learned at Chartres: the visible world is simply a manifestation of the invisible. One must do one's best to live well and to avoid evil while remembering that what we experience is not an end in itself. The cathedral, a structure so admired by his contemporaries, provided a concrete image of this stable system of belief. Even if one cannot rationally understand it, everything in Gothic architecture has a reason and a place in a greater system.

Readers would also do well to apply Durtal's reading techniques to Huysmans's text. In Chartres, he has very little knowledge about symbolism, but great admiration for medieval religious architecture. Like Victor Hugo or Viollet-le-Duc, who admired the cathedral's art but found its message mysterious, Durtal initially finds the stone images "difficult to decipher," "cumbersome because of the interpolated passages, repetitions, vanished or shortened phrases [. . .]"[149] These criticisms are not unlike those we direct to Huysmans's novels: why so much repetition? Why so much description? Where are we going? In the end, we learn that Durtal could not "read" the cathedral because his approach was incorrect; he was trying to "translate" the cathedral in words and sentences instead of looking for concepts.

As we progress in Huysmans's Durtal cycle, we learn to interpret the symbolism through Durtal's conversations with his friends, through his own reading and research into the cathedral, and through the descriptive passages in which he feels the effects of the cathedral. After studying books pertaining to symbolism, Durtal leaves his house to apply his knowledge to the stained glass or sculpture of Notre-Dame. If he runs into a friend while studying the cathedral, they discuss symbolism then continue their discourse during a shared meal. Like l'abbé Plomb, who introduced the cathedral to Durtal as an illustrated Bible in order to give him a point of departure for "reading" sculpture and stained glass, so Huysmans used Durtal's experience as a model for his readers. When we go to Notre-Dame de Chartres we know to look at the cathedral—as did Durtal—in terms of biblical stories, but also as a representation of the Catholic universe. We should reconsider Huysmans's Durtal novels. Although they do not approach the mastery of the Gothic cathedral, they constitute a valiant attempt to change the novel, to make it the cathedral's modern equivalent by populating a fictional universe with figures and art that reflect the Christian community and its values.

Huysmans and the Cathedral

Huysmans's magnificent praise of the cathedral as a sublime work of art that incarnates the beliefs of the Church adds many new significations to the repertory of early nineteenth-century stereotypes about Gothic architecture. He refers to Chateaubriand's well-known parallel between cathedral and tree by portraying Notre-Dame de Chartres in organic terms, as "a dense tree, whose roots plunged into the soil of the Bible itself; taking from it substance and drawing its sap," yet instead of accepting this impression, he pushes the analogy even further so that the tree image reflects the meaning the Middle Ages attributed to the cathedral: "the trunk was the symbolism of the Scriptures, the prefiguration of the Gospels by the Old Testament; the branches were the allegories of architecture, colors, gems, flora, fauna; the hieroglyphics of numbers; the emblems of Church objects and clothing [. . .]"[150] Where both Chateaubriand and Verlaine admired the cathedral as a nostalgic ruin, a vestige of an unrecoverable Catholic past, Huysmans proved that the mystical spirit was alive and well in nineteenth-century churches and monasteries. His descriptions of churches in the Durtal cycle reactivate Gothic architecture as a living, breathing creature whose soul depends on worshipers. The masterpiece of *La Cathédrale* is the extended opening scene during which the light of dawn enters the cathedral, waking the stone and glass inhabitants and bringing them to life, one by one. They step out of their frames and shadows to embrace the light. Such themes are echoed in a number of contemporary articles and essays about cathedrals by other authors; they followed the publication of *La Cathédrale*. In "Autour de Notre-Dame de Paris," a meditation about the cathedral illustrated with woodcuts by A. Lepère and Perrichon, Remy de Gourmont personifies the cathedral, whose voice accepts and echoes prayers, and who grows with the morning light.[151]

Huysmans's brilliance in the portrayal of the cathedral derived from the importance he placed on understanding it both as a work of art and as a reflection of a deeper Catholic meaning. In this way, he was able to use medieval symbolism to explain why we feel awe at the light shining through the stained-glass windows; it was l'abbé Suger's design. These are not miraculous structures sprung up magically, nor are they artistic ruins. The cathedral is a product of medieval thought and of medieval belief, a masterpiece created by man. His discussion of the medieval symbolism behind the cathedral allowed contemporaries to think about the aesthetic effect produced by the cathedral as they would one of Wagner's operas, so popular at the time. The cathedral builders, too, created a total work of art, in which each individual aspect contributes to an overarching central message. Huysmans's impact can be felt in Proust's praise of the cathedral as a "giant mirror," a living encyclopedia in which science, religion, and history mix through the arts of the Church.[152]

For Huysmans the cathedral is also a vessel, a harbor, a refuge for wounded souls. In 1944 Daniel Rops would credit Huysmans for this image in portraying the cathedral as "the basilica of returns, of conversion, the shelter of souls that seek themselves and that, beyond the cesspools of sin, the thickets of intelligence, the paternal renunciations, or even beyond the historical refusal of a people, arrive, in the silence of the stained-glass windows, to grasp once again the thread they thought they had broken."[153] Huysmans reinvents the cathedral according to l'abbé Suger's dream of "the essential oneness of liturgical celebration." This central idea of harmony in diversity appealed to modern Catholics, who attempted to purify their souls with prayer, and who welcomed those who felt lonely or isolated. This was not the "dangerous" Catholicism of the modern (or the medieval) world, in which priests battled for political power, but a purified, distilled version; it was the religion itself practiced in a communal setting and stripped of outside influences.

Huysmans used the novel, the most popular art form of his time, to link a misunderstood figure—the cathedral—to popular culture. He appealed to his contemporaries' interests—art, music, the occult, tourism—to introduce them to real Gothic churches. By showing that a cathedral—unlike a museum or monument— was able to take disparate elements and blend them into a united whole through a unifying belief, he provided an important emblem for a society torn apart by conflicting values. The cathedral had continued to function through six hundred years of social turmoil; the sheer bulk of its physical appearance was reassuring; it provided a stable link to both past and future.

Huysmans's portrayal of the cathedral as ordered, regulated, and still standing after many years overlaps with Zola's Republican admiration of the cathedral. But Zola preferred to consider the cathedral as a type, as a model to be achieved. Zola projected his "cathedral of the future world" as Michelet did his "cathedral of science," as a dream, an ideal for society to achieve; he stripped it of contemporary meaning and especially of associations with the political Catholicism that haunted Republicans at the end of the nineteenth century. Zola's cathedral adopted an idealized version of a secular medieval faith in which Catholicism had disappeared. Huysmans, in contrast, revered real cathedrals and focused on populating them. As François Mauriac noted, once he had converted, Huysmans "never wrote a line that was not for the defense and illustration of Catholic doctrine."[154] In a time of crisis, in a period he felt was being torn apart by increased individuality, Huysmans contributed to the rediscovery of a stable and highly intellectual system—symbolism—underlying the often stereotyped civilization of the Middle Ages. He brought out its historical origin as a way of uniting the Christian community. Though both writers invest the cathedral with very different and personal symbolism, they both claim it as a powerful figure for what French society could and would achieve.

FOUR

"Perpetual Adoration":
Proust and the Art Spirit

> Never was such a spectacle, such a giant mirror of science,
> soul, and history, offered to the sight and the intelligence of
> man. The same symbolism extends even to music, which can
> be heard in the immense nave and whose seven Gregorian
> tones represent the seven theological virtues and the seven
> ages of the world. It can be said that a performance of Wagner
> at Bayreuth [. . .] is not much compared to high mass in the
> cathedral of Chartres.
>
> —Marcel Proust, "La Mort de cathédrales" (1904)

Although he is traditionally categorized as a twentieth-century writer, one of the great innovators of the modern novel, we tend to forget that Proust was a contemporary of Zola and Huysmans. Like them he was profoundly influenced by fin-de-siècle tensions between Church and State and marked by the literary battles that pitted naturalists against symbolists. He was an active advocate of Captain Dreyfus during the Dreyfus Affair and throughout the 1890s he published essays and articles about high society and well-known writers. By 1908, when he began *Contre Sainte-Beuve,* the essay that would culminate in *A la recherche du temps perdu,* he had already published *Les Plaisirs et les Jours,* a book of collected essays that had appeared in Parisian reviews from 1892–1895; he had abandoned an autobiographical novel, *Jean Santeuil* (ca. 1895–1900); and he had published two annotated translations of John Ruskin's works: *La Bible d'Amiens* (1904) and *Sésame et le lys* (1906). Proust's early success as a scholar and a specialist on the Gothic cathedral have been overshadowed by *A la recherche du temps perdu.*[1]

Proust's fascination with cathedrals began almost twenty years before the publication of *Du côté de chez Swann;* he first read Ruskin in the *Bulletin de l'union pour l'action morale,* which published extracts of the English author's work from 1893–1903.[2] By 1897, Proust knew Ruskin's works well enough to debate his merits with a visiting English friend, and by 1899 he had begun "a project completely different from those I do generally, about Ruskin and certain cathedrals."[3] Although Ruskin's voluminous studies treat a variety of subjects, from art, history, and culture to writing, classical literature, and architecture, Proust chose the French Gothic cathedral as his focal point for studying the English critic. In 1899 and 1900 the insistence he placed on cathedrals punctuates his correspondence: "Does the *Poetry of Architecture* you mention by Ruskin contain anything about cathedrals? Which ones?"[4] Because of his overwhelming curiosity, he began embarking on voyages of discovery. Every summer from 1899 to 1903 he explored the churches of France in what he called "Ruskinian pilgrimages": he went to Amiens, Abbeville, Chartres, Provins, Saint-Loup-de-Naud, Saint-Leu-d'Esserent, Senlis, Laon, Coucy, Avallon, Vézelay, Dijon, and Beaune, either by himself or accompanied by friends. He would compare Ruskin's descriptions of saints, historical figures, and stained glass to the original architecture.[5]

Proust's passion for the French cathedral was so great that he came to the defense of it in 1904, just before the formal separation of Church and State, in an essay that reflects the capital importance he attached to medieval religious architecture. Proust was horrified to learn of a project for a law that would end state subsidy of church services; he thus wrote "La Mort des cathédrales," which was published in *Le Figaro* on August 16, 1904. Echoing Huysmans, Proust argued that cathedrals are living structures precisely because of the ceremonies performed in them. They are not simply beautiful shells, museums, or national monuments; a great part of the aesthetic impression they produce stems from their function, their "use value." Catholicism—the inspiration behind the construction of Gothic churches—gives everything in the cathedral meaning. Without the continued affirmation of the faith that built it, a cathedral would be nothing more than a beautiful museum or a lecture hall, devoid of spirit.

In order to prove the critical role church services played in the cathedral, Proust relied heavily on the theories of Emile Mâle (whom he had met several years earlier when Proust's brother rented a room next door to the Mâles).[6] He cited verbatim three pages of *L'Art religieux du XIIIe siècle*, in which the art historian describes the thirteenth-century symbolism underlying the Catholic mass. Each of the priests' actions, the lights, costumes, music, or timing have meaning, as do the sculptures, stained glass, and architecture of the Gothic cathedral: "The Catholic liturgy is one with the architecture and the sculpture of our cathedrals; the former, like the latter, derive from the same symbolism [. . .] there are hardly any sculptures in cathedrals, as secondary as they may seem, that do not have symbolic value. It is, in fact, the same for religious ceremonies."[7] Even the most trivial aspect of the ceremony contributes to the overarching meaning of the whole: to commemorate Catholic events and teachings from the Old to New Testament. The rites, which as Proust remarked, had remained virtually unchanged for six hundred years, correspond to underlying principles of Catholic theology.

Proust presents the cathedral as a "giant mirror" (the medieval *speculum*), a living encyclopedia in which science, morality, and history are disseminated through the arts of the church. It is a total work of art, akin to Wagner's *Gesamtkunstwerk*. The cathedral appeals to Proust not only for its composition in which each detail has its place, but also because it has universal attraction. Proust's play on the two senses of the word *entendre* reveals his admiration for this mixture of aesthetics and theology: one enjoys "hearing" the music, but one can also "understand" the seven Gregorian tones' scholarly reference to the seven theological virtues, which in turn, evoke the seven ages of the world. The art of the cathedral is pleasing to the uninitiated, yet it also disseminates a theological message about science, morality, or history to those who are familiar with it. Ultimately, both approaches converge on "the deep sentiment that animated the entire cathedral." Proust adopts Huysmans's embrace of "the soul of arches" by insisting on the importance of the system of "correspondences" that transform the cathedral from monument to macrocosm.

Despite his defense of religious services in "La Mort des cathédrales," however, Proust's vision of the "soul" of the cathedral is secular, as his comparison of high mass to a Wagnerian opera clearly demonstrates. He recommends the "spectacle" of the high mass in artistic terms, as he would a performance. Unlike Huysmans, Proust did not promote Catholicism itself. Instead, he attempted to convince his contemporaries that Catholic rites were worthy of artistic patronage. His mention of Wagner, the most popular musician of the late nineteenth century, is not coincidental. From 1880 to 1895 Wagner's works were so revered in France that Proust's contemporaries likened themselves to "worshipers" and made pilgrimages to the "sacred hill of Bayreuth."[8] Proust thus attaches the cathedral to his contemporaries' quasi-religious artistic preferences, while appealing to their nationalism; these are French—not German—concerts and they are superior. Proust felt religious services were inseparable from the cathedral's overall aesthetic effect— like Wagner's operas, each element contributes to a total impression—and must be understood in the context for which it was created. Proust thus explains symbolism in terms his contemporaries can understand, while voicing admiration for church services, which surpass even Wagner's compositions.

Although he entitles his essay "La Mort des cathédrales," Proust applies his praise to "all of the beautiful churches of France." This article, like his praise of the cathedral as "the highest and most original expression of the genius of France" (in the same article), came as an attempt at compromise, a call for tolerance in the midst of the increasing hostility between Republicans and Catholics. "The gap between your two Frances is intensifying at each new stage of anticlerical politics," he wrote a friend working for the government.[9] Proust's embrace of the cathedral as the genius of French art, in which spirituality and nationalism are inseparable, appealed to Republicans and Catholics, perhaps even more so because of his status: he was Jewish (though raised Catholic) and an active Republican supporter of Colonel Dreyfus. Paul Grunebaum-Ballin, the adjunct director of Aristide Briand during the promulgation of the law separating Church from State, cited Proust's defense of churches in a legal document commenting on each aspect of the Briand Law, while Catholic leader Maurice Barrès congratulated Proust for coming to the defense of the cathedral.[10] Proust's nationalistic praise of cathedrals in "La Mort des cathédrales" prefigures the ways in which, in *A la recherche du temps perdu,* the cathedral serves as a privileged image of the French nation, of artistic inspiration, and of spiritual discovery.

This chapter will link Proust's prolific nonfictional studies of cathedrals to the Gothic structures he introduces to the world of *La Recherche.* In his novel, Proust created a central character who, like Pierre Froment and Durtal, attempts to find his place in a society plagued by social and artistic crises; Proust, too, used the cathedral within the novel as a figure that reflects his protagonist's spiritual evolution.[11] In a first section, I will examine the cathedral's role in Proust's development of an aesthetic theory that allows him to break free of the literary battles that so influenced Zola and Huysmans. In a second section, I trace the ways in which the cathedral serves as both a guide for the hero and as a reflection of his evolving consciousness. From the child hero's onomastic appreciation of Saint-Hilaire and the Guermantes family to his anticipation of and disappointment with Balbec's supposedly Persian church, to his emotional discovery of Saint-Mark's basilica in Venice, the cathedral provides lessons about art. In a final section, I examine the ways in which Proust criticizes his contemporaries and their literary preconceptions through the characters of his novel. Where *Les Trois Villes* and the Durtal cycle have been largely forgotten today because of their sharp focus on contemporary issues, *La Recherche* remains one of the greatest works of French literature—often compared to a cathedral—because of Proust's ability to keep his didacticism in the shadow of his luminous art.

Instinct against Intelligence: Proust between Naturalism and Symbolism

Through his writings about John Ruskin and cathedrals, Proust developed an aesthetic theory that he would use to structure *La Recherche:* the belief in the importance of sensory impressions—the *petite madeleine,* Vinteuil's sonata, the steeples of Martinville—to trigger personal memories, to understand aspects of love or life, or to inspire the creation of works of art. The cathedral, which can be construed as a magnificent work of art that provokes an aesthetic response in the observer and as a structure that supports a complex theological system of references, lies at the heart of Proust's beliefs about instinct and intellect, materiality and spirituality, didacticism and rhetoric. He often used it to exemplify the importance of subjectivity in contemplating and creating works of art, as in the following draft for "Journées de lecture," the preface to Ruskin's *Sésame et le lys:*

> Such a day [visiting a cathedral when birds are singing in the surrounding trees . . .], seems [to a great man] something that exists inside of him and that he is not afraid to lose; he is linked to its reality beyond temporal changes or anything that could happen, including death, above which this

perfect feeling is somehow situated. But during this time, while the intelligence of the scholar [*lettré*] recognized each saint represented above the door, knowing that he who holds a head is Saint Denis [. . .] and murmuring the well known lines "St. Denis devançant ton martyre y supplée," the intelligence of the poet saw only the church, only as a confused mass of shadow and light. Just as [the scholar's] literature shuts him off from the emotion of true things, it can also ennoble mediocre things, as in society life where poetry has no place. [Literature] helps him take pleasure in [. . . discovering] on the duc of X's table the buttons that Mme de Bargeton had on her table the day she first invited Lucien de Rubempré to dinner [in Balzac's novel].[12]

In this rather condensed version of his theory, the reaction to the cathedral separates "poète" from "lettré": while visiting on a beautiful day, both may experience a special sentiment that seems to eclipse time and place. But while the poet perpetuates the feeling by embracing it as he sees it—"as a confused mass of shadow and light"—the scholar latches onto the material object, the cathedral, as the source of his emotion. The poet accepts "the perfect feeling" as a product of his vision, while the scholar uses his reason: he thinks about the links between cathedral and literature. Where the poet allows himself to be carried away by his aesthetic impression of the cathedral, the scholar closes himself off from his emotional response to the work of art by subordinating it to his literary knowledge. Like his counterparts in society, he will glorify even mediocre objects (buttons, for example) if they remind him of a work of literature (*Les Illusions perdues*).

Throughout his work and especially in *La Recherche*, Proust contrasts these two attitudes toward art. He interchangeably uses the terms *emotion, impression, sentiment, genius,* and *instinct* to evoke the response he admires in the poet, while applying the words *intelligence, intellect, reason,* and *knowledge* to the scholar's logical reaction to art. Throughout this chapter I will borrow his terms *instinctual* or *emotional* to refer to the poet's visceral response to art, while applying the adjectives *intelligent* or *reasoned* to the scholar's interest in material objects and their links to his scholarly learning.

For Proust it is "the emotion of true things," an instinctual response produced by works of art such as the cathedral, that opens the door to a "spiritual life" that inspires artistic creation. Such a "perfect feeling" raises man to a level of perception that, like a Christian afterlife, conquers death ("including death, above which this perfect feeling is somehow situated"). Proust (through Ruskin via Carlyle, Emerson, and Goethe), believed in a kind of transcendentalism: the world we think we see is distorted by our habits and preoccupations, which cloud our vision.[13] Accordingly, the truth our reason seems to perceive is generally an illusion. We must go beyond the level of the conscious—rational or intellectual thought— in order to discover the truth. But unfortunately, we cannot control such incursions into the unconscious: they arrive in the form of impressions, or epiphanies, when we are confronted with experiences that give us a fleeting sentiment or perception of beauty. Proust's famous madeleine episode is one such example. We instinctively feel something that cannot be captured by logic but that signifies an important idea or general law from the ideal world: "aesthetic pleasure is precisely that which accompanies the discovery of a truth."[14]

In *La Recherche,* cathedrals, books, paintings, and music are privileged ways of catching glimpses of the alternate reality in which Proust believes. Gilles Deleuze divides the hero's encounters with the world into sets of signs—about the world, about love, about sensory experience, and about art—but he distinguishes "signs of art" from other kinds of feelings because of their transcendental nature. Unlike experiences akin to that of the madeleine, in which a physical sensation brings back a personal memory, contact with a work of art such as the cathedral does not refer to anything known to the hero. Instead, it introduces him to a world of essences or impressions that put him in communication with the spirit of other artists, who in turn, give him the inspiration to create.[15]

Before beginning *La Recherche,* Proust used the cathedral as a privileged figure of this process, and in the following example from the preface to his translation of *La Bible d'Amiens,* he presents Claude Monet as an example of a "poète," the ideal observer who can tap into this special world in order to transform aesthetic impressions into art:

> When you see the western facade of Amiens for the first time, blue in the mist, dazzling in the morning, sun-drenched and liberally gilded in the afternoon, pink and already coolly nocturnal at sunset, no matter at what hour its bells ring in the sky, as Claude Monet captured it in his sublime canvases in which the life of this thing reveals itself—made by man but reclaimed by nature and submerged in it—a cathedral, whose life, like that of the earth in its double revolution, unwinds through the centuries while renewing itself and completing itself daily—at that moment, if you clear it from the changing colors of nature's envelope, you feel in front of this facade a confused but powerful impression.

Claude Monet's thirty paintings of the Rouen cathedral (1892–1894) correspond perfectly to Proust's ideal of attempting to reproduce impressions in art (see Figure 2.3). In fact, Proust's insistence on capturing the visual effects of the passage of time show his profound understanding of the painter's objectives. Monet attempted to paint "the envelop," the changing mixture of air and light that lay between the cathedral and himself.[16] This appreciation for capturing atmosphere in a work of art may also explain why Corot's "La Cathédrale de Chartres," in which the muted ochers and ambers transform the cathedral into a product of soil and sky, was one of Proust's favorites at the Louvre.[17]

As he continues his commentary about Notre-Dame d'Amiens, Proust insists that it is not enough to revel in the beauty of the cathedral or in Monet's interpretation of it; one must take the impression as an invitation to continue, as had Monet:

> Upon seeing this lacelike and monumental swarm of human-sized charac-
> ters in their stone stature rising toward the sky, holding in their hands
> crosses, banderoles, or scepters, this people of saints, these generations of
> prophets, this retinue of apostles, this multitude of kings, this procession of
> sinners, this assembly of judges, this flight of angels, side by side, one above
> the other, standing near the door and looking down at the city [. . .] no doubt
> you feel, in the heat of your emotion, as though this giant, immobile, and
> passionate ascension is a great thing. But a cathedral is not simply a beauty
> to be felt. Even if it is no longer for you a lesson to be followed, it is, at least,
> still a book to be understood. The portal of a Gothic cathedral, and more
> particularly the portal of Amiens, the Gothic cathedral par excellence, is the
> Bible [. . .] Give it a less literal religious meaning than in the Middle Ages
> or even just an aesthetic meaning, you could nevertheless link it to one of
> those sentiments that appear to us beyond our life as the true reality, to one
> of those "stars to which we should hitch our wagon."[18]

Proust argues that impressions lead to the truth and show the path to creating art. The artist must take the sentiments as an invitation, "a lesson," "a book to be un-derstood," and must translate them. Such beliefs develop from a Platonic theory of essences, yet Proust's focus on the artist's response to such impressions distances him from Plato.[19] The "poète" must interpret his unique impression of the cathe-dral through style, as did Monet in his studies of the Rouen cathedral; he paints the "confused mass of shadow and light," thus creating a work that may evoke an emotional response in his viewer, who will translate his unique impression into a completely different form of art (a symphony perhaps, or a poem). Thus the cycle continues and a personal impression can be raised to a universal level.

Proust's focus on the cathedral and the Bible corresponds to Ruskin's belief in Amiens as "*the* Bible," a book of symbols to be deciphered, but it also reveals the extent to which Proust equated aesthetic inspiration with religious. Even if we do not understand the erudition behind the cathedral (as would a "lettré" like Ruskin), its "aesthetic meaning" still provides a way of experiencing another kind of perception. Once Proust had developed a theory to explain the importance of such "powerful impressions," he placed it at the heart of the preliminary novel he had conceived in 1909. He divided the book in three sections, "Combray," "L'Adoration perpétuelle," and "Le Bal des têtes." In these passages, which corre-spond roughly to the first and last parts of *La Recherche* as we know them today, Proust contrasted his hero's beliefs about literature to those of his contempo-raries.[20]

The phrase *adoration perpétuelle* comes from Proust's work on Ruskin, to whom Robert Sizeraine had attributed a cult of beauty (he called his 1897 book

Ruskin et la religion de la beauté). Proust disagreed with this appellation, arguing that while the adoration of beauty may have been Ruskin's "perpetual act," the British author truly loved "just religion."[21] By adopting the title "L'Adoration perpétuelle" for the section in which he presents the revelation of his own aesthetic theories, Proust linked his character to the religion of beauty that he refused Ruskin. His use of the term *adoration* (the Adoration of Christ, the Adoration of the Magi) also gave religious resonance to his aesthetic theories. In "L'Adoration perpétuelle," the hero experiences a spiritual revelation, which Proust parallels to that of the Christian mystics by using words that evoke visions and spiritual transport: "felicity," "vision," "elation," "celestial." When the hero arrives at his moment of epiphany, he finally understands that "art is what is most real, the most austere school of life and the true Last Judgment."[22] The constant repetition of the word *resurrection*—with its important Christian resonance—illustrates the extent to which Proust wanted to portray his hero's spiritual enlightenment in religious terms: he reaches the eternal realm of "spiritual life" through the "rite" of translating his aesthetic impressions into art.

Proust's aesthetic system can be considered a religion not only because of his appropriation of religious vocabulary, but also because he uses it to link man to a higher spiritual order. Proust's theories about such a superior force correspond to Larousse's definition of religion, in which "man recognizes his weakness and recognizes his submission to something superior." In all of his essays about the spiritual transport of art, man is linked to an external force, "a reality beyond temporal changes or anything that could happen." It is little surprise that Proust often portrays art as a replacement for organized religion such as Catholicism and that scholars praise his "religion of art."[23] Yet like Huysmans, Proust does not take solace from the world by cloistering himself in these beliefs; he actively attempts to win others over to his cause.

In fact, not only does Proust single out the emotion and religious feelings conveyed by a work of art, he also insists on the importance of intelligence for translating and perpetuating these impressions. Style is at the heart of Proust's belief in the power of art. He dwelled on this concept in his letters to Anna de Noailles, but most clearly expressed it in a 1913 interview with *Le Temps:* "Style is by no means an embellishment [. . .] it is not even a question of technique; it is— like color for painters—a quality of vision, a revelation of the particular universe that each of us sees and that others do not. The pleasure an artist gives us is from showing us another universe."[24] Within his system, Proust replaces the theologian with the artist, who captures the divine truth through symbols or metaphors. Metaphors are the key to Proust's aesthetic theory: they are the stylistic element that allows the writer to capture the space in between the two realities he perceives.[25] Intelligence is not to be rejected, because it is the means by which the artist "translates" the impressions perceived by his instinct: "But on the one hand, the truths of intelligence, if they are less precious than feelings [. . .] also have their interest. Even the greatest thinkers of our century [. . .] linked jewels of feeling through an intelligent framework so they only appear from time to time."[26] The true value of a work of art for Proust thus lies neither in composition nor in subject matter but in style, in the way a writer portrays his impressions of the world. Proust argues that surface aspects perceived by intelligence—the composition, subject matter, or biographical details that critics often use to evaluate a work—have little relationship to its beauty: "The beauty of a painting does not depend upon the things that are represented in it."[27]

Proust's terminology, which pits the impressions of "poète" against those of the "lettré," echoes the vocabulary used in the 1891 Huret interviews. Proust followed the debates and felt that the writers' arguments were on the order of politics. He lamented the "materialism" of contemporary literature.[28] Throughout his essays and notably at the end of *La Recherche,* Proust criticized the writers of the 1890s who made the subject matter of their art more important than their style:

> *True art has better things to do than make so many proclamations and it achieves itself in silence.* Moreover, those who theorized [. . .] used stock expressions that strikingly resembled those of the imbeciles they insulted [. . .] Quality of language [. . .] is something that theoreticians think they can do without [. . .] because they need to see it expressed directly, they cannot discern it from the beauty of an image. Hence the crass temptation for a writer to write intellectual works. What great dishonesty. *A work in which there are theories is like an object on which one leaves the price tag.*[29]

Proust's hero decides that he should not be concerned by critics—like those who pushed Zola and Huysmans to champion social causes in their works—because they believe that "literature is a spiritual game destined progressively to disappear."[30] Such writing is inferior to true art because it is concerned only with subject matter. In this section of *La Recherche,* which he had, at one time, intended to call "L'Adoration perpétuelle," Proust condemns most nineteenth-century writers, with the exception of Chauteaubriand, Baudelaire, and Nerval, who attempted to translate their vision through style. Because they succeeded in depicting their own perspective, their spirit continues to live on in their works.[31] Good art, for the hero, is thus a kind of salvation: the truth expressed in such works conquers death because it continues to reach out to generations of readers or spectators.

Through his studies of the cathedral, by 1900 Proust had articulated—and published—the major outlines of the aesthetic theory that he would continue to develop at the heart of *La Recherche:* it is through contemplating art, then "hitching one's wagon" to the sentiments evoked by it, that one can attain a kind of spirituality. He planned this section, one of the first he had written, to go at the end of his novel: "after finishing the book, one will see (I would like it to be so) that the entire novel is a working model that illustrates the artistic principles expressed in the last section, a kind of preface, if you will, placed at the end."[32] This segment would be the key to Proust's literary masterpiece.

While Proust's aesthetic theories created a theoretical framework for his novel, they also provided contemporaries with an extremely approachable vision of the cathedral. Huysmans encouraged readers to learn about symbolism as a way of understanding the cathedral from the medieval (and theological) Catholic point of view, but Proust insisted that the aesthetic feeling inspired by the cathedral was also of crucial importance. In "La Mort des cathédrales," he cleverly persuaded contemporaries to shift support for religious services to the Fine Arts budget by arguing that Catholicism was essential for maintaining the aesthetic qualities we admire in the cathedral. By imagining a world in which the cathedral is a just another tourist attraction that archeologists have attempted to re-create, and by paralleling it to other, similar cultural attractions (notably Wagner's operas at Bayreuth), Proust proves how far superior the 600-year-old church services of French cathedrals are to anything the Germans could concoct. Proust appealed to artistic sensibilities and to patriotic sentiments by championing the cathedral as "the highest and most original expression of the genius of France."

Pilgrim's Progress: From Idolatry to the Religion of Art

"There is no better tourist guide than Proust." The publication of volumes entitled *Voyager avec Marcel Proust* and *How Proust Can Change Your Life* represent a new tendency to appreciate Proust as a travel companion and counselor.[33] Proust as guide may be a far cry from the stereotyped image of the sickly author scribbling his manuscript from the impenetrability of his cork-lined bedroom, but he did hope to influence readers: "It would be inexact, in thinking of those who would read [my work], to say my readers. For in my opinion, they would not be my readers, but really the readers of themselves, my book only being a kind of magnifying glass [. . .] with its help I would furnish them with the means of reading inside themselves."[34] The hero proposes this ideal at the end of *Le Temps retrouvé* and it provides an apt summary of the subtle psychological force that Proust's novel exerts on readers. He does not tell readers how to visit Venice or how to improve our lives, but gives us the means—notably through *exempla*—of discovering our own truths. He uses his hero's progressive understanding of the world as a model for us to emulate. The cathedral, privileged tourist destination and pilgrimage center, is an important figure for the hero; he is fascinated by Gothic architecture—like a tourist—but only understands the dynamics of the attraction—as do readers—when he reaches the epiphany of "l'Adoration perpétuelle. "

The work's title—*In Search of Lost Time*—implies travel and Proust himself envisaged his hero's "journey" as "the evolution of a mind." *La Recherche* is less the story of an apprenticeship than of a voyage of discovery. In fact, when the hero asks the painter Elstir about understanding art, he receives a cryptic response that reinforces the idea of life as a quest: "We do not receive wisdom, we must discover it for ourselves, after a journey that no one can make for us, that no one can spare us, because wisdom is a point of view about things."[35] By the end of the novel, as Proust explained to Jacques Rivière, the director of *La Nouvelle Revue Française*, readers will have discovered the author's conception of the truth—"the Truth [. . .] and what it means to me"—and will, hopefully, have discovered truths of their own.

In his novel, the cathedral marks the stages in the hero's artistic evolution, much as, in his essays, it served as a model for the different ways in which a "poète" and a "lettré" interpret art.[36] After the opening passage, in which an older narrator comments on his disorientation at awaking in strange places (a moment that corresponds to the end of *Le Temps retrouvé*) and after *Un amour de Swann*, *La Recherche* follows the hero more or less chronologically as he travels through fin-de-siècle society encountering different kinds of people—bourgeois, aristocrats, artists—who expose him to a variety of attitudes and mentalities. The narrative structure—in which an older "I" periodically intervenes to comment on the observations of the young hero with phrases of the "Later I would learn . . ." variety—provides a beautifully subtle commentary on what the hero is witnessing. He is marvelously blind to most of what he sees, accepting experiences at face value; it is only in retrospect or through rare flashes of understanding that he comprehends the "rules" or "psychology" behind what he has observed. Progressively adopting and rejecting the practices of his contemporaries allows Proust to criticize them while masking the severity of his comments. In *La Recherche* the hero's reaction to each cathedral provides a measure by which readers can gauge his progressive understanding of art, and by extension, compare his beliefs to our own.

The Idolatry of French Monuments

Throughout *La Recherche* cathedrals produce aesthetic impressions in the hero; the style of the three major descriptive passages of churches in *La Recherche*—Saint-Hilaire, Balbec, and Saint Mark's—reveals each stage of his progressive understanding of art. In Combray, the hero is awed by darkness, the size, and the profusion of ancient objects in l'Eglise Saint-Hilaire. For him, the church is a place of French history, where tombstones, stained glass, and tapestries make him think of the stories he has been told about Esther, Dagobert, or Saint-Louis. The most important attribute of the following single-sentence description of the church is the legendary, dreamlike atmosphere it evokes with its breathless attention to historical detail:

All of this [the atmosphere] and even more the precious objects bequeathed upon the church by people who were nearly legendary figures for me (the golden cross fashioned, it was said, by Saint Eloi and offered by Dagobert, and the tomb of the sons of Louis the Germanic in porphyry and enameled

copper), because of which I moved forward into the church as we reached
our seats, as in a valley visited by fairies, where the peasant is filled with wonder at the sight of a rock, a tree, a pool, the tangible traces of these objects'
supernatural passage, all of this, for me, made the church something entirely
different from the rest of the city: an edifice occupying, if it can be said, a
four-dimensional space—the fourth being Time—, unfurling its nave across
the centuries, which, bay after bay, chapel after chapel, seemed to conquer
and cross not just a few meters, but successive eras from which it emerged
victorious; concealing the rough and ferocious eleventh century in the
thickness of its walls, from which its heavy coarse arches and large rough-
hewn stones appeared only through the deep cleft that the steeple staircase
hollowed out near the porch, and even there, concealed by gracious Gothic
arcades that grouped together coquettishly in front of it like older sisters who
smilingly place themselves in front of their surly, loutish badly-dressed
younger brother to hide him from strangers; raising into the sky above the
Square its tower, which had contemplated Saint Louis and seemed to see him
still; and plunging with its crypt into a Merovingian darkness where, feeling
our way along under the dark and powerfully ribbed vaulting that was like
the membrane of an enormous stone bat, Théodore and his sister would light
with a candle the tomb of the little daughter of Sigebert, on which a deep
hollow—like a fossil's mark—had been dug, it was said, "by a crystal lamp,
which, on the night of the Frankish princess' murder, had detached itself
from the golden chains that suspended it at the site of the current apse, and
without breaking the crystal, without extinguishing the flame, had buried
itself in the stone, making it give way weakly underneath."[37]

Proust's consistent use of the imperfect and present perfect tenses combined with
present participles creates a place that has been freed from the restraints of time:
past and present mingle in eternal suspension. This effect is enhanced by words indicating different periods: "centuries," "eras," "Merovingian." Although this passage is recounted in the novel by an adult narrator who is remembering his childhood experience, he recaptures his youthful perspective by mentioning legends,
fairies, and the ghost stories that Théodore told the other children in the crypt, all
of which are linked to the Merovingian child, Sigebert's daughter.[38]

The profusion of objects contained in the church add to its impression of
leaving a palpable trace of the past. From the crosses and tombs to the Gothic
arches, the hero links each part of the church to a famous historical personage who
had seen or touched it. The cathedral seems haunted by the spirit of the past, as
the phantoms of Saint Eloi, Louis the Germanic, Saint Louis, and the daughter of
Sigebert guide the viewer through the church. Proust evokes his hero's wonder at
this legendary space through verbs such as "unfurling," "conquer," and "cross,"
which expose the cathedral's dynamic connection to the past, while evoking the
child's roving eye as he penetrates the layers of the cathedral. The hero's awe at his

proximity to the characters of myths replaces the religious sentiment one would expect in the description of a house of worship, and reinforces the child's perspective of marvel.

Proust spent a great deal of energy on the construction of this passage. Richard Bales has shown that six of Proust's sixty-two *Cahiers* devote lengthy passages to the Combray church. Each of the versions of this sentence, the earliest dating from 1909, placed emphasis on historical characters and the religious objects that populated the church.[39] Like the other major segments evoking churches in *La Recherche,* Proust carefully planned this one, the first scene revealing the hero's relationship to art. L'église Sainte-Hilaire provides a baseline from which to gauge an evolving artistic sensibility.

The hero is profoundly affected by being near so many objects from the past: he feels as if he has been projected into a fourth dimension constituted by time. This overwhelming feeling of wonder is similar to the aesthetic impression that will inspire him to write after seeing the Martinville steeples, yet the youthful hero misinterprets these instincts. He thinks that his impression of inhabiting a valley of fairies is a result of his proximity to objects that once surrounded famous people. Instead of realizing, as he later will, that his sense of the marvelous is an invitation to create, his reason tells him that his impressions are intellectual. He links the church's ornamentation to history.[40] Similarly, the hero thinks he admires Saint André-des-Champs, the church near Roussainville, primarily for its Frenchness: "How this church was French." He later calls it *opus francigenum* and believes that it is the incarnation of Françoise's credos—the physical representation of a vernacular peasant tradition that continues to thrive in France.[41] The church affects him, yet he interprets his emotions through people such as Françoise, Théodore, and Albertine.

The hero's reaction, however, is not instinctual; he has learned it from contemporaries like Swann, Norpois, and Legrandin, who appreciate paintings not for their style, but for the historical figures or themes represented in them. These are the same people who, as tourists, visit cathedrals guidebook in hand, curious to link these historic artifacts to stories they know. In the tradition of Viollet-le-Duc, who represented cathedrals as rational French monuments, they attempt to "read" sculptures and analyze the techniques used to build them. In his essays on John Ruskin published in newspapers, Proust encouraged this tradition by referring to the cathedral as a scholarly book and French monument whose stories could be translated (he provides a lengthy "summary" of the ways in which the cathedral figures the Bible). Proust invited his readers to go to Amiens with Ruskin's book in hand, and recommended that they closely follow one of the two paths to the cathedral described in *The Bible of Amiens.* Like Ruskin, Proust asked readers to use their intelligence (their knowledge of Ruskin, of history, and of the Bible) to read the cathedral. He did not ask them to trust their own impressions of its beauty.

Despite his initial enthusiasm for following in the footsteps of Ruskin, Proust would later condemn his attitude as "idolatry," a concept he first defined during his work on cathedrals; it was Ruskin's term. In *Lectures on Art* the art historian presented idolatry as "the serving with the best of our hearts and minds some dear and sad fantasy which we have made for ourselves, while we disobey the present call of the Master, who is not dead, and who is not fainting under His cross, but requiring us to take up ours."[42] Proust argued that for his contemporaries, idolatry consisted of giving preference to what they intelligently deemed beautiful (according to intertextual or scholarly criteria), instead of trusting the sincerity of their aesthetic impressions ("the present call of the Master"); they relied too much on scholarship and not enough on their immediate response to the art itself. Idolatry is the hero's dominant mode of interpreting the world in *La Recherche,* especially throughout his childhood. He tries to envision the world as he thinks his cultured adult friends might. Accordingly, he likes things only if he has previously heard or read about them: he hates going to the Champs-Elysées, for example, and wishes that Bergotte had described them in a book.

Proust was the first to admit his own idolatry of Ruskin. He was intrigued by Ruskin's stories about the characters figured on cathedrals much as his hero was attracted to l'église Sainte-Hilaire because of its links to the stories he had been told. He so enjoyed such "Ruskinian pilgrimages" that he highly recommended them to his readers: "I would like to give the reader the desire and the means of spending a day at Amiens on a kind of Ruskinian pilgrimage." Later, he added, "I do hope that you will go to Amiens after having read my article."[43] Early on, Proust, too, was an idolater, who loved cathedrals because they had been visited by Ruskin.

Proust returns over and over in his work to the concept of committing idolatry, especially when referring to contemporaries who subordinate art to their own treasured preoccupations or critical ideals. Unfortunately, this tendency was particularly pronounced in literature. Sainte-Beuve's "excellent method," which evaluated writers according to their biography, beliefs, logic, or financial situation, had recently been rediscovered by contemporaries.[44] In 1908 Proust started a lengthy essay entitled "Contre Sainte-Beuve," dedicated to disproving the system and to showing "how [Sainte-Beuve] sinned [. . .] as a writer and as a critic."[45] Proust's use of vocabulary generally reserved for the sacred—"idolatry" and "sin"—set such scholarly "idolaters" apart from his own religion of art. Unlike the "poète," these idolatrous "lettrés" fail to perpetuate the spirit of art because they focus on the material world; they discount the higher plane of aesthetic satisfaction.

Later, Proust heavily criticized Ruskin's idolatry of the cathedral by taking issue with the idea that only those versed in symbolism can truly comprehend the beauty of Gothic architectural forms.[46] In *The Bible of Amiens,* half history lesson and half guide to the cathedral, Ruskin translates the intricacies of Notre-Dame d'Amiens for his readers: he gives them a history lesson about the cathedral and the personages associated with it or portrayed in it, from Clovis and his family to Saint Firmin, Saint Martin, and Saint Jerome; then he interprets the figures portrayed in the sculpture and stained glass of the cathedral by way of diagrams and commentary. Proust disagreed with Ruskin's intellectualizing approach because he insisted that cathedrals were great works of art precisely because of their ability to evoke an aesthetic impression that transcended rational thought. For him, specialists are not "the only people for whom the living cathedral, that is to say the sculpted, painted, song-filled cathedral, is the greatest of spectacles. It is for this reason that we can feel music without understanding its harmony."[47] Proust insisted that even the most unschooled people, if they rely on their emotions when entering a cathedral, will feel an aesthetic response—"a vague but powerful emotion"—that reflects the church's religious message, just as people who cannot read music can still feel what it expresses.

Through the hero, who is seduced by the pull of his emotions but feels compelled to rationalize them, Proust tells his readers not to neglect art by limiting perceptions to the confirmation of what they have seen in books. Proust may be a guide, but his goal is not to cater to the average tourist; his guidebook dismisses authority and asks readers to trust their instincts.

Balbec and the Disappointment of Tourism

A secondary hurdle lying between the hero and his acceptance of the power of art results from preconceived notions fueled by reading and reverie. The narrator often anticipates meeting a person or traveling to a place by linking the sound of its name to stories his has read or pictures he has seen; he is thus disappointed when he finally encounters the real thing. The hero's experience with the church of Balbec exemplifies the disappointment that accompanies such expectations; he is unable to see the church itself because of the power of his preconceived ideas. Years before he goes to Balbec, the hero begins dreaming about the city, largely because of its name, whose sound conjures up visions of "a nearly Persian church" with waves lapping up against its porch. In his imagination, the town itself is the church:

> Certain town names, Vézelay or Chartres, Bourges or Beauvais, are used to designate, by abbreviation, their principal churches. This frequent tendency—if applied to places we do not yet know—ends by sculpting the entire name, which henceforth, whenever we want to introduce the idea of the town into the name—the town we have never seen—we impose upon it— like a mold—the same engravings, and the same style, transforming the town's name into a kind of great cathedral.[48]

His dream of a great cathedral is confirmed by adults, Swann and Legrandin, who praise the mystical "Persian" attributes of the church and tell him that it is more beautiful than anything in Siena. When he arrives in Balbec, however, instead of finding a cathedral city bordered by waves, he is horrified to see the church of Balbec surrounded by signs, omnibuses, and cafés:

> And the church—catching my attention at the same time as the café, the passerby of whom I asked directions, the train station to which I would return—blended with all the rest, seemed an accident, a product of this late afternoon, in which the cupola, mellow and engorged against the sky, was like a piece of fruit, bathed in the same light as the chimneys of neighboring houses that ripened its melting pink and golden skin. But I wanted only to think of the eternal meaning of the sculptures when I recognized the Apostles, the statues of which I had seen casts at the Trocadéro museum, and which, on the two sides of the Virgin, in front of the deep bay of the porch, waited as if to honor me. With their sweet, kindly, blunt faces and stooped shoulders, they seemed to advance with an air of welcome while singing the Alleluia of a beautiful day. But it was clear that their expression was as immutable as that of a corpse, changing only if I walked around them. I said to myself, "This is it, this is the Church of Balbec [. . .] All that I have seen so far are just photographs and casts of the famous porch, this church, these Apostles, this Virgin. Now here is the church, the statues themselves, here they are, the originals, something much greater." Perhaps it was also something less.[49]

This passage, like the one describing l'église Saint-Hilaire, is narrated by an older hero, who recounts the anticipatory perspective of his youth and remembers his crushing disappointment when the church did not live up to his hopes. He had imagined the church by itself, with the statues of the Apostles and the Virgin that he had remarked in photographs and in the Musée des monuments historiques. Instead of the "immortal work so long desired," however, he sees the statue of the Virgin, like the church itself, as "filthy" with the "same soot as the neighboring houses [. . .] a little old lady of stone whose height I could measure and whose wrinkles I could count."[50] The apostles, whose "eternal meaning" he had so anticipated, look dead. Instead of the timelessness he had expected to find, everything in Balbec is scarred by objects from the present. The hero can hardly bear to look at the church, whose photographs he had admired, whose name he had adored, and to which Swan had given his highest praise: "It is delicious, as beautiful as Siena."

The hero leaves the city dejectedly. His experience has violated the purity of his dream: "I had partially opened a name that I should have kept hermetically sealed and into which, exploiting the passage I had imprudently created in dispelling all of the images that had previously inhabited it, a streetcar, a café [. . .] had rushed into the syllables, which closed upon themselves, letting the new images frame the porch of the Persian church, and would no longer cease to contain them."[51] But as in his appreciation of l'église Saint-Hilaire, the hero has misinterpreted his own reaction to art. He too quickly dismissed his aesthetic response to the church—"a product of this late afternoon, in which the cupola, mellow and engorged against the sky, was like a piece of fruit, bathed in the same light as the chimneys of neighboring houses that ripened its melting pink and golden skin"—by focusing on what he had already learned about the statues—"I wanted only to think of the eternal meaning of the sculptures." Because of his desire to find confirmation of his dream image, "the Persian church" of pictures, books, and imagination, the hero was unable to concentrate on the church itself: he discounts the impression it inspires in him as he attempts to confirm his preconceived notions.

As for l'église Saint-Hilaire, Proust devoted a number of drafts to the Balbec scene, every version of which presented the experience in terms of anticipation, disappointment, and retrospective understanding.[52] In *La Recherche*, the hero's experience with the Balbec church illustrates the triumph of imagination over "the emotion of true things." For l'église Saint-Hilaire, an attachment to historical objects prevented him from recognizing his immediate, instinctual response to art. Similarly, the imagery the hero associates with names creates a shield that blocks out his true encounter with art. He can think of nothing but finding confirmation of his preconceived image. The hero experiences similar disappointments throughout *La Recherche*, when his dreams about names conflict with their reality. His fascination with the Guermantes family as ethereal characters from a stained-glass window is shattered, for example, when he sees that the Duchess has a large blemish on her nose, just as his anticipation for La Berma dissolves when he sees her act. He is unable to perceive the true value of such people or places because of the power of his imagination. Dreaming, although not the act of a "lettré," is linked to the intertextual games that the scholar plays: it covers the true object with a cloud of associated references.

Through his character, Proust criticizes the attitude of contemporary tourists who, like the hero, or like Zola's Pierre Froment, are disappointed by churches—the basilicas of Lourdes and Rome, for example—because they do not live up to their reputation. This type of disillusionment occurred more frequently as tourism grew into a major leisure activity and as advertising offered "dream worlds" that could not be matched by reality. Literature itself was implicated in this phenomenon as nineteenth-century writers traveled all over the world and wrote works based on their adventures. In *Contre Sainte-Beuve*, Proust uses the example of Nerval's *Sylvie*, which his contemporaries praised for what they saw as a patriotic glorification of the French countryside. Because writers Barrès and Voguë evoked the names in Nerval's work—Chââlis, Pontarmé, îles de l'Ile-de-France—as full of "the divine sweetness of flickering daylight candles" or "bells swathed in October mist," readers anticipated that both Nerval's text and these cities would reflect such magical qualities.[53] Proust's contemporaries accepted the dreamlike images promoted by others instead of realizing that each person has his own vision of the world and that expectations about real places nearly always lead to disappointment:

"All of the praise given to us about famous lands leaves us cold."[54] The crushing dismay of Proust's hero, when he finds that Balbec is not a cathedral city perched on the edge of the sea, provides a touching illustration of the nefarious effects of excessive anticipation. For Proust, imagination is a useful and important tool, but it can obscure the even more important artistic inspiration that can result from encounters with beautiful objects or sites. He provides yet another warning to his reader: do not let your own impressions get overwhelmed by expectations.

Beyond Idolatry: Balbec and Impressionism

The church of Balbec provides a turning point for Proust's hero because he has the opportunity to reassess it. Later in the novel, he meets the impressionist painter Elstir, who helps him understand the importance of Balbec for art history and for the artist. The hero finally understands that to enjoy a work of art he must trust his own emotions. Proust, himself, made such a discovery. As he began annotating *La Bible d'Amiens,* Proust turned to other experts—Viollet-le-Duc and Emile Mâle—through whom he realized that he had adopted Ruskin's vision of the cathedral instead of trusting his own impressions. Mâle served as an aesthetic guide for Proust, much as Elstir does for the hero of *La Recherche:* he suggested churches to visit in a new series of cathedral explorations that Proust began in 1907 and he answered his questions about the symbolism and history of medieval religious architecture.[55] Proust devoured *L'Art religieux du XIIIe siècle,* which he called a "pure masterpiece and the last word in French iconography."[56] He used the book to elucidate and correct Ruskin's remarks when he annotated the translation he and Marie Nordlinger had made of Ruskin's *The Bible of Amiens.* Bales and Autret have shown that many of Proust's passages about medieval architecture and iconography in *La Recherche*—notably the descriptions of the Combray and Balbec churches above—are inspired directly from Mâle.[57] The two remained in lifelong contact, and under Mâle's tutelage Proust learned about Gothic cathedrals and their construction: the notes to his translations of Ruskin's works, in which he corrects comments made by Ruskin, Viollet-le-Duc, and Huysmans, reveal his familiarity with medieval symbolism and the cathedrals of France.[58] While Ruskin had whetted Proust's appetite for Gothic churches, Mâle, France's specialist of medieval architecture, explained their intricacies and led Proust to a more complex understanding of cathedrals' form and function.

Mâle's work, while dealing primarily with the ways in which the cathedral reflects the symbolism of the Middle Ages, produces a fascinating blend of erudition and praise. Mâle was both "lettré" and "poète" and his obvious admiration for the cathedral shines through the work in claims such as "When shall we understand that in the domain of art France has accomplished nothing greater?" or

"It is not only the genius of Christianity which is revealed, but the genius of France."[59] Through an elaborate analysis of the medieval thought incarnated in the cathedral, Mâle proves Victor Hugo's claim that the cathedral is a stone book. Mâle conceives of the cathedral as the equivalent of a *speculum* (mirror/encyclopedia) and he "reads" the cathedral against this framework. Proust was clearly influenced by the didactic function of the *speculum;* in "La Mort des cathédrales," he presents the cathedral as "a giant mirror" in which every element is profoundly in harmony with the cathedral's symbolism.

But even more important, perhaps, for Proust, Mâle evokes the ways in which the artist and architect used their intelligence to create forms that would impress or delight the spectator; the art of the cathedral goes beyond the intellectual messages inscribed throughout it. Even someone insensible to the scholarly messages or to the religion underlying the cathedral's art can appreciate the call to meditation and sanctuary produced by the grandeur and purity of the cathedral's form:

> Conviction and faith pervade the cathedral from end to end. Even the modern man receives a deep impression of serenity, little as he is willing to submit himself to its influence [. . .] Seen from afar, the church with her transepts, spires and towers seems like a mighty ship about to sail on a long voyage. The whole city might embark with confidence on her massive decks [. . .] On entering the cathedral it is the sublimity of the great vertical lines which first affects his soul. The nave at Amiens gives an inevitable sense of purification, for by its very beauty the great church acts as a sacrament [. . .] The cathedral like the plain or the forest has atmosphere and perfume, splendour, and twilight, and gloom [. . .] Here indeed is the indestructible ark against which the winds shall not prevail. No place in the world fills men with a deeper sense of security.[60]

Mâle's enthusiasm for the ways in which the cathedral's form inspires confidence, security, and meditation, corresponds quite closely to the sense of wonder, peace, and serenity that Huysmans attempted to express in his descriptions of Notre-Dame de Chartres. Proust, too, borrows the image of the cathedral as a ship, traveling through time, in his description of Saint-Hilaire. By 1904, Proust had gone well beyond Ruskin and his advocacy of scholarly tourism. He had come to see the cathedral as did Huysmans and Mâle, as a total work of art that inspired a religious or spiritual response: "this artistic realization, the most complete that ever was because all of the arts collaborated in it, of the greatest dream to which humanity ever aspired."

But where Mâle's public was somewhat limited by the scholarly focus of his work, both Huysmans and Proust presented theories about medieval architecture through the novel, thus reaching an even greater audience and disseminating scholarly theories to an uninitiated public. Proust furthers knowledge of the cathedral through his hero, who increasingly learns about medieval symbolism. He, too, changes his perspective. Two hundred pages after his visit to the Balbec church, the hero meets Elstir. Like Mâle, he is the perfect tutor because he conceives of art in both intellectual and instinctual terms. Accordingly, when the hero asks him questions about the statues of the apostles that had disappointed him on the Balbec porch, "those great statues of saints, who, perched on stilts, form a kind of avenue," Elstir explains that this "avenue" represents history:

> "It starts from the beginning of time to end with Jesus Christ," he told me. "On one side you have his ancestors of the spirit, on the other, the Kings of Judea, his ancestors of the flesh. All of the ages are there. And if you had better examined what seemed stilts to you, you would have been able to name the figures perched up there. Under the feet of Moses you would have recognized the golden calf, under Abraham's the ram, under Joseph's, the demon advising Potiphar's wife."[61]

In Balbec, the hero had been disappointed to find that the giant, immortal statues of the Apostles he expected to see were tarnished by the soot of the present. Elstir, however, teaches him that their procession does represent eternity; it symbolizes their continued march through time. The facade of the Balbec church, in which all of Christ's ancestors are figured, returns, at the end of *La Recherche,* as an image of time. The hero sees himself staggering on his own pair of stilts, like the Apostles atop the Balbec cathedral, a figure perched precariously on the years separating him from Combray and his own ancestors: Swann, Bergotte, Elstir, and his family.

In *A l'ombre des jeunes filles en fleurs,* however, the hero looked up at the giant statues without understanding their symbolism; he saw them as curious figures with no link to history. Proust uses the Balbec church to provide a marker for the shifting perspective of his hero, who, by the end of *La Recherche,* has acceded to a superior height: he no longer perceives reality from the same base. In the conclusion, it is the hero himself who looks down from the vertiginous heights, dizzied by the physical sensation of elapsed time.

Elstir leads the hero beyond a material conception of art by explaining symbolism to him. But his conversations with the artist also convince him that to find his own vision (to avoid disappointment), he must subordinate knowledge to instinct.[62] Elstir is a "lettré," yet unlike characters—Bloch is one—who want art to represent "life as it is, recomposed as we see it," Elstir attempts to put aside his judgments about reality when he paints, so he can see things in terms of his individual and immediate sensorial impressions. Elstir teaches the hero that it is important to rely on one's instinct before thinking about what others may have said. It is only then that one can use intelligence to translate one's vision. The hero realizes this only later: "Things that we have not had to decipher, to clarify through our own efforts, things that were clear before us, are not ours. Only the things that others do not know and that we pull from the darkness inside of us truly belong to us."[63]

Elstir's enthusiasm for the art of the Balbec church is like Mâle's powerful tribute to the cathedral at the end of *L'Art religieux du XIIIème siècle:* it stirs up an aesthetic exhilaration more powerful than his explanations of its didactic symbols. He mixes the two, yet his enthusiasm for the art triumphs. He describes it as "the most beautiful illustrated Bible the people have ever been able to read [. . .] the most tender and most inspired expression of that long poem of adoration and praise that the Middle Ages dedicated to the glory of the Madonna [. . .] it is a gigantic unified theological and symbolic poem. It is tremendous, it is divine, it is a thousand times superior to anything you will see in Italy." For Elstir, the church is a multitude of gorgeous fragments produced by a sculptor of genius. He praises the church for the ways in which the sculptor was able to translate his ideas about biblical scenes into visual form: "Believe it when I say that the fellow who sculpted that facade was every bit as talented, his ideas just as profound as those of the artists that you admire the most today [. . .] There are certain words from the Office of the Assumption that are translated with a subtlety of expression that even a Redon has not been able to match."[64] Elstir admires the ways in which content and style merge in a work of genius. If the hero had been able to subordinate his expectations and his knowledge to an experience of aesthetic immediacy, he too, would have been able to appreciate his initial enthusiasm for the beauty of the church, which had impressed him as a soft, lush fruit in the afternoon sky.

Such great enthusiasm often comes from catching a glimpse of "the emotion of true things" through beautiful style like that of the anonymous sculptor of the Balbec church. It provides a kind of epiphany conducive to creating a work of art. In "Journées de lecture," the aesthetic sentiment produced by a cathedral transcended even death itself. In notes for *Contre Sainte-Beuve,* Proust wished that the part of him that had experienced such ecstasy could write his novels: "He finds an even higher connection, his joy grows even more. For he dies instantaneously in the particular, and immediately starts floating and living in the general. He lives only from the general, the general animates and nourishes him, and he dies instantaneously in the particular."[65] By comparing and contrasting the attitudes of his characters, Proust takes the theories of spiritual communion he developed while working on Ruskin, and incorporates them gracefully into his novel.

The hero finally experiences this exalted communal art spirit near the end of *La Recherche,* when he travels to Venice. The sunlight and shadows of Venice remind the hero of Combray, but unlike Combray or Balbec, where he could not get past the names or objects that seemed to bring him aesthetic sentiments, in Venice he allows his impressions to wash over him without trying to analyze them: "There, I felt impressions similar to those that I had often felt at Combray, but transposed according to an entirely different and richer form."[66] His experience is no longer fixed to the "particular"—the objects he sees—but to the "joyous promise" he feels in Venice's atmosphere: the impressions cradle him as he "immediately starts floating and living in the general." Even Saint Mark's basilica is transformed into a reflection of the ideal world of sensations to which it belongs: "The church did not present itself to me as a simple monument, but as the terminus of a journey over spring-like marine waters, with which, I felt, Saint Mark's formed an indivisible and living whole."[67] In this third defining experience the hero sees Saint Mark's, like Venice, in terms of the general: Gothic arches, light, water, and air. Unlike Balbec and Combray, however, in which Proust described the churches at length, devoting long passages to evoking their realistic details and linking them to the French nation, in Venice he reduces the hero's experience to a series of metaphors that evoke light, water, and air: the church is no longer attached to time or place.

Proust progressively modified his style to evoke the hero's evolving perspective of art. In his description of l'église Saint-Hilaire, he concentrated on the physical details of the church—its tapestries, stained glass, nave, apse, and stones—a stylistic technique that reflects the hero's interest in objects that coexisted with famous people of the past. Similarly, in Balbec, he represented the modern elements—the posters, omnibuses, and grime—that clash with the hero's preconceived notion of the church as immortal, thus leading to his disappointment. In Venice, however, Proust describes the basilica entirely through metaphor: there is little physical description of the church—the hero mentions only its horsemen and the mosaics of the baptistery—which he evokes through its atmosphere. Comparing Saint Mark's to "the terminus of a journey" raises it from the particular—physical aspects—to the general: it is the end of his gondola trip, but also the resolution of his spiritual pilgrimage. The hero's quest, which has taken his whole life, is summarized in the words "Saint-Marc."

It is striking that Saint Mark's is the only real church evoked at length in *La Recherche*.[68] As Autret, Bales, and Yoshida have shown, Combray and Balbec are fictional composites that Proust progressively adapted from descriptions he had made of real churches such as Beauvais, Bayeux, Chartres, and Amiens.[69] Much as Elstir attempted to paint what he felt, not what he thought he saw, Proust constructed his churches from a number of translated aesthetic impressions: "Individuals (human or not) are, in a book, made from numerous impressions, which, taken from many young girls, from many churches, from many sonatas, serve to create an entire sonata, a single church, a single young girl [. . .]"[70] Unlike Bloch (or Zola), who conceived of art as a tool capable of giving an accurate and scientific representation of reality, Proust believed that true works of art came from converting aesthetic impressions into fictional equivalents. Despite his insistence on the need to transform the reality we see, Proust retained Saint Mark's in his work. Why would he name and portray this church while creating composites from other real places?

For one, Proust's choice of Saint Mark's is yet another reaction against his contemporaries and their response to tourism. In a 1906 preface to his cousin's translation of *The Stones of Venice,* Proust subtly criticized his contemporaries' fondness for dreaming of Venice: "The agonizing Venice of Barrès, the carnivalesque and posthumous Venice of Régnier, Mme de Noailles's Venice of insatiable love, Leon Daudet's Venice [. . .] exert upon every well-born imagination a unique fascination."[71] Contemporaries had praised Nerval's *Sylvie* as a poem about the misty French countryside and they idolized Venice along similar lines; they accepted the authors' perspectives and flocked to find confirmation of their reading instead of accepting their own vision of the city. Proust's description of Venice is singularly disappointing for the reader who anticipates a repeat of the realistic descriptions of Combray and l'église Saint-Hilaire, with their proliferation of relics and famous names. Instead, Proust evokes the church and the city in terms of impression: the hero's entire Venetian trip is evoked by a web of metaphors linking the city and its artwork to light, water, and air. His experience reflects nothing of the surface details constituted by typical descriptions of travel because it is comprised of personal interpretations and memories.

There may be no better tourist guide than Proust, but he seeks to undermine traditional tourism by weaning his contemporaries from their bad habits. He creates fictional churches in order to discourage his readers from visiting "the Proustian church of Combray" or the "eternal Apostles of Balbec" (though modern readers have managed to do this anyway by identifying real models for the fictional churches). He presents the only real church—Saint Mark's—in terms that refuse to provide the specificity of guide books like Ruskin's *Saint Mark's Rest* or *The Stones of Venice.*

Second, Saint Mark's was symbolically central to Proust's project in *La Recherche.* Edward Bizub has shown that visiting Saint Mark's constituted one of the inaugural episodes of *La Recherche,* a segment that linked Venice, Ruskin, Madame Proust, reminiscence, art, and rebirth as well as *Saint Mark's Rest,* the book that the hero's mother originally read in Combray (Proust replaced it with *François le champi* in the final version).[72] Given the importance of Saint Mark's for Proust's personal mythology, it was crucial that the event that triggered the hero's final epiphany about art be a memory of the basilica. At the beginning of *Le Temps retrouvé,* the hero has just come back to society after years in a sanatorium. He is discouraged by his lack of literary talent, and has given up on writing as a vocation. As he walks across the courtyard in order to attend a concert at the home of the Princesse de Guermantes, he steps on an uneven stone in the courtyard, which begins a series of three "réminiscences" or "sentiments" that allow him to relive moments from his past. This event inaugurates *l'adoration perpétuelle,* where the hero finally understands his contemporaries' conception of art and is able to formulate his own theories about a religion in which the worship and creation of art grant immortality.

As he stumbles on the uneven stone, he sees "a deep azure [. . .] impressions of coolness, of dazzling light"; his impressions of Venice return to him.[73] The uneven stone corresponds to a moment when he slipped in the baptistery of Saint

Mark's while he and his mother were studying the mosaics depicting the baptism of Christ in the waters of the Jordan river. The baptismal motif, recalled just at the moment that the hero discovers the power of art, brings strong religious resonance to *l'adoration perpétuelle.* This scene has generated an enormous amount of critical commentary, most of which compares the hero to Christ and equates the baptism to a consecration of the hero's new vocation.[74] The experience in Saint Mark's is capital for *l'adoration perpétuelle,* in which the hero finally accepts writing as his true calling.

This retroactive discovery of his vocation is even more important since the entire novel explores the ways in which contemporaries and their beliefs discouraged the hero from becoming a writer. His spiritual crisis began when, as a child, he was attracted to art only to have his faith in his ability shattered. In an impression similar to that described by Proust in "Journées de Pèlerinages," a church produces in him a feeling that reveals "the emotion of true things." On a carriage ride in Combray, he remarks his changing perspective of the Gothic steeples of l'église de Martinville and that of the steeple of Vieuxvicq, as the speed of the horses carries him forward. This impression inspires him to write: "What was hidden behind the steeples of Martinville had to be something analogous to a pretty sentence because it was in the form of pleasing words that they appeared to me."[75] He composes a prose poem in which he attempts to translate the "special realities" that haunt him. The hero follows his instinct in writing, and feels a great sense of accomplishment from having done it; he exemplifies Proust's belief that great artists attempt to translate their individual vision of the world through art.

Like Monet's studies of the Rouen cathedral, the hero's description of the steeples focuses on his shifting impression of them in changing light and color. He sees them as "three birds perched on the plain, motionless and distinct against the sun," then watches their transformation with the movement of the carriage—"they turned into the light like three golden pivots and disappeared"—before catching a last view of them in the setting sun: "I glimpsed them a final time from far away, seemingly no more than three flowers painted upon the sky [. . .] young ladies from a legend, abandoned in a solitary setting where night had already begun to fall."[76] Like the "poète" of "Journées de pèlerinages," the hero accepts his vision as "a confused mass of shadow and light." Had he trusted his instincts, the child hero would likely have continued to write much more. But instead, he allowed himself to be convinced of his lack of a talent by a "lettré" modeled on Sainte-Beuve and Bourget; he incarnates the prevailing aesthetic beliefs of Proust's time.

Monsieur de Norpois, an ambassador and renowned literary personage, shatters the hero's confidence by insisting that literature has more important things to do than to be beautiful: "Today we have more urgent tasks than harmoniously arranging words."[77] He chastises the hero's poem for its lack of subject matter and compares it to the works of Bergotte, which he dislikes: "Even here it is already the same defect, this nonsense of aligning harmonious words without thinking about the content." Norpois's criticism is a pastiche that summarizes all of the elements of contemporary literary criticism against which Proust had protested since the 1896 *Jean Santeuil,* and that uncannily anticipates the criticism that would be leveled against Proust after publication of parts of *La Recherche.*

Norpois's condemnation discourages the hero from trusting his instincts: "Until now, I had concluded only that I had no talent for writing; now M. de Norpois took away from me even the desire to write."[78] Although his whole life has been a series of aesthetic disappointments in which his logic told him he was a failure, the memory of Saint Mark's of Venice makes the hero realize that he was wrong to have believed Norpois. He suddenly understands that he should have relied on the instincts of his childhood, which promised him happiness through art. At the end of *La Recherche,* the hero finds his salvation in art by comprehending the lessons of his life, which retroactively damn the society whose inaccurate beliefs kept him from following the right path. But luckily, he also realizes that all of his false starts will provide the material for his book; time was not lost after all.

Perpetual Adoration: Immortality Through Art

"L'Adoration perpétuelle"—the theology of *La Recherche*—argues that art is crucial for the afterlife; an artist's work—sculpture, stained glass, book, poem, sonata, painting—lives on in the aesthetic impressions of the people who come in contact with it. It is for this reason that the hero felt the same kind of impulse to create when he read certain passages of Bergotte's work and looked at Elstir's paintings as when he noticed the Martinville steeples. When Bergotte died, the hero felt confident that he was not "forever dead" because his spirit would continue to thrive in his books and in the people, like him, who read them: "He was buried, but all that dismal night, his books, laid out three by three in the lighted shop windows, kept vigil like angels with their wings spread, and seemed for he who was no longer, the symbol of his resurrection."[79] At the end of *La Recherche,* as the hero has begun writing his book, he worries about not having the time to finish it and thinks of the great works of literature that have remained incomplete at their authors' death. Significantly, the cathedral is just such a work: "How many great cathedrals remain unfinished! We nurture [the book], we fortify its weak parts, we preserve it, but afterward it is the book that grows, that designates our tomb, that protects it against rumors and for awhile against oblivion."[80] The cathedral, like the book, is a work of art that harbors and transmits the spirit of its artists. Bergotte's works symbolize his resurrection, just as the cathedral immortalizes the soul of its builders, whether or not they were able to see their projects to completion. This concept provides a secular equivalent to the Christian community so advocated by Huysmans; in both communities artists and the faithful (living and dead) live eternally in a system of mutual support.

Proust's belief in the ability of art to preserve the spirit of its artist dates from 1900, when he wrote an article in eulogy of John Ruskin. Even if works of art have been forgotten for years, he insists, they still come back to life the minute a spectator or reader stumbles on them. Thoughts, which people the ideal realm beyond the surface of life, live forever, often lying dormant until the right reader comes to wake them by casting his eye on them. When Proust visited the cathedral of Rouen in order to find a sculpture described by Ruskin, he felt that his focus on the figure had brought back to life not only the medieval sculptor's vision, but also Ruskin's preservation of it: "And it is one thought of the sculptor, in fact, that was captured here in its movement by the immobility of stone [. . .] nothing dies then, of what has lived, no more the thought of the sculptor than that of Ruskin."[81] Ruskin's genius revived the tiny sculpture from obscurity, as Proust animated Ruskin's thought while reading him, and as we resuscitate Proust's spirit by opening *La Recherche*.

Proust argues that art stabilizes and captures history, a theory Antoine de Compagnon equates to the function of a *lieu de mémoire*.[82] Opening the cover of a great book is like going into a cathedral: it reveals an immense expanse of time, caught within a molded frame. The hero never enters a church without feeling the past emerge from its walls. In Saint-Hilaire, for example, it was as if he were in a "valley of fairies," where the stone nave, like a time machine, projected him to the past. Its tombstones seemed molded by time—"time had softened them, and made them run like honey, flowing in a golden stream beyond their borders."[83] The arcades of Saint Mark's are similarly honey-like: "The wide arcades whose flared pink surface was lightly marked by time, thus giving the church, where [time] had respected the freshness of the coloring, the impression of having been modeled from a soft and malleable material like the wax of giant alveoli; where, on the contrary, [time] had hardened the material and artists had polished and enhanced it with gold, of being the precious Cordova leather binding of the colossal gospel of Venice."[84] The stone itself is acted on by time, but also bears its marks, captured in the vaulting of a cathedral as in the binding of a book.

If Proust insisted so much on his hero's spiritual journey from idolater to creator, it is because he felt that it was essential to preserve the chain of *l'adoration perpétuelle*. The great danger is that readers will not believe in the power of art: they will never rise to the level of "poète" by attempting to go beyond the "particular," the aspects constituted by composition, subject matter, or doctrine. In *La Recherche* Proust reclaimed the aesthetic function of literature in order to perpetuate the spiritual life he believed it constituted: he wanted to save it from those contemporaries who saw literature as "a game, destined to disappear"—a popular way to present political or theoretical issues. Without the religious services that preserve the soul of the past, the cathedrals, and France's soul will die. So, too, books preserve France's spirit, which will die if readers do not look beneath the subject matter. It was thus imperative for Proust that people go beyond their superficial contact with art in order to perpetuate its religion. "One of the great and marvelous characteristics of fine books [. . . is that . . .] for the author they can be called 'Conclusions' and for the reader 'Incentives.'"[85] The art spirit can only be continued by those who take aesthetic sentiments as an invitation to create.

Ironically, we have not learned Proust's lesson and we have canonized him for exactly the things he discouraged. In our pantheon of collective French memory, Pierre Nora's *Lieux de Mémoire,* Proust's novel has been accorded a pedestal near that of the cathedral. In France, Proustiana abounds, from Illiers-Combray (a "sacred pilgrimage site") to the sales of T-shirts, watches, and baked goods emblazoned with his likeness, to the reduction of all of his complex theories into the well-known episode of the madeleine, which transforms *La Recherche* into a rather long book about memory. Like Nerval's *Sylvie,* which Proust shuddered to imagine as a glorification of the French countryside, *La Recherche* (and especially "Combray") has been anthologized into nostalgic tableaux that represent a now vanished way of life and Proust has become "a champion of countryside and family, a poet of 'old France.'"[86] Yet even fragmented and misinterpreted, the enthusiasm of Proust's writing does produce the kind of aesthetic encounters that he hoped would prolong his spiritual life, from the narrator's awestruck description of Saint-Hilaire—"the valley of fairies" to his appreciation of Venice as a floating dream, the "terminus of a journey over spring-like marine waters." We shiver at his lyricism and if we learn our lesson we will perpetuate our emotion by taking it as an incentive to create.

Proust truly intended his book as a guide, through which he hoped to assist wayward readers. His goal, albeit secular, is not so far from that of Huysmans. He, too, wants to bring converts to the religion of art: via the cathedral or the book. Richard Shattuck has described the didactic aspect of *La Recherche* as "training our sensibilities," as helping the reader follow the hero's experiences so as to anticipate the kinds of real-life situations that the character himself failed to recognize until later in life. Proust thus shortens for his readers the learning curve experienced by the hero of the book.[87] At the end of *La Recherche,* the hero has reached the status of "poète": he writes his own work, in which he teaches about human psychology and he perpetuates the religion of art by resuscitating the works of the artists who preceded him. Proust thought of Ruskin as the fifth apostle of the porch of Notre-Dame d'Amiens because of his devotion to this church, and so the hero, like Christ, becomes the figure at the top of *La Recherche.* For him, each great author creates his own invisible cathedral, in which his life experiences are reflected and stacked through time and space, waiting for readers to bring them to life.

Proust and the Cathedral-Novel

Given readers' limited attention span, however, why would Proust have adopted a structure that traces his hero's psychological development for some 3,000 pages before finally revealing the theory—*l'adoration perpétuelle*—that explains everything that came before it? A somewhat disingenuous answer would be "time itself." In fact, Proust had originally intended the novel as a single volume, without so much as paragraph breaks; the conclusion would have come quickly. By 1913, he had decided to publish three volumes about the size of Zola's *Travail* (*Du côté de chez Swann, Le Côté des Guermantes,* and *Le Temps retrouvé*).[88] When World War I halted the publication of *La Recherche,* the revelation of *l'adoration perpétuelle* was postponed, thus allowing the middle of Proust's book to develop.[89] In fact, the recently discovered manuscript of the last volumes of *La Recherche,* revised just before Proust's death, reveals the extent to which he would have continued to expand the middle of the novel had he not died.[90] Without the temporal disturbances in publication, *La Recherche* would have been strikingly different. It probably would have much more closely resembled *Les Trois Villes* and the *Durtal cycle,* both in length and in terms of its overt critical message.

Time and chance thus provide a preliminary answer, but the question of composition is an important issue for this study because the structure of *La Recherche* is often compared to that of a cathedral. In his correspondence, Proust insisted on the precision of his plans and used the cathedral as a metaphor for books. It is thus tempting to attach each part of *A la recherche du temps perdu* to an aspect of the cathedral. After all, the royal portal of a Gothic church depicts the life of Christ or the Virgin and Proust's hero is the focus of *La Recherche,* the central figure around which all else takes place. Throughout *La Recherche,* Proust equates characters to church sculpture and figures from stained-glass windows or he evokes them in terms of biblical and allegorical personages. Characters Françoise, Théodore, Albertine, and Gilberte have their place in the portal of Saint-André-des-Champs, just as the Guermantes family belongs in the stained-glass windows of Saint-Hilaire. The scullery maid in Combray is referred to as Giotto's figure of Charity in the Arena Chapel of Padua, and Legrandin is the "Saint-Sebastian of snobism." Similarly, some characters—Gilberte and Swann, for example—are Old Testament figures who prefigure the New—Albertine and the hero.

It is thus conceivable to envision Proust, like a medieval artist, constructing a church in which the stories portrayed in the art present scenes for the spectator to interpret. Proust often described his composition in terms of the architectural techniques of repetition and stacking familiar to the Gothic cathedral, in which he purported to fill the spaces between the columns with *exempla* illustrating vices or virtues. A 1920 letter to Jacques Rivière reveals this conception of the novel:

> Because it is a construction, there are, inevitably, filled sections, pillars, and in the space between two pillars I can indulge in meticulous paintings. The entire volume about the separation with Albertine, her death, forgetting it, leaves far behind it the argument with Gilberte. In this manner there are three sketches of the same subject (separation of Swann with Odette in *Un*

amour de Swann—argument with Gilberte in *Les Jeunes filles en fleurs*—separation with Albertine in *Sodome et Gomorrhe,* the best part).[91]

Like the cathedral-builders, Proust developed the overarching plan of his work (the initial three volumes), then filled in the spaces. Such characters often signify more than their presence in the text would suggest and Proust alludes to general laws about behavior through his individual characters.[92] *La Recherche,* whose outward structure of time lost and regained stood fast although its interior remained incomplete at its author's death in 1922, has inspired a rich critical tradition analyzing the metaphorical relationships between Gothic architecture and Proust's novel.[93]

Despite the temptation of equating the novel to a cathedral, Proust himself never explicitly referred to his work as a cathedral-novel and even discouraged the appellation. When Jean de Gaigneron wrote to Proust in 1919, complimenting him on his work, Proust made clear his ambivalence about the cathedral metaphor:

> Your intelligence goes so deeply to the heart of things that you do not simply read the printed book that I published, but the unknown book I would have liked to have written. And when you mention cathedrals, I can only be moved by an intuition that permits you to guess what I have never said to anyone and what I write here for the first time: that I had wanted to give each part of my book the title: Porch I. Stained glass of the apse, etc. to reply in advance to the stupid criticism made about the lack of construction in my books in which I will show you that the only merit is in the solidity of the smallest parts. I immediately gave up these architectural titles because I found them too pretentious, but I am touched that you found them by a kind of intelligent divination.[94]

In this often incompletely cited letter, Proust makes a distinction between the book he published and the one he would have liked to have written, between what he thought about doing and what he chose not to do. Above all, it reveals the extent to which Proust was irritated with his critics, who attacked him for a lack of construction, and who demanded that he spell out his master plan for them. He refused to stoop to their "pretentious" tactics. After all, this is the man who had written that "True art has better things to do than make so many proclamations and it achieves itself in silence [. . .] A work in which there are theories is like an object on which one leaves the price tag."

Although he was flattered that Gaigneron could grasp the hidden architecture of his novel, he voiced displeasure about the ostentation of such an analogy. Although he had used it as a way of reassuring friends about the book's complex composition before the publication of *Du côté de chez Swann* (1913), he later rejected it (possibly because Romain Rolland had publicized the term *literary cathe-*

dral in conjunction with *Jean-Christophe:* "its proportions are as firm and strict as in gothic architecture.")[95] Rolland was particularly loathsome to Proust because he incarnated the ideals and attitudes against which Proust argued in *La Recherche:* like Norpois or Bloch, he advised using literature for utilitarian purposes. Proust took aim at Rolland in *Contre Sainte-Beuve* by describing him as the least artistic author of their time: "The steeples of his churches, which are like long arms, is [*sic*] inferior to everything that M. Renard, M. Adam, and maybe even M. M. Leblond have done. In addition, this art is the most superficial, the most insincere, the most material (even if its subject is the spirit, because the only way for spirit to be in a book is not for it to be the subject but for it to have participated in the writing), and also the most frivolous."[96] Proust continued to use building as an analogy for his work, but mixed it with the less fastuous "constructions" practiced by Françoise: sewing and cooking.[97]

Few readers realize the extent to which Proust's novel grew out of his frustration with contemporary attitudes toward literature.[98] Intellectual arrogance lay at the heart of his project, which he had originally wanted to begin with the words "Each day I attach less value to intelligence." He struggled for years to find a form that could reconcile his two principle goals: criticizing his contemporaries and creating a beautiful work of art free from theory. The most celebrated French novelist of the twentieth century anguished over whether he should even write a novel.[99] "Retroactive unity," keeping his explicit criticism of contemporaries hidden until "l'Adoration perpétuelle," was the key that allowed him to turn his project into a novel.[100] As he told Jacques Rivière when he began publishing *La Recherche,* this structure would allow him to achieve his goals without publicizing his topic:

> I found it more honest and more delicate as an artist not to show, not to announce that I was, in fact, departing on a search for truth, nor to say what that meant for me. I so hate ideological works where the story is always nothing but a failure of the author's intentions that I preferred to say nothing. It is only at the end of the book, once the lessons of life have been understood, that my thought will be revealed.[101]

By refusing to put a "price tag" on his novel, Proust allows readers to discover his theories for themselves. The hero's experiences teach them not to read books primarily for content: as the hero discovers, it is more rewarding to gain personal inspiration from the truths indicated by the enthusiasm of a beautiful style. The genius of Proust's structure is to postpone the intellectual's discovery of the book's overarching didactic message in order to highlight the novel's artistic value (the very quality glorified by *l'adoration perpétuelle*). Providing a key at the end of his work transformed *La Recherche* into a synthesis of instinct and intelligence, art and analysis.

The cathedral was, in fact, the perfect analogy for Proust's structure, but he could not admit this without seeming pretentious.[102] As with a cathedral, readers can revel in the beauties of Proust's style, or they can look more closely for figures that provide a lesson or that tell a story. Proust's discovery of a way to fuse art and didacticism is, in fact, one of the major reasons why his novel, which began as a work extremely similar to *Les Trois Villes* and the *Durtal cycle,* succeeded, while Zola's and Huysmans's have been largely forgotten. Instead of announcing his polemical project in the opening pages of the book, as Huysmans did in *Là-Bas,* Proust revealed his beliefs progressively, never allowing theory to overcome art. Unlike Zola and Huysmans, who sandwiched their criticism of society and their didactic expositions within their characters' conversations and activities, Proust saved his lessons for the end. It is only in retrospect that the hero's "lessons of life" take on the critical meaning Proust intended and allow readers to apply them.

Although Proust concludes *La Recherche* with his hero's retrospective understanding of "the lessons of a life," he invites readers to reconstruct the truth by rereading the book in terms of style: once we know how to read, we must take *La Recherche* as our own "preface," an "incentive" to create. Proust's success in building his unfinished novel into what posterity has called a "cathedral-novel" paradoxically derives from his implicit structure. It is the reader who must discover the Gothic arches that hold the novel together. The ultimate cathedral-novel is the one that extends us an invitation to create the cathedral for ourselves.

Proust's Legacy

To borrow Proust's analogy, once the framework of a cathedral has been constructed, artists can spend years filling in the blanks between pillars. Thanks to the expanded time created by World War I, Proust reworked his project and multiplied characters, situations, and descriptions. His novel went well beyond his initial criticism of the pretentious and flawed theories of Bourget, Sainte-Beuve, and Rolland, to create a much richer, much more nuanced vision of the world and the psychological forces that motivate individuals. In 1919, Proust republished his 1904 essay, "La Mort des cathédrales." In the preface, he evokes the extent to which his perspective—about books and cathedrals—has changed over the years of his postponed publication of *La Recherche:*

> It is under this title ["The Death of Cathedrals"] that in the past I published in *Le Figaro* a study that was intended to argue against one of the articles of the Law of Separation. This essay is quite mediocre; I'm giving only a brief extract that shows how much, with several years' distance, words change sense and how often, on the turning path of time, we cannot perceive the future of a nation any better than that of a person. When I discussed the death of cathedrals, I feared that France would be transformed into a shore

where giant chiseled conches seemed to have run aground, emptied of the life that inhabited them and no longer bringing to an attentive ear the distant murmur of the past, simply museum objects, themselves frozen. Ten years have passed, "the death of cathedrals" is the destruction of their stones by the German armies, not that of their spirit by an anticlerical Chamber that is now united as one with our patriotic bishops.[103]

This passage reveals the profound comprehension of time and human nature that courses through *La Recherche.* It also shows that Proust recognizes his idolatry of cathedrals. In 1904, he had delivered an aggressive and persuasive manifesto about the national importance of preserving church ceremonies as a link to the past and as a manifestation of French genius. His arguments convinced contemporaries to maintain the support of church services, the "soul" of the cathedral. Like his later descriptions of Saint-Hilaire and Saint Mark's, in which time has molded stones like wax, Proust devoted his writing to bringing attention to art, the privileged means of preserving collective memory. In 1919, however, Proust realized that although he had fought to preserve the life that animates these works (church services, attendance, readers), he had neglected to fully consider the fragility of the work of art itself. Born at a time no longer preoccupied by the physical destruction and vandalism of cathedrals, he had paid more attention to their "spirit."

Proust's profound sorrow about "the death of the cathedrals" shows, however, that he had not changed entirely. Throughout his work the cathedral served as a guiding image, a place of both spiritual revelation and of education. It is no coincidence that he used it here as the ultimate example of a lesson learned about the fragility of art and the mutability of human sentiments. No one could have guessed that the violent arguments that tore France in two throughout the 1890s would culminate in the long-desired union of all Frenchmen, in which the cathedral, "the highest and most original expression of the genius of France," would become the symbol of a martyred nation.

FIVE
Conclusion

Combray was no more than a small town like many. But our
ancestors were represented as donors in some of the stained-
glass windows, in others our coat of arms was inscribed. We
had our chapel and our tombs there. The church was destroyed by the French and by the English because the Germans were using it as an observation post. All that mixture of
surviving history and art that was France is being destroyed,
and this is not the end. And of course I am not so foolish as
to compare, for family reasons, the destruction of the church
of Combray to that of the cathedral of Reims, that miracle of
a Gothic cathedral that seemed naturally to discover the purity of ancient statuary, or to that of Amiens. I do not know
whether the raised arm of Saint Firmin is broken today. If this
is the case, the highest affirmation of faith and energy has disappeared from this world.

—M. de Charlus to the hero in *Le Temps retrouvé*

Charlus and the hero of *La Recherche* discuss the plight of French churches near
the end of *Le Temps retrouvé,* when the hero has come back to Paris for a few days
in 1916. Charlus, who sees the destruction of Saint-Hilaire and other cathedrals
as synonymous with the disappearance of France's history, art, faith, and national
energy, reflects the change in the cathedral's social status since the mid-nineteenth
century. By World War I, the cathedral, which Zola had evoked as a vision that
helped one in a time of trouble—"this constantly evoked vision gave him the
courage to fight, in the middle of the silent murder in which he felt himself enveloped,"—which Huysmans had called "a harmony, a synthesis, it encompassed
everything,"—and which Proust had referred to as "the highest and most original
expression of the genius of France"—had become a symbol of a united French nation, a figure embraced by Republicans and Catholics alike.

The meanings attached to the Gothic cathedral in France had remained relatively limited until the nineteenth century: it was essentially a symbol of the Middle Ages and the Catholic Church. With the publication of *Notre-Dame de Paris,*
however, the popularity of Hugo's message about the cathedral as a democratic
product created a secondary and competing vision of Gothic architecture as a style
in revolt, a work of secular French art that prefigured the Revolution. Throughout

161

the century these two competing versions of the cathedral appeared and reappeared with relative frequency. It was only in the last decades of the nineteenth century, however, that the symbolic registers of the cathedral were reopened once again, as writers and artists began to add personal meanings to the recognized ones. Victor Turner has argued that a symbol's distinguishing characteristic is its semantic flexibility. Because its signification is not fixed, individuals may transform a symbol's accepted sense by bringing new associations to it or by "including it in a complex of purely private fantasies." Given enough power or prestige, the individual can thus reshape the symbol.[1]

Zola and Huysmans provide good examples of celebrity influence. They were both established novelists before they began *Les Trois Villes* and the Durtal cycle; their books were serialized in widely read periodicals and sold in the tens of thousands of copies. As they expanded the subject matter of their novels in order to provide readers with an alternative to the pessimism of their time, their works became press sensations that caused them to be hounded by reporters. Before movie, radio, and television, they were national celebrities, whose opinions greatly interested contemporaries. Proust, too, influenced his peers by publishing his essays in widely read newspapers and by making arguments that were used as examples in legal debates about the value of Gothic architecture.

For Zola, the cathedral had been an oppressive reminder of the Catholic Church, yet in the 1890s he began to remodel it into the temple of a secular God, dedicated to the worship of science and the values of a Republican France. In *Les Trois Villes* the cathedral incarnates Pierre Froment's dream of social harmony. Huysmans originally admired Gothic architecture as a kind of museum that harbored French artifacts, yet his increasing interest in the Catholic liturgy spurred him to represent the cathedral as the perfect link between material and spiritual worlds, between worshipers and God. Proust built the cathedral into an ideal figure in which art superceded conflicts between Catholics and Republicans; he considered it a privileged form of art that triggered the desire to create. These authors associated the cathedral with extremely different concepts—Zola with science, work, and the architecture of the future; Huysmans with Catholicism, symbolism, and religious conversion; and Proust with nationalism, art, and didacticism—yet all returned repeatedly to their admiration for the cathedral as a stable and enduring human structure built to affirm spiritual beliefs. Above all, they admired the ways in which Gothic architecture harmoniously embraces disparate fragments, incorporating them into a single system.

In fact, the widely read works of these authors exerted a profound influence on a society hungry for messages about harmony in diversity. They "romanced" the cathedral not only by incorporating it in their novels and by praising it, but also by convincing their readers to fall in love with it: they transformed Gothic architecture into an attractive universal figure that satisfied the needs of their stories and their society. "In order to understand Cathedrals," wrote Charles Morice,

"[. . .] do we not have to compose in our minds, an immense and unique Cathedral, made up of all the Cathedrals?"[2] The cathedral appealed to contemporaries precisely because of its status as a unifying concept. It provided a comforting response to fears about the fragmentation and dispersion of society and the loss of tradition; it was a stable, still-functioning system of belief that organized and gave meaning to all of the disparate elements in and around it. "Unity!" exclaimed Charles Morice, "This is what produces the incomparable splendor of Christian art, this indissoluble union of all of the elements that compose it. Architecture, painting, stained glass, sculpture, gold and silver work, tapestry, embroidery [. . .] it all originates from the One, it all comes down to the One."[3] The political battles between Catholics and Republicans, the government scandals, and the growing individualism and materialism of an increasingly secular country resulted in a marked nostalgia for a stable social order. This search for harmony is evident in Zola's desire to bring contemporaries together in the embrace of a new religion based on the cardinal virtues of Christianity, in Huysmans's goals to renew the extremely ordered worldview of medieval Catholicism, and in Proust's embrace of art as a vessel that preserves communal values. It is also apparent in contemporary movements to reassemble dispersed elements from the past by creating institutions—museums, libraries, and schools—dedicated to better understanding the nation's history.

The cathedral as the ultimate figure of the community, as a reminder that unity can exist in diversity, appealed to the turn-of-the-century's nostalgia for what Michel Foucault has called "total history," a desire to envisage history as an unbroken chain from past to present by "[. . .] draw[ing] all phenomena around a single centre—a principle, a meaning, a spirit, a world-view, an overall shape." Foucault has argued that the late nineteenth century was at the edge of an epistemological shift from "total history" to "general history." While some craved the order of a society anchored firmly to the past, others embraced history as waves of fragmentation and dispersion.[4] Such a crisis is evident in the 1891 Huret interviews or in what Mallarmé called "La Crise de vers." While many authors sought a single voice (like that of Hugo) to bring order to the seeming diversity of opinions and literary schools, others embraced the creative opportunities afforded by being cut off from tradition. The cathedral, which can respond to both impulses, became a powerful model of compromise. Its links to symbolism and Catholicism anchor it to traditional French history, while the diversity of its artwork can be interpreted as a fascinating reflection of the artist left to his own devices. The sheer variety of artwork and theology contained in the cathedral offered something for everyone; it provided a figure of social stability and community spirit that could simultaneously represent conflicting values: medieval Catholic spirituality and symbolism, secular artistic masterpieces, or the historical longevity of the French nation itself.

As the fledgling Third Republic struggled to find an identity after years of imperial rule, politicians, writers, artists, and scientists questioned French institutions and beliefs while trying to find a way of bringing order to a world of seeming degeneration. In the wake of the inferiority complex provoked by the Franco-Prussian war, scholars like Fustel de Coulanges had argued that better understanding the French past, beginning with the Middle Ages, would bring an end to the squabbles between Catholics and Republicans and would restore confidence in the French nation. Indeed, in the long run he was correct. By the end of the nineteenth century, nearly everyone was in agreement that France's medieval heritage was key to its identity as a country that had consistently produced not only great works of art, but also works of art far superior to that of many other European countries. As Charles Morice put it in 1914, cathedrals "are the common patrimony of Catholic Europe [. . . but] the other Cathedrals of the Christian world, all of which came after ours, did not know how to say so many things, nor to say them with such graceful orderliness."[5] With the near-universal recognition of the importance of the French—and especially medieval—patrimony, came pride in French art and monuments as a reflection of the brilliance of French spirit.

The Cathedral's Legacy

The works of Zola, Huysmans, and Proust continued to influence contemporaries in the years preceding World War I, especially with the publication of Catholic and Republican works that championed medieval religious architecture as both theme and symbol: Debussy's "La Cathédrale engloutie" (1910), Péguy's *Tapisserie de Notre-Dame,* Claudel's *L'Annonce faite à Marie* (both published in 1912), Barrès's *La Grande Pitié des Eglises de France* (1913), and Rodin's *Les Cathédrales de France* (1914). All of these works link nationalism, spirituality, and art to the cathedral, a figure of French genius and faith. Rodin's work, especially, summarizes the points of Zola, Huysmans, and Proust, and serves as a consecration of the fin-de-siècle Gothic revival, not the least because it was prefaced by what is nearly a book of its own, Charles Morice's 110-page homage to the history, signification, and criticism of the Gothic cathedral. In this work, the author describes the late nineteenth century as the "fruition of the discovery of the Cathedral, the resurrection, as it were, of the religious art of the Middle Ages."[6] Morice helped Rodin begin assembling his notes for *Les Cathédrales de France* in 1910, the year after the exhibition of Rodin's sculpture, "La Cathédrale," at the 1909 Paris Exposition.[7] For the book, the sculptor had made "my pilgrimages to all of the Cathedrals of France," both to modest Gothic country churches and to major city cathedrals. He was horrified to have stumbled on "this great art" so late in his career; he had always ignored Gothic sculpture because he had been taught that it was unworthy of his attention.[8] *Les Cathédrales de France* is a lyrical tribute to his belated discovery of Gothic

Figure 5.1. Rodin. *Cathedral of Nantes. Les Cathédrales de France.* Art and Architecture Division. Miriam and Ira D. Wallach Division of Art, Prints and Photographs. The New York Public Library. Astor, Lenox and Tilden Foundations.

architecture; he expresses himself through essays, notes, aphorisms, and sketches (Figure 5.1). Rodin proposed the cathedral as *the* symbol of the French nation—"Cathedrals are France." His fondness for Gothic architecture repeats and amplifies descriptions of it as an awe-inspiring figure of harmony in diversity: cVariety in unity, we cannot let ourselves tire of repeating these words."[9]

Zola, Huysmans, and Proust had reconfigured the conflicting religious, democratic, and nationalistic ideals of Chateaubriand, Hugo, and Viollet-le-Duc; Rodin summarized them all in describing the cathedral both as the epitome of French faith and genius, and as the masterpiece of French architecture, a highly ordered and scientific structure that was France's equivalent of Greece's Parthenon.[10] What a difference from the Second Empire, when professors at the Académie des Beaux-Arts dismissed Gothic architecture as having nothing to do with French genius! It was only by the beginning of the early twentieth century that the cathedral was widely recognized as a French masterpiece that rivaled the treasures of Greece.[11]

Rodin often compared the cathedral favorably with Greek art, while glorifying the French national style for creating a community, a French family, in which even the most wayward members were linked. "The Cathedral is a fastener that reunites everything: it is the knot, the pact of civilization."[12] Like Zola, Huysmans, Proust, and Maurice Barrès (who evoked Notre-Dame de Bourges as "a house of the collective"), for Rodin the cathedral—a mother and protector—was at the heart of the "family" that constituted the French nation:[13]

> I must tell you what riches you scorn. [Cathedrals] belong to all, each Frenchman owns a share, as he does, in the depths of his soul, his share of moral life. Taking the people to the Cathedral is taking them home, to its house, to the citadel of its strength. The country cannot perish as long as Cathedrals are here. They are our Muses. They are our Mothers.[14]

A symbol of the Virgin Mary for Catholic authors like Huysmans and Péguy (whose 1914 *Quatrains,* resound with prayers to Chartres, "O Princesse cathédrale"), the cathedral was also a secular figure (mother and muse) for Zola, Rodin, and Barrès.[15] Like Joan of Arc, whose rehabilitation was occurring at the same time, the cathedral was championed by Catholics and Republicans alike as a martyr and powerful supernatural female protector of the French nation.[16]

Pride in the French collective explains the paradox about the rise of the cathedral's popularity during a time of increasing anticlericalism; medieval religious art had become a prized aspect of the national patrimony. Disrespect of this French heritage thus became a point of contention. Although activists since Hugo had attempted to pass legislation protecting French monuments, the first official act of conservation dates only from 1887. After the Separation of Church and State, France fell into a period of vandalism and administrative turmoil. Because the anticlerical government made churches the property of the state, dissolved religious orders, liquidated their assets, and chased other congregations from France, empty churches and abbeys remained largely unguarded, thus falling prey to antique dealers and collectors, who pillaged them. Monks and nuns, too, sold the property they had rescued in order to finance their exile.[17] Though little discussed, many of the objects amassed by American antiquarians including George Grey Barnard—the original collector of many of New York's Cloisters Museum holdings—were obtained during this period, purchased from farmers and antique dealers and distributed to Paris dealers or illegally exported to the United States.[18] Morice, in his introduction to Rodin's book, protests against the lack of laws prohibiting such activities: "We have no law forbidding the sale of our artistic treasures overseas, and America snatches them up with the power of the dollar."[19]

Although the French government abolished the national budget for churches and their services during the separation of Church and State, it is a testimony to the influence of Zola, Huysmans, and Proust and their contemporaries—who had succeeded in convincing the public of the value of cathedrals—that a category was specially established within the Fine Arts budget for cathedrals. Other monuments selected as "historical" would eventually be conserved by another special office designated for historical monuments (in 1910). Instead of turning cathedrals into museums, conference rooms, or casinos, as Huysmans and Proust had feared, the government allowed them to continue serving as houses of worship and protected many of them as national monuments. These laws, however, protected only those churches designated as cathedrals (seats of bishops) and classified monuments. Not every Gothic church was thought important enough to be classified. Many rural churches thus began to fall apart as their communities could not pay for their upkeep. Maurice Barrès came to the defense of these houses of worship through political speeches, through articles published in *l'Echo de Paris,* and through books. His *Tableau des églises rurales qui s'écroulent* (1913) and *La Grande Pitié des églises de France* (1914) argue for the importance of what Riegl calls "use value." Preserving churches is crucial to the collective memory of the French nation:

> Others may distinguish between the beautiful and ugly, humble and glorious churches of France: but I do not make such distinctions. In my eyes all of our churches are beautiful and glorious, all merit salvation: because all of them have been ringing for centuries with the same deep soulful accents, they are a visible link between the living and the dead [. . .] churches are the voice, the song of our land.[20]

His belief is like that of rural Frenchmen, who profoundly objected to the government's new administration. For them churches and their bells *were* part of the family.[21] Barrès's enthusiasm contributed to the promulgation of more stringent legislation in 1913 (the text of today's law), but the country was still ill equipped to deal with the pressing needs of so many financially abandoned churches.

Rodin, too, worried about desertion, both spiritual and monetary, which he felt would lead to the "death" of cathedrals, and by extension French spirit. "No one defends them."[22] He even wrote a chapter of eulogy, entitled "Last Testament," so resigned was he to the disappearance of the national treasure. "[The Cathedral] is dying; it is the country that is dying, abused and insulted by its own children. We can no longer pray before the humiliation of our replaced stones [. . .]"[23] His glorification of the cathedral as a national symbol adds an apocalyptic undercurrent linking the fate of the country to that of its medieval religious architecture. His focus on the soul and its death echoes images suggested by Zola, Huysmans, and Proust of the cathedral as a threatened place of artistic and patriotic sentiment. For Rodin, the cathedral is the ultimate symbol of both nation and faith; it is a living symbol of France. When this book was published, on the eve of World War I, it solidified the cathedral's links to the entire French nation and its varying beliefs: "The cathedral is the synthesis of the country."

The importance the cathedral had come to play in the national consciousness is evident in the country's reaction to World War I. Under the pretext that Notre-Dame de Reims would make a good observation post, the Germans bombed the cathedral almost incessantly, from September 3, 1914 to October 5, 1918, dropping over 350 mortars on it by the end of the War.[24] Such brutality, directed against what had become a major symbol of French achievement, had a profound effect on religious and secular groups alike. In a 1917 article, Emile Mâle described his country's mourning: "When France learned that the cathedral of Reims was in flames, every heart was stricken. Those who cried for a son found fresh tears for the saintly church."[25] In 1921, when he visited the ruins of the church, he was appalled by the extent of the damage and proclaimed the cathedral a tormented martyr: "I have seen the cathedral of Reims after its most recent injuries: a phantom church in the middle of a phantom city. At first, the charred cathedral, covered with deep wounds, was horrifying [. . .] the cathedral resembled a martyr who had just endured agonies that his torturers had not been able to complete."[26] News of the atrocities of the war damage reached even the United States. In a 1916 lecture in Boston, Ralph Adams Cram discussed the abominations inflicted on this, "the crowning symbol of a great culture":

> The glass that rivalled Chartres is splintered in starry dust on the blood-stained pavement and its fragments made the settings in soldiers' rings. Its vault is burst asunder by bombs, its interior calcined by the conflagration, the incredible sculptures of its portals blasted and burned away. Yet it stands in its infinite majesty, gaunt and scathed in a circle of ruin, still the majestic fabric of a great people, a great epoch, a consummate art.[27]

The world was aghast by the bombing, even more so when German leaders declared that they valued one of their soldiers more than the entire cathedral. Notre-Dame de Reims became a rallying point for French patriotism, and emerged as a figure of strength under siege.[28] In spite of the political, religious, and aesthetic debates that had racked fin-de-siècle France before the war, all of France came together in defense of the cathedral, their national symbol. As Proust had put it, the anticlerical Chamber had "united as one" with the "patriotic bishops."

Just after the bombings at Reims, Edmond Rostand, the playwright, attempted to boost public morale by capitalizing upon the cathedral as a positive symbol of France's ability to overcome adversity. He thus composed a poem entitled "La Cathédrale," devoted to Notre-Dame de Reims. This sonnet, which the schoolchildren of France learned by heart,[29] evokes the cathedral as a strong and proud figure—a testament to French genius—whose grace under siege only renders it more proud and "a little more immortal." "The Fortress dies when dismantled/But the Temple, shattered, lives more nobly; and suddenly/Its eyes, remembering its roof with disdain,/Prefers to see the sky through a lacework of stone." Instead of cursing the Germans, he suggests thanking the "stupid artillery" for shaming their nation while giving France something it did not have before: its own Parthenon.[30]

The patriotic pride attached to the cathedral during and after World War I transformed the spiritually rich cathedral images of Zola, Huysmans, and Proust into a symbol of the French nation and its cultural heritage; for all but Catholics, religion was evacuated to make way for what could be called "Frenchness." Romain Rolland, who proclaimed the attack on Reims an irreparable blow to the French soul, illustrates the extent to which the cathedral was synonymous with French spirit: "He who kills this work murders more than a man, he murders the purest soul of a race."[31] Outrage like Rolland's echoes Proust's conversation between Charlus and the hero about the destruction of Combray's Saint-Hilaire: "The highest affirmation of faith and energy has disappeared from this world." Charlus, like Rolland, feels that the destruction of cathedrals, by either French or German troops, kills the French spirit itself. The hero of *La Recherche,* however, criticizes such materialistic attitudes. He argues that the cathedral is a symbol of the French spirit; it is not the nation:

> I adore some symbols as much as you do. But it would be absurd to sacrifice to the symbol the reality it symbolizes. Cathedrals must be adored until the day when, to conserve them, we will have to renounce the truths they teach [. . .] Do not sacrifice men to stones whose beauty comes precisely from having captured, for a moment, human truths.[32]

While the hero loves cathedrals, he also understands that the human truths they represent are eternal; he is speaking for the Proust of 1919, who recognized, in the republication of "La Mort des cathédrales," his former idolatry of cathedrals. Human spirit transcends the material entity constituted by the cathedral's stones. One should not thus sacrifice men to protect art. Charlus grudgingly agrees with the hero, mentioning that Barrès said the same thing, the day after the bombardment of Reims began. Indeed, Barrès's contrast of humans and stones strikingly resembles the words of Proust's hero: "Let the marvels of French genius perish, rather than French genius itself! Let the most beautiful stones be annihilated, and let the blood of my race remain! At this moment I prefer the most humble, the most delicate French infantryman to our artworks worthy of immortality."[33]

The writings of Zola, Huysmans, and Proust played a vital role in detaching the cathedral from the Middle Ages and transforming it into a flexible semantic figure. In the midst of the Dreyfus Affair and the Separation of Church and State, vicious battles that pitted Catholics and Republicans, these authors used their novels to portray the cathedral as a place of cooperation, where science, religion, and art worked together. It was artists, not politicians or art historians, who were responsible for bringing attention to medieval religious architecture and for transforming the cathedral from the beautiful and mysterious structure praised by Chateaubriand and Hugo into a sophisticated symbol. As Charles Morice remarked, the end of the nineteenth century "inaugurated the synthetic period. Synthesis: reconstruction. Innumerable works, heretofore few and far between, take shape and, in recomposing the ancient whole, give it life."[34] In the novels of Zola, Huysmans, and Proust, the cathedral becomes an engineering marvel, a repository of French history, a community center, an illustrated Bible, a spiritual nexus, a macrocosm, and a masterpiece of art, all contained in one structure. But as different kinds of values came to be attached to medieval ones, the cathedral developed into a model for the French nation itself. If a cathedral could bring order to so many conflicting values, then the French nation, too, could tolerate different religious beliefs, political theories, and social classes. "French spirit" encompassed a variety of different beliefs, all organized around the supporting pillars of maintaining and preserving the traditions of the past.

By World War I the long-sought unity had been posited in an embrace of the past, and the cathedral had become, as André Vauchez has put it, "the darling of the secular Republic." After World War I the government rapidly devoted funds to rebuilding damaged churches, even accepting large monetary grants from the United States (Rockefeller was a major contributor). After World War II, in which a number of Normandy churches including the cathedral of Rouen, were damaged or destroyed, the cathedral continued to serve as national symbol. The German surrender was signed in Notre-Dame de Reims and De Gaulle celebrated a *Te Deum* in Notre-Dame de Paris. To the end of the twentieth century, Ministers of the Interior from opposite sides of the political spectrum consistently proclaimed the conservation of cathedrals an issue of "national urgency."[35] More recently, Pierre Nora's *Les Lieux de Mémoire,* which traces French fascination with its patrimony, devoted several articles to individual churches and their components. The once-maligned cathedral has truly grown into a *lieu de mémoire,* a treasured place of French collective memory.

Although the French conception of the cathedral after World War I became increasingly linked to patriotism, the complex semantic meanings attached to the cathedral by Zola, Huysmans, Proust and their contemporaries lived on and continued to expand, especially in the United States.[36] In 1913 the publication of a book about the Middle Ages—Henry Adams's *Mont Saint-Michel and Chartres*—created an explosion of American interest in Gothic architecture. The book, which Adams had written and published privately in 1904, is widely considered to have been inspired by (and based on) Huysmans's *La Cathédrale.*[37] Nearly all of Adams's sources were French—Viollet-le-Duc, l'abbé Bulteau, Huysmans, and Mâle—and he relied very little on his own analysis.[38] Adams thus introduced a generation of American scholars and medieval enthusiasts to French conceptions of Gothic architecture and to the medieval scholarship underlying it. Above all, he praised the cathedral's unity, as had Zola, Huysmans, and Proust. The book was a resounding success that broke publishing records and remains in print today.

Mont Saint-Michel and Chartres was made public at the insistence of Ralph Adams Cram, the leader of the medievalist movement in the United States. An American "Gothic restoration" had been underway in architectural fields since the 1890s, notably through Cram's work.[39] Examples of his designs can be seen in the cathedral of Saint John the Divine (begun in 1892) and Saint Thomas's Church (1911–1913) in New York, in the Graduate College of Princeton University (completed 1913), and in the Saint George's School Chapel in Middletown, Rhode Island (1924–1928). He did not simply build Gothic structures because he liked the form, but because he admired their spirit: "an instinctive mental affiliation with the impulses behind the older art and with the cultural and educational principles for which they stand."[40] Cram did not advise the Gothic style for all buildings, however. He felt it was best suited to the spiritual and intellectual goals of churches and universities, because "a building must look like what it is, express visibly the energy that informs it, and declare its spiritual and intellectual lineage."[41] Because of what he called his "Gothic propaganda," Gothic architecture began to be associated with education in the United States.[42]

Cram was particularly impressed with Adams's book and had begged him to release it to the public because he felt it was "a revelation [. . .]" about the goals of the medieval theologians and architects: "[. . .] all the theology, philosophy, and mysticism, the politics, sociology, and economics, the romance, literature, and art of that greatest epoch of Christian civilization became fused in the alembic of an unique insight and precipitated by the dynamic force of a personal and distinguished style." While Cram had disseminated his theories in lectures and books, he felt that Henry Adams had clearly outlined the cultural context surrounding the construction of Gothic cathedrals, especially in a form that would appeal to the general public. Cram called it "one of the most valuable adjuncts to the study of mediaevalism America thus far has produced."[43]

As medievalism came into vogue—Calder Loth and Julius Trousdale Sadler, Jr., speculate that more American buildings in the Gothic style may date from after the publication of *Mont Saint-Michel and Chartres* than in all of the rest of American history[44]—Americans claimed it for a variety of purposes, as had Zola, Huysmans, and Proust. A variation on Zola's legacy can be seen in skyscrapers, perhaps the true secular cathedrals of the "future." The 1913 Woolworth Building, in particular, was modeled on Gothic forms and was labeled "The Cathedral of Commerce." So, too, was the 1926–1929 "Cathedral of Learning" at the University of Pittsburgh. Perhaps one of the most interesting acknowledgments of the skyscrapers' debt to Gothic architecture is on display at Notre-Dame de Chartres. In 1954, the Institute of American Architects commissioned a stained-glass window to replace one damaged in 1791. Paid for with some of the proceeds of *Mont Saint-Michel and Chartres*, it represents Saint Fulbert, the builder of the Romanesque cathedral at Chartres. In the bottom series of images is his church—Notre-Dame de Chartres—set between two American skyscrapers, which, in a sign of tribute and homage to their ancestor, balance it.[45]

Through the influence of aesthetic theories disseminated by Huysmans, Adams, and Cram, even non-Catholic denominations, formerly leery of the "idolatry" and symbolism of Catholic churches, were won over by Gothic architecture's form, which seemed to invite one to prayer. Saint John the Divine and Washington National cathedral (begun in 1907), are perhaps the best known examples of this non-Catholic renewal of Gothic church architecture in America. These marvelous modern Gothic cathedrals truly celebrate the community: they embrace artist colonies, nuclear disarmament rallies, AIDS awareness outreach, historical tours, and even Halloween celebrations, all of which are sustained and united by worship. National Cathedral, a contradictory construct for a country so clearly dedicated to maintaining the separation of church and state, provides an excellent example of what "cathedral" means today. A word that originally signified "chair," the seat of a bishop of the Catholic Church, "cathedral" has developed into a rich concept that can absorb many seemingly conflicting values: although maintained by the Episcopal Church, National Cathedral was built with government funds to welcome people of all beliefs. It is a modern artistic and architectural achievement modeled on a medieval structure; it inspires powerful religious meditation; it maintains and encourages community groups, educational and social outreach programs; and it serves as a stage for important national ceremonies. In the years following the glorification of the cathedral as a positive symbol of community, artists continued to add secular values to the cathedral's Catholic base. It grew into a new spiritual model for France and for the world, a timeless pantheistic temple capable of embracing and absorbing Zola's secular religion, Huysmans's Catholicism, and Proust's art spirit.

NOTES

In citing works in the notes, short titles, indicated by the following abbreviations, have generally been used.

ARTP   *A la recherche du temps perdu*
Corr.   *Correspondance*
CSB   *Contre Sainte-Beuve*
OC   *Oeuvres complètes*
RM   *Les Rougon-Macquart*

Introduction

1. He used this expression in the 1890 preface to an unpublished collection of religious poems, *Chorus mysticus,* to describe his motivation for writing a collection devoted to "liturgical poetry." *Paul Valéry–Gustave Fourment: Correspondance 1887–1933,* ed. Octave Nodal (Paris: Gallimard, 1957): 218–219. Unless otherwise indicated, all translations from the French are mine.

2. The only major study about late-nineteenth-century literary interest in the Middle Ages is *The Middle Ages in French Literature 1851–1900,* by Janine Dakyns. She traces the myriad medieval obsessions of Catholic and symbolist writers throughout the 1880s and 1890s. The phenomenon is much better known in art history, especially through studies of symbolist art. See Laura Morowitz, "Consuming the Past: The Nabis and French Medieval Art." Christian Amalvi discusses the medievalism of the nineteenth and twentieth centuries in *Le Goût du Moyen Age,* but he does not distinguish one era from another.

3. The term *fureur gothique* comes from Maigron's description of this trend in *Le Romantisme et la mode* (Paris: H. Champion, 1911). Though dated, Dorothy Doolittle's 1933 dissertation, "The Relations between Literature and Mediaeval Studies in France from 1820 to 1860" (Bryn Mawr, Pennsylvania) remains one of the most valuable reference sources for the medievalism of this period. Patricia Ward gives a succinct overview of the romantic infatuation with the Middle Ages in *The Medievalism of Victor Hugo* (Pennsylvania University Press, 1975).

4. At the beginning of the twentieth century, Charles Morice criticized the "falsity" and "accessory shop" aspects of the romantic Middle Ages, lxxvii. In *Re-*

constructing Camelot: French Romantic Medievalism and the Arthurian Tradition (Cambridge: D. S. Brewer, 1995), Michael Glencross exposes the more serious historical and scholarly influence Arthurian legends exerted over the period from 1812 to 1860. Michel Espagne has linked the birth of medieval philology to the growth of interest in positivism following the Franco-Prussian war in "A Propos de l'évolution historique des philologies modernes: l'exemple de la philologie romane en Allemagne et en France." *Philologiques I* (Paris: Editions de la maison des sciences de l'homme, 1990: 159–183): 174–175.

5. The term *cathedral* literally designates any church that serves as the seat of a bishop, but by the late nineteenth century the word *cathedral* also signified Catholic churches built in the Gothic style. Today, as then, many small churches in France bill themselves as cathedrals because of Gothic attributes such as pointed arches and buttresses. The association between cathedrals and Gothic style developed at the beginning of the nineteenth century, and unless otherwise indicated I use the two terms indistinguishably. See Alain Erlande-Brandenburg's excellent study of the nineteenth century's conception of the cathedral as a primarily Gothic structure, 1–14.

6. Cited in Amalvi, *Le Goût du Moyen Age,* 158.

7. "Guidé par la folie unique de la Croix/Sur tes ailes de pierre, ô folle Cathédrale!" *Sagesse. Oeuvres poétiques complètes* (Paris: Editions Gallimard/Bibliothèque de la Pléiade, 1962): X 249.

8. Robert de la Sizeraine introduced the French to Ruskin's theories of art and "guides" to French cathedrals in 1897, with *Ruskin et la religion de la beauté* (The *Bulletin de l'Union pour l'Action Morale* had published extracts of Ruskin from 1893 to 1903). Albert Robida's multivolume series entitled *La Vieille France* (*La Bretagne, La Normandie, La Provence, La Touraine*) was published from 1890 to 1893 and introduced contemporaries to the highlights of France's cultural heritage, while a 1917 publication, *Les cathédrales de France,* contained twenty-five lithographs of French cathedrals. Emile Mâle published *L'art religieux du XIIIe siècle en France,* his doctoral thesis, in 1898. Henry James's *Little Tour in France,* originally issued in 1884, was printed with a new preface in 1900, while Henry Adams's *Mont-Saint-Michel and Chartres* was published publicly in 1913.

9. Pierre Nora introduced the term *lieu de mémoire* in the eponymous seven-volume work he directed from 1984–1992 (*Les Lieux de Mémoire.* Paris: Gallimard). The expression has now entered major dictionaries such as *Le Grand Robert de la langue française* to refer to people, places, things, and events that have been consecrated as part of the national heritage. See Nora's preface to the English edition, in which he defines the term and compares the work itself to a cathedral (*Realms of Memory.* New York: Columbia University Press, 1992): xv–xxiv.

10. For a brief summary of ideas about Gothic style see Louis Réau, "Le mépris pour l'art du Moyen Age," in *L'Histoire du vandalisme,* 136–38. The extent to which Gothic remained a derogatory term into the eighteenth century can be

gauged by reading Goethe's 1772 "Von deutscher Baukunst," in which he describes Gothic as misshapen and deformed before visiting the Strasbourg cathedral. *Essays on Art and Literature* (New York: Suhrkamp Publishers, 1986): 5–6.

11. Tina Waldeier Bizzarro provides a magisterial overview of the primarily negative French attitudes toward Romanesque and Gothic architecture from the sixteenth to the nineteenth centuries in *Romanesque Architectural Criticism: A Prehistory*, 1–2, 7–8. She argues that Vasari is the first known writer to link "Gothic" with the Barbarians, but that he was obviously inspired by earlier writers. Françoise Choay shows that in the seventeenth century nearly all religious architecture from the sixth to the fifteenth centuries was dismissed as "Gothic," though subsequent writers specified between "old" and "modern" Gothic (today's distinction between Romanesque and Gothic), 57–58. Paul Frankl's summary of the major architectural theories circulating in nineteenth-century Europe clearly reveals the confusion surrounding the Gothic style.

12. Choay attributes the continued English appreciation of the Gothic to late exposure to Italianate forms and to the triumph of the Reform. The disaffection of religious monuments under Elizabeth I and the laws created to protect them established enough historical distance for people to appreciate the innate artistic qualities of the monuments, 59.

13. In *L'Allégorie du patrimoine*, Françoise Choay attributes the proconservation "mentality" in France to the post-Revolutionary era. She also reveals the stunning ignorance of architects and art historians at this time. Because their training had focused primarily on classical architecture, they were unable to recognize valuable medieval architecture, let alone understand how it had been constructed or how it could be repaired, 111–112. Jean Mallion provides an overview of early nineteenth-century attitudes toward medieval architecture in *Victor Hugo et l'art architectural*. He shows how one of the first French archeologists, Charles-Alexis-Adrien Duhérissier de Gerville, trained in England, became so frustrated by the limited information and vocabulary pertaining to medieval architecture that he did all he could to assist Caumont in his endeavor to compile a scholarly treatise about medieval architecture, 27–32.

14. Cited in Robert Mane. *Henry Adams on the Road to Chartres* (Cambridge: Harvard University Press, 1971): 146.

15. In *France Fin de Siècle*, Eugen Weber distinguishes the 1880s and 1890s, which called themselves the fin de siècle, from the decade or so preceding World War I. Later, the entire period came to be known as the *Belle Epoque*, 1–2.

16. *The Gothic: Literary Sources and Interpretations through Eight Centuries*, Paul Frankl's overview of the ideas linked to the Gothic cathedral in Europe since the Middle Ages, provides an indispensable survey of individual attitudes toward the Gothic, but the scope of his project did not allow room for detailed analysis of these ideas. He does not draw many conclusions about specific periods and their relationship to the Gothic.

17. The period after the Franco-Prussian war saw what Michel Espagne has called "a sort of institutional consecration of the discipline [of philology]": the creation of chairs of medieval French and medieval French history at the Collège de France and La Sorbonne and the election of medievalists to such prestigious organizations as L'Académie Française ("A Propos de l'évolution historique des philologies modernes: l'exemple de la philologie romane en Allemagne et en France." (*Philologiques I.* Paris: Editions de la maison des sciences de l'homme, 1990: 159–183): 175. Gaston Paris and Paul Meyer founded La Société des Anciens textes français (1875) and the journal *Romania* (1872), while Godefroy published *Le Dictionnaire de l'ancienne langue française* (1881) and Petit de Julleville wrote *Histoire du Théâtre en France* (1880–1889) and *L'Histoire de la langue et de la littérature françaises* (1896).

18. In my historical understanding of the nineteenth century's relationship to the Middle Ages I am indebted to Janine Dakyns, whose *The Middle Ages in French Literature 1851–1900* is a seminal text for nineteenth-century medievalism. Her study convincingly argues that throughout the century shifts in attitude toward the Middle Ages mirrored political transition. Dakyns's general conclusion, however, which equates the fin-de-siècle nostalgia for the Middle Ages to that of the romantic period, does not go far enough. While the symbolist enthusiasm for the Middle Ages was generally cosmetic in nature and could be described as an escapist desire for a lost past, the passion for the Middle Ages in the 1880s and 1890s also inspired intellectual interest in the Middle Ages and laid the foundation for modern medieval studies. The blend of patriotism and positivism that followed the Franco-Prussian war brought new scholarly attention to the origins of the French nation and to its artistic heritage.

19. Cited in Amalvi, 149. See Weber, "Curism and Tourism," for more about the growing interest in travel at the end of the century, 176–194. Remy Saisselin, *The Bourgeois and the Bibelot,* gives an overview of the consumer and museum culture of the late nineteenth century.

20. In *Les Quatre Vents de l'Esprit,* Hugo wrote: "J'aime la cathédrale et non le Moyen Age." Cited in Paul Zumthor, "Le Moyen âge de Victor Hugo," xxx.

21. The windows were designed by Victor Champignuelle. See Morowitz, 289–290.

22. The term "vitromanie" came from L. Ottin's 1896 history of stained glass (*Le Vitrail*). See Morowitz, "Consuming the Past," for descriptions of the prevalence of medieval stained glass and tapestries as well as nineteenth-century imitations of such works (283–342).

23. I will discuss the turmoil of the 1880s and 1890s in greater detail in chapter 1.

24. In *Littérature et Architecture,* Agnès Peysson-Zeiss makes a valuable contribution to understanding Hugo's, Huysmans's, and Zola's representations of architectural monuments in terms of social stability, yet she does not consider cathedrals as inherently different from other monuments from the past. Her

anachronistic presentation of Zola's 1872 *Le Ventre de Paris* as the "logical conclusion" to Huysmans's failed spiritual journey in the 1898 *La Cathédrale* also illustrates her tendency to consider all nineteenth-century medievalism on the same level. The study does not mention Zola's fascination for cathedrals in the 1880s and 1890s. Similarly, Ségolène Le Men's brilliant study of links between illustrated books and cathedrals in the nineteenth century does not sufficiently emphasize shifting attitudes to the cathedral.

25. The word church—*église*—comes from the Greek *ekklêsia* and means gathering or assembly. Above all, houses of worship belong to the community. Philippe Hamon examines the importance that architectural models held for nineteenth-century novelists in *Expositions,* but he, too, places the cathedral on a par with buildings such as castles, glass houses, or ruins. Such parallels produce extremely valuable structural readings of literary works, but considering religious architecture on the same terms as secular architecture downplays the cultural role churches played in a France struggling to reconcile Church and State.

26. See Riegl, 39–42. Choay underlines the fact that the religious nature of churches continues to influence our attitudes to them, even as increasingly secular societies ascribe more and more weight to their historical and aesthetic aspects. Note 1, 191.

27. Until 1905, the government provided the Church with a budget to cover the upkeep of churches and the performance of religious services. See Jean-Michel Leniaud, *Les Cathédrales au XIXe siècle,* Françoise Choay, *L'Allégorie du patrimoine,* and Pierre Dussaule, *La Loi et le Service des monuments historiques français* (Paris, La Documentation française, 1974) for descriptions of these critical laws that set in place reforms that would evolve into France's current legislation regarding historical monuments.

28. Alain Erlande-Brandenburg clearly acknowledges Hugo's impact on a generation of specialists in the chapter of *The Cathedral* entitled "Myth or Reality." Ségolène Le Men reveals how a profusion of illustrated editions of the novel kept Hugo's theories current throughout the century. Françoise Choay also shows how writers mobilized and fought alongside administrators in the battle to make the public recognize and preserve historical monuments.

29. In his *Cahiers,* Barrès speaks often of the cathedrals he visits during his travels and worship. His fondness for Gothic architecture would culminate in 1913, with his defense of disaffected churches, *La Grande Pitié des Eglises de France.* Léon Bloy's journal reflects a similar interest in cathedrals. Paul Claudel, in *Art Poétique* (1907), reveres the cathedral as mother and muse.

30. Their conception of the cathedral is similar to Wagner's conception of a *Gesamtkunstwerk der Zukunft,* a total art of the future, of which Wagner first wrote in 1849. For an analysis of the effect of Wagner's theories on France, see Richard Sieburth, "February 1885, The Music of the Future." *A New History of French Literature.* Ed. Denis Hollier (Cambridge, MA: Harvard University Press, 1989): 789–798.

31. See Weber 22, 67. Other reasons for increased interest in religion stem from the humiliating defeat of the Franco-Prussian war and the sense that this event was a punishment for the years of sacrilege following the French Revolution. As Thomas Kselman has pointed out, both Marian apparitions and pilgrimages jumped sharply in 1872 and 1873, the years immediately following the Franco-Prussian war, as pilgrims attempted to atone for the sins of their contemporaries. (*Miracles and Prophecies in Nineteenth-Century France.* New Brunswick, NJ: Rutgers University Press, 1983): 113–116. René Rémond has argued that the Assumptionist Fathers, responsible for establishing the national pilgrimage at Lourdes in the wake of the Franco-Prussian loss, used this event to mobilize believers in the late part of the century. See *The Right Wing in France from 1815 to de Gaulle,* Trans. James M. Laux (Philadelphia, 1966): 184–188.

32. *Grand dictionnaire universel du XIXe siecle,* 904–905.

33. D. G. Charlton provides a comprehensive overview of the beliefs of the secular "religions" of the nineteenth century (4–35) before describing in detail their beliefs and practices in *Secular Religions in France.*

34. He commented on Zola's works in his letters to his mother and incorporated him into *La Recherche.* In his translation of Ruskin's *The Bible of Amiens* Proust admires and criticizes Huysmans's *La Cathédrale.*

35. Although Zola, Huysmans, and Proust began composing *Les Trois Villes,* the Durtal cycle, and *La Recherche* at roughly the same time, and despite the fact that these works share striking formal and thematic similarities, scholars rarely examine the three together. Proust began publishing *A la recherche du temps perdu* in 1913, but the principal themes and aesthetic theories of the novel developed from his work of the 1890s: *Les Plaisirs et les Jours* (1893); the abandoned novel, *Jean Santeuil* (1895–1899); and his translations of John Ruskin (1898–1906). For more about the reception of Zola's and Huysmans's works, see René Ternois and Michael Issacharoff.

36. *Expositions: Literature and Architecture in Nineteenth-Century France,* 46–47. Hamon's remarks, though applied specifically to architecture, echo Victor Turner's comments about the anthropological use of symbols, whose semantic "openness" allows them to be rewritten. "Symbolic Studies" (*Annual Review of Anthropology* 1975): 145–161: 150–151.

37. Cited in Robert Mane. *Henry Adams on the Road to Chartres* (Cambridge: Harvard University Press, 1971): 143. "La cathédrale" is feminine in French and is often portrayed as a woman, especially the Virgin Mary.

1. The Synthesis of France

1. For a general overview of shifting European attitudes toward the Gothic from the Middle Ages to the twentieth century, see Paul Frankl, *The Gothic.* Chapters 3–5, "The Period of the Turn Toward Gothic," "The Scientific Trend," and

"The Study of Art as a Scientific Discipline" are most helpful for the late-eighteenth and early nineteenth-century context. See also Fernand Baldensperger, *Le Mouvement des idées dans l'émigration française (1789–1815). I: L'Expérience du présent* (Paris, 1924) and Choay, *L'Allégorie du patrimoine.*

2. See Penelope Hunter-Stiebel, *Of Knights and Spires: Gothic Revival in France and Germany* (New York: Rosenberg and Stiebel, 1989): 8.

3. Kenneth Clark describes this fad in *The Gothic Revival* and traces its origin to the "Gothic mood" of Spenser, Milton, and Thomas Gray. One of the most impressive commentaries he cites about this time comes from W. Whitehead, an author who remarks the mid-century vogue for Gothic in 1753: "Everything was Gothic; our houses, our beds, our books, our couches were all copied from some parts or other of our old cathedrals," 70.

4. Gray's letters to his mother praise the "lightness" and "delicacy" of the cathedrals they visited in Rheims, Amiens, and Siena. Kenneth Clark devotes a number of pages to Gray's subsequent appreciation of Gothic cathedrals, 43–53.

5. Megan Aldrich provides a succinct overview of the relationship between the Gothic novel and the taste for Gothic architecture in eighteenth-century England in "Gothic Sensibility: The Early Years of the Gothic Revival." In *A. W. N. Pugin: Master of the Gothic Revival* (New Haven: Yale University Press, 1996): 13–29.

6. See Georg Germann, 53–54 and 81–82.

7. *The Cathedral,* 2–3.

8. In fact, Goethe wrote two essays entitled, "Von deutscher Baukunst," one in 1772 (about the Strasbourg cathedral) and one in 1823 (about the Cologne cathedral). The translators of *Goethe. Essays on Art and Literature* (vol. 3) distinguish between the two by calling the first "On German Architecture," and the second "On Gothic Architecture," as Goethe had erroneously labeled the Gothic style "German" in 1772 (New York: Suhrkamp Publishers, 1986). Goethe's choice of title also reveals the ambiguous status of the term *Gothic* at the end of the eighteenth century. It had not yet been detached from its "barbaric" connotations. Paul Frankl discusses Goethe's emotional response to the cathedral and traces his inspiration to Abbé Marc Antoine Laugier and Jean François Félibien des Avaux (1658–1733): 417–427.

9. Georg Germann establishes Goethe's importance for the nationalist project furthered by the Boisserées, Ludwig Tieck, and Josef Görres, 89–98.

10. Paul Frankl discusses Germany's debt to Goethe at great length in *The Gothic.* Even though Goethe later repudiated his 1772 essay, his theories still exerted influence on his contemporaries, 423–425. Frankl also shows how the Schlegel family's lectures, writings, and travel were instrumental in building interest for the construction of the Cologne cathedral, 451–464.

11. See Pierre Moisy, *Les séjours en France de Sulpice Boisserée (1820–1825), Contribution à l'étude des relations intellectuelles Franco-Allemandes* (Lyon-Paris,

IAC, 1956). Boisserée's book continued to exert such a strong impact that Hugo recommended it as a model for what the French should do while restoring Notre-Dame de Chartres in the 1840s. Jean Mallion traces Hugo's affinity for Boisserée in *Victor Hugo et l'art architectural,* notably on 468, 552, and 671.

12. Volume 2, part 2, chapter 32 (Paris: Garnier-Flammarion, 1968): 79.

13. See Frankl and Choay.

14. For a detailed description of Lenoir's activities, the development of the museum, and its impact on contemporaries, see Dominique Poulot, "Alexandre Lenoir et les musées des monuments français." *Les Lieux de mémoire* (Ed. Pierre Nora. Paris: Editions Gallimard, 1986): II, 2, 91–127.

15. Cited in Mallion, 427. See Le Men for more about the history and impact of Taylor and Nodier's work.

16. Part 3, book 1, chapter 8 (Paris: Garnier-Flammarion, 1966): 23.

17. Part 4, book 5, chapter 1 (Paris: Garnier-Flammarion, 1966): 73.

18. Part 3, book 1, chapter 8 (Paris: Garnier-Flammarion, 1966): 27.

19. *Histoire de l'art depuis les premiers temps chrétiens jusqu'à nos jours,* volume 2 (Paris: Librairie Armand Colin, 1906): iv. In fact, the tree myth is even older and was used by Goethe, among others. Charles Morice also credited Chateaubriand as the first to recognize the value of the Gothic style, xi.

20. Cited in Germann, 78.

21. Montalembert is cited in Choay, 100. See Dom Louis Soltner. *Solesmes and Dom Guéranger 1805–1875* (Trans. Joseph O'Connor. Orleans, MA: Paraclete Press, 1995) for more about the early influence of Chateaubriand on Dom Guéranger.

22. Janine Dakyns describes the controversy set off by Gaume's passionate embrace of the Middle Ages as an alternative to the "retrograde" Renaissance. She also describes other debates related to the rediscovery of the Middle Ages by Catholics at this time, 75–77. See also Christian Amalvi, 203–209.

23. Art historian Camille Enlart describes this attitude in the introduction to his *Manuel d'archéologie française,* vol. 1 (Paris, Auguste Picard, Editeur, 1919): 20.

24. "C'est vers le Moyen Age énorme et délicat/Qu'il faudrait que mon coeur en panne naviguât,/Loin de nos jours d'esprit charnel et de chair triste/. . . Haute théologie et solide morale,/Guidé par la folie unique de la Croix/Sur tes ailes de pierre, ô folle Cathédrale!" *Sagesse* x, 14 (Paris: Gallimard, Bibliothèque de la Pléiade, 1962): 249.

25. "Introduction," lxxxiii.

26. For more about the Catholic revival of literature that occurred in the nineteenth century, see Richard Griffiths, *The Reactionary Revolution* and Gugelot, *La Conversion des intellectuels au catholicisme.* Verlaine's *Sagesse* was read by nearly all new artist converts.

27. "La Bande noire" was published in 1824 in a journal called *La Muse*

française, then republished in *Odes et Ballades.* He printed a passage against vandalism in *La Revue de Paris* in July–August 1829, and his essays against demolition
appeared in *Le Nouveau Keepsake français, La France littéraire,* and *La Revue des
Deux Mondes* from 1831 to 1832. See Jean Mallion, 425–444.

28. *Expositions,* 26.

29. OC IV, 95.

30. This metaphor would also become one of Chateaubriand's favorites,
notably in *Les Mémoires d'Outre-Tombe,* whose long construction he compares to
a cathedral. See Michel Riffaterre's "Chateaubriand et le monument imaginaire"
for an analysis of Chateaubriand's verbal obsession with the word monument.
Chateaubriand Today (Ed. Richard Switzer. Madison, WI: The University of Wis-
consin Press, 1970): 63–81.

31. See the conclusion of Claudie Bernard's "De l'Architecture à la littérature: la topographie parisienne dans *Notre-Dame de Paris* de Victor Hugo" for an
analysis of the three levels of interpretation upon which the title, *Notre-Dame de
Paris,* hinges. Because Hugo reuses the name, Notre-Dame de Paris, he empties it
of its original meaning. The title thus becomes metonymical (the cathedral is included in the book); metaphorical (the cathedral is a book, yet the book is a cathedral); and generative (the cathedral inspires the book, which gives back life to the
cathedral by immortalizing it). (*La Revue des lettres modernes* 1: 1984): 103–137.

32. OC IV, 122. See also Ségolène Le Men, for a history of the illustrated
editions of the novel and the inspiration they took from the text. Célestin Nan-
teuil's lugubrious 1832 frontispiece is one that best captures this spirit (Reproduced in Le Men, 69).

33. Cited in Mallion, 444. Mallion discusses contemporary reactions to
Notre-Dame de Paris and remarks upon reviewers Paul Lacroix, Sainte-Beuve, and
Théophile Gautier's enthusiasm for the great erudition and love of the cathedral evident in the book, 61. In 1863 Théophile Gautier continued to praise Hugo's role
as instigator of the public interest in medieval art: "[Hugo] saved medieval art in
France and gave archeology lyric impetus." Cited in Mallion, 8. Le Men traces the
prevalence of illustrated editions of *Notre-Dame de Paris* throughout the century.

34. See Jean Mallion's analysis of the evolution of the *Comité des Monuments historiques* and its social function. He provides a thorough summary of the
minutes from the meetings of the *Comité,* in which Hugo often insisted upon the
importance of putting pressure on local governments to preserve historical monuments, 445–479. He reprints Hugo's interventions in the appendix. Mallion also
shows Hugo's commitment to preserving monuments throughout Europe, even
until a few months before his death, 481–512. *Les Cathédrales de France au XIXe
siècle,* Jean-Michel Leniaud's magisterial work on the functioning and financing of
restoration projects in nineteenth-century France, also provides an overview of the
administrative details pertaining to the *Comité.*

35. See Mallion, 62–67 and 533–552, for a discussion of theories that in-

spired Hugo. Many of his beliefs about the development of the Gothic style and the Crusades were borrowed from the art historical works of Henri Sauval, Sulpiz Boisserée, Charles Robelin, Auguste le Prévost, and Ludovic (Louis) Vitet.

36. OC IV, 95.

37. Despite the formal differences between Notre-Dame de Paris and fully Gothic structures such as Notre-Dame de Rouen, Hugo argues that all Gothic cathedrals are essentially the same: they are built on a Romanesque base: "The trunk of the tree is immutable, the vegetation is capricious." OC IV, 96.

38. OC IV, 138.

39. Without Quasimodo, "Notre-Dame was [. . .] deserted, inanimate, dead [. . .] This immense body is lifeless; it is a skeleton; the soul has left it [. . .] It is like a skull that still has holes for the eyes, but no gaze." OC IV, 122. The English title of the book—*The Hunchback of Notre-Dame*—signals the importance of Quasimodo.

40. We see Claude Frollo's chambers at the top of one of the towers, but only briefly catch glimpses of the interior of Notre-Dame, which is presented in terms of emptiness, darkness, and shadow.

41. "Victor Hugo." In OC XI, 597.

42. In the *Dictionnaire raisonné de l'Architecture* VIII, 144. Cited in Mallion, 604.

43. See Louis Réau, *Histoire du vandalisme* for a description of such violent acts. Françoise Choay argues that the appreciation of the patrimony is above all a mentality that had to be developed.

44. Speech given upon his election to the Académie des Beaux-Arts on 27 July 1880. Cited in Mallion, 512.

45. Jean Mallion reprints this dedication in the appendix of *Victor Hugo et l'art architectural,* 643.

46. See Germann, 135. The other major publications of the European Gothic revival were *The Ecclesiologist,* in England, and *The Kölner Domblatt,* in Germany. Germann notes the impressive communication among the editors of these three publications; they shared contributors, wrote for each other, and consulted about forthcoming issues, 99–104.

47. A. W. N. Pugin, a Roman Catholic Englishman with family in France, was another extremely interesting and influential persona in the European dissemination of information about medieval architecture. Son of an antiquarian, he was a connoisseur of medieval art and architecture by the age of eight. He traveled throughout Europe writing and studying medieval art and corresponding with fellow Gothic enthusiasts such as Didron. His publications about medieval decor and furnishings were widely distributed throughout Europe and America. See Clive Wainwright, "A. W. N. Pugin and France." In *Master of Gothic Revival.* Ed. Paul Atterbury (New Haven, Yale University Press, 1995): 62–77.

48. See Jean Mallion for a discussion of the repercussions of Hugo's work

throughout the nineteenth century. Erlande-Brandenburg evokes Viollet-le-Duc's debt to Hugo, 11–26.

49. The *Dictionnaire historique d'architecture* (1832) of Quatremère de Quincy came under particular fire by proponents of the Gothic because of the art historian's vicious attacks on what he considered "decadent," "illogical," and "dangerous" construction techniques used in building cathedrals. The article "Exagération" took particular aim at what he perceived as the cathedral's excesses.

50. For more about the battle over the Gothic in the mid-nineteenth century, see Barry Bergdoll, "The Ideal of the Gothic Cathedral in 1852," 108–110. He shows that though this disparate group collaborated in publicizing the importance of Gothic style, they almost split over issues of restoration and modern construction. Georg Germann also stresses Viollet-le-Duc's animosity toward L'Ecole des Beaux-Arts, the institution responsible for the formation of architects in France. Viollet-le-Duc had attempted to shift power from the school by asking Napoléon III to create independent teaching positions in architecture, and he billed his *Entretiens sur l'architecture* as the first time medieval architecture had really been taught, 136–138.

51. *Dictionnaire raisonné de l'architecture française du XIe au XVIe siècle* (Paris: V. A. Morel, 1875): I, 71. Viollet was also influenced by Vitet, whose *Monographie de l'église Notre-Dame de Noyon* (1845) constituted a seminal step away from romantic attitudes to the cathedral.

52. Albert Lenoir and Léon Vaudoyer, "Etudes de l'Architecture en France" (*Magasin Pittoresque* 12: 1844): 262. Cited in Bergdoll 114. Beulé is cited in André Michel, *Histoire de l'art depuis les premiers temps chrétiens jusqu'à nos jours,* vol. 2 (Paris: Librairie Armand Colin, 1906): iii.

53. Bergdoll deftly summarizes the competition between the two groups and their conceptions of the Gothic, 106–115.

54. "Mouvement archéologique en Prusse." *Annales archéologiques,* XI (1851): 129.

55. See Dakyns, 31–186 and Bergdoll, 110.

56. *Histoire de France* II, 130, 694.

57. Ibid. II, 642.

58. See Jean Pommier, 19–22.

59. For links between Hugo and Michelet see Lucien Refort, "L'Art gothique chez Victor Hugo et Michelet" (*Revue d'histoire littéraire* 1926): 390–394. Laurence Richer acknowledges Michelet's debt to Hugo in *La Cathédrale de feu,* and shows how the two shared a vision of the cathedral as a new step in architecture, the result of the people's liberation from Church and monarchy. In his journal, Michelet would describe the Gothic style as "a burst of liberty toward the sky" (I, 94) and the cathedrals as a construct of the Freemason, not the priest (I, 208). Cited in Richer, 242.

60. See Paul Bénichou, *Le temps des prophètes: doctrines de l'âge romantique*

(Paris: Gallimard, 1977), regarding Michelet's changing identification of the medieval church with humanity, 519–523. The 1861 edition of *Histoire de France* cut much of the end of volume two, in which Michelet had praised Gothic architecture.

61. Laurence Richer studies Michelet's complicated relationship to cathedrals in *La Cathédrale de feu*. In the chapter she consecrates to architecture, Richer likens Michelet's anguish to a love affair ("Questions d'architecture," 224–302).

62. Richer, 265–269.

63. *Histoire de France,* vol. vii, 110. Cited in Richer, 278. Richer also examines Michelet's antagonistic relationship to Viollet-le-Duc. Despite the fact that they shared a common view of medieval architecture, Michelet probably distanced himself from Viollet-le-Duc because of the architect's close ties to Napoléon III, 229.

64. July 1, 1862: 483.

65. *Journal,* vol. 1, 208. Cited in Richer, 293.

66. In the 1857 *Etudes d'histoire religieuse,* vii, 28. Cited in Dakyns 64–65.

67. 1 July 1862 (Vol. 40: 203–228): 216.

68. She gives many examples of the links between Renan's change of heart and freedom of the press. She attributes his virulence to the state condemnation of *La Vie de Jésus* in 1863 and the resulting persecution he suffered, 61–62.

69. Cited in Dakyns, 64–65.

70. *Ahasvérus* was written in 1833, but republished in 1843 and 1858. Dakyns gives a number of examples of Michelet-inspired images of the cathedral, notably Taine's essays, Louis-Xavier de Ricard's *Le Crépuscule des dieux* and Ménard's "Euphorion." See 70–75, and 117–123.

71. See François Furet, *Revolutionary France 1770–1880.* Trans. Antonia Nevill (Cambridge, MA: Blackwell, 1992). The entire book is devoted to the continued tensions between Right and Left following the French Revolution.

72. "Une Nouvelle Histoire de France, de M. Guizot," 439.

73. See Colleen Beth Hays, "Literary History and Criticism of French Medieval Works in the Nineteenth Century: The Phenomenon of Medievalism" (1993 dissertation: The University of Oklahoma) for a lengthy discussion of the development and dissemination of these issues of origin from the sixteenth to the nineteenth century.

74. From the third installment of "L'Organisation de la Justice dans l'antiquité et les temps modernes" (1 August 1871: 538).

75. "La fausse interprétation du passé est à l'heure où nous sommes le plus dangereux des poisons," 441.

76. See Elizabeth Emery, "The 'Truth' about the Middle Ages."

77. August Reichensperger, the editor of the *Kölner Domblatt,* praised the essential Germanness of the cathedral in the 1840 issue, 25 (Cited in Germann,

152). Josef Görres is cited in Germann, 94. Michelet, for one, was reluctant to embrace the Gothic cathedral as a French invention because of the heavy symbolic claims made on it by Germany. See Richer, 283–285.

78. Germann traces the propaganda attached to Cologne Cathedral from the time of Goethe and analyzes art historians' attempts to cope with the new discovery about Amiens Cathedral, 89–95, 151–165.

79. See Claude Digeon, *La Crise allemande de la pensée française, 1870–1914* (Paris: Presses Universitaires de France, 1959; 1992), for an analysis of the revenge movement and its defining impact on French identity.

80. These are the words of a bill proposed on January 11, 1872, thirty-three years before the official separation of Church and State. The original bill's wording was changed, largely because of the conservative Catholics who were worried that "universal Christ" might include the Christ of the Protestants. Cited in Elliott M. Grant, "Zola and the Sacré-Coeur" (*French Studies* 20. 1966: 243–252): 243.

81. The symbolic resonance of Montmartre is rich. It was the original hill on which Saint Denis, one of France's first martyrs was supposedly beheaded, but was also the site of bloodshed during the Paris Commune. See David Harvey, "Monument and Myth: The Building of the Basilica of the Sacred Heart," for a lengthy explanation of Montmartre's history, including the events leading to the construction of the Sacré-Coeur.

82. For these and more statistics pertaining to the subscription and construction of the basilica of the Sacré-Coeur, see Raymond A. Jonas, "Monument as Ex-Voto, Monument as Historiosophy. The Basilica of the Sacré-Coeur," and *France and the Cult of the Sacred Heart.*

83. Pierre Froment's opinion in Zola's *Paris* (OC VII, 1486).

84. See Raymond A. Jonas, "Monument as Ex-Voto, Monument as Historiosophy," 497–499. He reproduces one of these illustrative comparisons and the propagandizing discourse that accompanied it.

85. David Harvey, "Monument and Myth: The Building of the Basilica of the Sacred Heart," 222–227.

86. See Alexander Sedgwick, *The Ralliement in French Politics: 1890–1898* (Cambridge: Harvard University Press, 1965) and David Shapiro, "The Ralliement in the Politics of the 1890s," in David Shapiro, ed. *The Right in France 1890–1919* (London: Chatto and Windus, 1962). Raymond Jonas reproduces various designs submitted to the competition in *France and the Cult of the Sacred Heart.*

87. *Journal* 2 (Paris: Mercure de France, 1956–1963). 22 May 1907: 234.

88. OC XIV, 1, 342–348

89. See Jennifer Birkett, *The Sins of the Fathers: Decadence in France 1870–1914* (London: Quartet Books, 1986), Robert A. Nye, *Crime, Madness and Politics in Modern France* (Princeton, NJ: Princeton University Press, 1984), and Eugèn Weber, *France Fin de Siècle* for more about this sense of impending doom.

René Ternois provides an in-depth view of the philosophical writing of the time in *Zola et son temps*.

90. See Eric Cahm, *The Dreyfus Affair in French Society and Politics* (New York: Longman Publishing, 1996), for a thorough investigation of the impact the Affair exerted on all walks of society: from politicians and writers to families and students.

91. *La Cathédrale* OC XIV, 1, 117.

92. *The Gothic Image* (trans. Dora Nussey), vii.

93. Huysmans presents these ideas in "La Symbolique de Notre-Dame," an article published shortly after Mâle's doctoral thesis. This article repeats the theories contained in his 1898 novel *La Cathédrale* (OC XI: 170, 192).

94. *La Cathédrale* OC XIV, 1, 84–85.

95. *Aesthetics*, 687.

96. CSB 776–77.

97. Despite the lack of novels describing real architectural structures, many authors devote passages to fictional churches. In Stendhal's work, for example, churches play an important role as spaces of love and death: Julien first sees Madame de Rênal in the church at Verrières in *Le Rouge et le noir;* its red curtains prefigure his own bloodshed and execution; and he shoots her in the same church. Fabrice, in *La Chartreuse de Parme,* also makes contact with his lovers in the churches Saint-Jean and Sainte-Marie de la Visitation. These churches serve as theaters in which Fabrice seduces with his virtuoso performances (sermons). See Edward Engelberg's "The Displaced Cathedral" for an analysis of the ways in which nineteenth-century novelists replaced the unifying or communal values of the cathedral with erotic counterparts, 245–246.

98. For a description of the genesis of this story, see the introduction and notes of Madeleine Ambrière for the 1979 Pléiade edition of "Jésus-Christ en Flandres." *La Comédie Humaine,* vol. 10 (Paris: Editions Gallimard. Bibliothèque de la Pléiade): 297–310 and 1353–1374. "L'Eglise" was originally published in *La Caricature* in 1831. Balzac incorporated his narrator's vision of "La Danse des Pierres" in this work. His narrator, despondent over the 1830 revolution, visits the fictional Couvent de la Merci, in which sees a vision of the cathedral that transports him to the time of its construction by true believers. For a study of the cathedral as metaphor for Balzac's work, see Stéphane Vachon, "Construction d'une cathédrale de papier."

99. "Saint-Julien l'Hospitalier," which Flaubert had begun in 1856, then abandoned for twenty years (published in 1877), was also inspired by the cathedral of Rouen (as was "Hérodias"). He adapted a story represented in a stained-glass window. He had unsuccessfully attempted to have his editor publish a reproduction of the stained glass alongside his tale. Flaubert's modern hagiography was influential in inspiring symbolist writers such as Marcel Schwob (see Dakyns 190–91), and was criticized by Huysmans for its lack of spirituality (*En Route* XIII,

39–40). While Flaubert's *La Tentation de Saint-Antoine* and "Saint-Julien l'Hospitalier" provide rich links to the fin-de-siècle Gothic revival and merit further study, they exceed the bounds of this work, which focuses on the ways in which fin-de-siècle novels represent the entire cathedral.

100. As we will see in chapter 2, fictional churches appear often in the Rougon-Macquart series.

101. The number of critical works devoted to the literary "crisis" of the 1890s provides an idea of the prevalence of this idea at the time. Michel Raimond, *La Crise du roman,* shows the ideological unrest of the time, while Claude Digeon, *La Crise allemande de la pensée française:* 1870–1914 (Paris: Presses Universitaires de France, 1959), reveals the period's obsession with Germany. Christophe Charle, *La Crise littéraire à l'époque du naturalisme* (Paris: Presses de l'Ecole Normale Supérieure, 1979), links the sense of crisis to economic difficulties within the publishing industry. See especially the statistics he gives in chapter 2, "Les producteurs et le marché, expansion et crise," 41–60.

102. The contentious atmosphere of this time has been likened to a "seething melting pot of ideas" by Philip Walker. He goes on to describe the philosophical and religious complexity and confusion of this time, provoked by anticlericalism, the advances of science, and the failure of many of the early nineteenth-century modes of positivist thought (eclecticism, secular religions, metaphysical systems). The introduction of the works of foreign philosophers and scholars, coupled with France's own self-questioning, combined to produce a huge number of conflicting doctrines, 90–91.

103. Paul Bourget was one of the major proponents of this theory. His 1885 *Essais de psychologie contemporaine* accused Zola and the Goncourt brothers of portraying their contemporaries as powerless—"weakening of the will," "sickness of the will," "incapacity to act"—thus perpetuating a sense of depression in readers (Vol. 2. Paris: Alphonse Lemerre, 1886): 159, 161.

104. Ferdinand de Brunetière's famous 1887 attack on Zola announces "La Banqueroute du naturalisme" (a term previously used by Bourget). For a good analysis of this expression and its use in science and literature, see Harry W. Paul, "The Debate over the Bankruptcy of Science in 1895" (*French Historical Studies* 5, 1968): 298–327.

105. Bourget, "Etudes et Portraits, le pessimisme de la jeune génération." *Le Journal des débats* 16 June 1885.

106. Venita Datta shows the extent to which Zola bore the brunt of the attacks; the younger generation had even founded a magazine, *Les Entretiens,* to dispute his theories, 47. The magazines and journals of the time ran many negative caricatures of Zola. *Birth of a National Icon: The Literary Avant-Garde and the Origins of the Intellectual in France* (Albany: State University of New York Press, 1999).

107. *Là-Bas* was published in *L'Echo de Paris* until April 20. The interviews were from March 3 to July 5.

108. Huret, "Avant-propos," 19.

109. Huret, 41.

110. Ibid., 20.

111. Among the "Psychologues" were Anatole France, Edouard Rod, and Maurice Barrès; the "symbolistes et Décadents" included Stéphane Mallarmé, Paul Verlaine, Jean Moréas, and Charles Morice; the "naturalistes" comprised Edmond de Goncourt, Emile Zola, J.-K. Huysmans, and Guy de Maupassant.

112. "La littérature ici subit une exquise crise, fondamentale." *Igitur. Divigations. Un Coup de dés* (Paris: Editions Gallimard, 1976): 239.

113. See Elizabeth Emery, "Zola, Disciple of Huysmans?" (*Excavatio* 9, 1997: 44–52) for a longer description of these theories and an analysis of the ways in which Huysmans was instrumental in Zola's decision to abandon the "experimental novel" for the "new religion of science."

114. OC XII, 655.

115. To Edmond de Goncourt. See *Journal,* vol. 3, 402, 491. See also Dorothy E. Speirs and Dolorès A. Signori, *Entretiens avec Zola* (Ottawa: Les Presses de l'Université d'Ottawa, 1990). On pages 56 and 61, they reproduce a 14 February 1890 interview with Zola in *Le Siècle* and a 2 April, 1890 interview with *Le Figaro* in which he explains his desire to finish quickly: "J'ai hâte d'avoir achevé ma carrière d'écrivain. Il faut que j'aille vite," 61.

116. Although Zola continued to admire Huysmans and his work, they were barely on speaking terms after *Là-Bas,* and Huysmans virtually disappeared from Zola's correspondence after his attack on naturalism. Zola was apparently exasperated by *Là-Bas,* as Huysmans explained to Arij Prins in a 24 January 1892 letter: "Je ne vois plus Zola que Là-Bas a exaspéré" (24 January 1892, letter, 114: 235).

117. It is often argued that Huysmans is the most misanthropic of the decadents because of phrases such as the one that closes *A rebours:* "Est-ce que cette fange allait continuer à couler et à couvrir de sa pestilence ce vieux monde où ne poussaient plus que des semailles d'iniquités et des moissons d'opprobres?" I believe that such frustration indicates a desire to change society; Huysmans's characters criticize it instead of resigning themselves to its degeneration. By the end of *L'Oblat,* the inveterate loner Durtal has come to accept the company of others and has even embraced monastic living.

118. Huret, 19.

119. See Zola's *Oeuvres complètes,* vol. 7, for a dossier about the media's obsession with Zola's activities. The numerous caricatures are of particular interest. Huysmans's correspondence to Arij Prins is also telling in this regard. He has to hide in order to throw journalists off his track. See especially letters 108–09, 118, 122, 139, 313, 370.

120. "Introduction," xcv–xcvii.

121. Jean Lorrain's 25 January 1891 article about medieval mysticism in *Le*

Courrier français adopts Verlaine's "enormous and delicate Middle Ages" with its "wingèd cathedral" as the key concept for his contemporaries' love of cathedrals, medieval art, and saints' lives, 4. Laura Morowitz traces the fascination for cathedrals and medieval motifs in late nineteenth-century French art.

122. "La Littérature contemporaine" (*Mercure de France,* 1905: 284). Cited in Dakyns, 206.

123. *The Age of the Cathedrals,* 101.

124. See the interesting chapter entitled "Narrate, Describe, or Catalog?" (109–142).

125. *Lettres à une amie,* 5. In *Jean Santeuil* the narrator describes Casaubon as having "travaillé toute sa vie pour une oeuvre insignifiante et absurde," and compares his failure to that of many artists with high aspirations, 489.

126. *Aspects of the Novel.* (New York: Harcourt, Brace, and World, 1954).

2. "The Immense Cathedral of the Future World"

1. He often leveled this criticism directly at Théophile Gautier, as here, in a July 1879 article for *Le Voltaire* (OC XII, 367).

2. "Nos poètes" (OC X, 932). See Robert Finch, "Ivory Tower" (*University of Toronto Quarterly,* 24, 1955–1956: 23–37) for the genesis of this term, originally used by Sainte-Beuve to deprecate what he saw as Alfred de Vigny's tendency to hide in the past. The expression came into vogue at the end of the century to evoke the escapist tendencies of symbolist writers.

3. Many critics, most notably Philip Walker and Evelyne Cosset, have focused on Zola's tendency to discredit the past while focusing on the future. Walker discusses this trend with particular regard to *La Débâcle* in "Prophetic Myths in Zola," while Cosset treats the utopian time valorized in *Les Quatre Evangiles* (*Les Quatre Evangiles d'Emile Zola: Espace, Temps, Personnages.* Genève: Librairie Droz S.A., 1990): 55–58.

4. RM III, 1347. In spite of his enthusiasm, Pluchart is not an entirely trustworthy figure in *Germinal.* He is a visionary whose practical treatment of workers does not live up to his promises. It is thus ironic that Zola comes to resemble Pluchart in *Les Trois Villes* and *Les Quatre Evangiles;* his enthusiasm also overwhelms practical considerations. His cathedrals, like those of Pluchart, are largely ideal.

5. RM III, 1379–1381.

6. RM III, 1347.

7. 20 September 1891, letter 159: V, 199. His choice of Lourdes was most likely unpremeditated since the trip to the Pyrenees was intended to distance Madame Zola from Paris while his mistress gave birth to their son. The Zolas stayed in Lourdes from September 13–17. See *Correspondance générale d'Emile Zola,* OC VII, 199, note 1.

8. Zola had stumbled on his topic during a trip to the Pyrenees in September 1891, two years before completing the last two novels of the Rougon-Macquart series. In fact, *Les Trois Villes,* and notably *Lourdes,* its first volume, can be seen as a precursor to the last two novels of the Rougon-Macquart series: *La Débâcle,* whose composition he had begun in July, before his trip, and *Le Docteur Pascal.*

9. Aix MS 1591, fol 209.

10. OC VIII, 1468.

11. Armand Lanoux, "Discussion" (*Europe* 1968, 468–69): 158.

12. *Zola et son temps,* 650.

13. RM IV, 826. Zola's research folders for this novel are conserved in the Bibliothèque Nationale, nouvelles acquisitions françaises (Paris, BNF MS 10,323). Most of his notes about religious architecture come from *Le Grand Dictionnaire universel du XIX siècle* and from Viollet-le-Duc's writings about Notre-Dame de Paris (MS 10,323 fol. 50–52, 103–138, 260). See Henri Mitterand's "Etude" of *Le Rêve* for a description of the contents of these folios (RM IV, 1610–1617).

14. See "Le Jeune Zola et les prêtres," in Pierre Ouvrard, *Zola et le prêtre* (Paris: Beauchesne Editeur, 1986). Philip Walker shows that by the age of nineteen Zola was already beginning to break with Catholicism. By the end of 1864 or earlier, he had lost faith in it entirely (*Germinal,* note. 10, 103). See also OC IX, 409, 871–893; OC X, 881; and Corr. I, 223–227.

15. *Les Apprentissages de Zola* (Paris: Presses Universitaires de France, 1993): 92.

16. For more about Michelet's influence on Zola see Marcel Cressot, "Zola et Michelet. Essai sur la genèse de deux romans de jeunesse: *La Confession de Claude, Madeleine Férat,*" in the *Revue d'Histoire Littéraire de la France,* 35 (July–Sept. 1928): 382–389. David Baguley also discusses Zola's debt to Michelet in *Fécondité,* 53–59, as does Allan Pasco in "Love à la Michelet in Zola's *La Faute de l'abbé Mouret," Nineteenth-Century French Studies* 7 (Spring–Summer 1979). Zola, himself, discusses his fondness for Michelet in two "Causeries" (OC XIII, 112–117, 274–277) and an article entitled "M. Jules Michelet" (OC X, 218–221).

17. *Zola et les mythes ou de la nausée au salut* (Paris: Editions du Seuil, 1971): 216–252.

18. For a thorough discussion of Zola's tendency to portray religious architecture as a place of oppression, emptiness, and death, see Chantal Bertrand-Jennings, "L'Ecrasement," chapter 3 of *Espaces romanesques,* 41–50.

19. RM I, 1462.

20. RM I, 1473.

21. RM II, 916; RM IV, 989–990.

22. See Borie, *Zola et les mythes ou de la nausée au salut* (Paris: Editions du Seuil, 1971) for an interesting discussion of the sexual and economic relationships among women, churches, and the Catholic Church, 216–252.

23. Matthew 21: 12–13.

24. "Étables" (RM I, 1215; OC VII, 221–222), "halles au blé" (OC VII, 222), "salles d'attente" (OC VII, 650, 816), "musées" (OC VII, 650), and "gares" (OC VII, 616).

25. OC III, 175–176.

26. Jean Borie calls them slot machines for the Catholic Church in *Zola et les mythes ou de la nausée au salut* (Paris: Editions du Seuil, 1971): 221.

27. One of Zola's most scathing condemnations of churches, women, and money occurs in his 1870 satire, "La Petite Chapelle," where every stylish woman buys a chapel and has it installed in either the greenhouse or her boudoir, in order to play at worshiping a Virgin of her own making (*Contes* 388–392).

28. RM IV, 826.

29. Ironically, Zola learned about *La Légende dorée* from Huysmans, whose embrace of this book led him to write *Là-Bas,* the book that would destroy their working relationship. He lent Zola his personal copy.

30. See Rosalind H. Williams for a discussion of the prevalence of "dreams" at this time, especially 154–209.

31. Bibliothèque Nationale MS. 10.323, fos 217–218, cited in RM IV, 1626. See Elizabeth Emery, "'A l'ombre d'une vieille cathédrale romane': The Medievalism of Gautier and Zola" (*The French Review* 73:2. 290–310) for a more detailed analysis of the links between the intellectual context and Zola's decision to write the novel.

32. Laura Morowitz explores the ways in which Mérovak is a personification of the symbolist artists' obsession with the Middle Ages. For more about Mérovak's exploits see Maurice Hamel's "Mérovak: l'homme des cathédrales," *La Gazette des Beaux-Arts* (January 1962): 53–60; Léon Riotor's "L'homme des cathédrales," *La Plume* (September 1898): 527. Michael Driskell's *Representing Belief: Politics, Religion and Society in Nineteenth-Century France* (University of Pennsylvania Press, 1992) explores the nineteenth century's concept of medieval artists from the eleventh to fifteenth centuries as "primitifs."

33. RM IV, 826.

34. For Zola's unenthusiastic role in this production, see Laura Morowitz, "Zola's *Le Rêve.*"

35. Jean-Max Guieu describes the genesis of this lyrical opera, whose libretto was not written by Zola, 39–45. Lawson A. Carter describes its production and reception. It was considered an important event for French opera (*Zola and the Theater.* Westport, CT: Greenwood Press, 1963): 176–179.

36. Adolphe Brisson in *Les Annales politiques et littéraires* (21 October 1888). Other reactions to *Le Rêve* were mixed. Critics admired its subject matter or congratulated Zola for having written a successful prose poem, or they mocked his lack of attention to style and genre (RM IV, 1650–1657). Jules Lemaître was one of the few to understand that the novel was a blend of fairy tale and naturalist novel (RM IV, 1656).

37. The critic from *La Paix* (23 October 1999). See RM IV, 1651–1657 for selections from contemporary reviews of *Le Rêve*.

38. RM IV, 824.

39. RM IV, 1621.

40. Much of the information about his research for the book is contained in the preparatory documents conserved at the Bibliothèque Nationale. Henri Mitterand has published details about them in his "étude" for *Le Rêve* (RM IV, 1646).

41. See Elizabeth Emery, "Bricabracomania: Zola's Romantic Instinct," for a detailed description of the medieval artifacts in Zola's homes. Yvan Loskoutoff thoroughly traces Zola's fascination for heraldry in "Médan. L'héraldique d'Emile Zola" (*Les Cahiers Naturalistes* 71: 1997): 349–369. Huysmans's correspondence to Arij Prins, notably letter 116, discusses Zola's tendency to be taken in by overpriced fakes attributed to the Primitives.

42. *Journal,* 20 juin 1881. Frederick Brown publishes a number of photographs of Zola in his various offices, surrounded by stained–glass windows, tapestries, and suits of armor in *Zola: A Life.*

43. See Frederick Brown, 37, and Colette Becker, ed. *Dictionnaire d'Emile Zola* (Paris: Laffont, 1993): 273.

44. RM IV, 924; RM IV, 862; RM IV, 989.

45. RM IV, 826.

46. RM IV, 862.

47. Hegel, *Aesthetics* II, 685.

48. Zola corresponded with Monet. His links to the Impressionists have been treated by a number of scholars, notably Joy Newton ("The Influence of the Impressionist Movement on Emile Zola." 1964 doctoral thesis at the University of London) and Sophie Monneret (*Cézanne, Zola: la fraternité du génie.* Paris: Denoel, 1978).

49. RM IV, 862. Monet is cited in Pissarro, 21.

50. RM IV, 863.

51. *Monet's Cathedral,* 22. In 1914, Charles Morice went even further in linking the Impressionists' goals to those of the cathedral builders, especially in their impression of nature, art, and science, xc–xciv.

52. Pissarro, 23–27. Morice, "Introduction," xc–xci.

53. "She left the dream" (RM IV, 993).

54. RM IV, 1627.

55. Larousse defines utopia in the *Grand dictionnaire universel* as "du grec *ou,* non; *topos,* lieu" (XIV, 704), but from the beginning Thomas More left the word's sense ambiguous by leaving off its first letter. See Bronislaw Backzko, *Lumières de l'Utopie* (Paris: Payot, 1978) for a discussion of the double sense latent in the etymology of utopia.

56. OC XIV, 704.

57. *Les Misérables.* OC IV, 770.

58. See Albert Laborde's 1969 interview with Henri Mitterand, "Emile Zola à Médan. Un entretien avec Albert Laborde" (*Les Cahiers naturalistes* 38: 1969): 146–68. He considers dreaming as Zola's favorite distraction and recalls a conversation with Zola to that effect, 160.

59. In two 1860 letters to his friend Jean-Baptistin Baille, Zola explained that a poet is a "regenerator [. . .] who devotes himself to the progress of humanity" (OC XIV, 1250). Two months later he wrote: "above all, art must be useful [. . .] The artist,—poet, painter, sculptor, musician,—is a truly great priest. I have often compared him to a prophet: this is the best possible comparison" (OC XIV, 1250).

60. Zola's lifelong admiration and hatred for Hugo has been treated in a number of articles examining the relationships between *Notre-Dame de Paris* and *Le Ventre de Paris,* in which Zola implies that naturalism has killed romanticism: David Baguley, "Le Supplice de Florent: à Propos du *Ventre de Paris,*" *Europe, revue littéraire mensuelle* (avril-mai 1968): 91–96; Auguste Dezalay, "Ceci dira cela: Remarques sur les antécédents du *Ventre de Paris,*" *Les Cahiers Naturalistes* 58 (1984): 33–42; Ilinca Zarifopol-Johnston, "'Ceci Tuera Cela': The Cathedral in the Marketplace," *Nineteenth-Century French Studies* 17, 3–4 (1989): 355–368; Roger Ripoll, in "Zola juge de Victor Hugo," *Les Cahiers Naturalistes* 46 (1973): 182–204; and Marie-Sophie Armstrong, "Hugo's 'égouts' and *Le Ventre de Paris,*" *The French Review* 69:3 (February 1996): 394–408.

61. *Les Rayons et les Ombres.* OC VI, 27.

62. OC VII, 308.

63. For a discussion of the anticlerical tracts of the time and their resemblance to Zola's views, see René Ternois, *Zola et son temps,* Chap. 4, "La Religion. Idées et mots d'une époque" (69–114); Joseph Moody, *The Church as Enemy* (Washington: Corpus Books, 1968, 155–222) and Pierre Ouvrard, *Zola et le Prêtre* (Paris: Beauchesne Editeur, 1986, 165–183), who trace Zola's links to the literary *topos* of the bad priest.

64. It is possible that Zola borrowed his idea from Huysmans, who, in the Huret interview, had mentioned the study of a priest's soul as an innovative topic for the naturalist novel. Pierre Froment also shares striking similarities with Ernest Renan, whose tensions between Catholicism and science were well known to contemporaries.

65. Sandra Zimdars-Wartz, *Encountering Mary from La Salette to Medjugorje* (Princeton: Princeton University Press, 1991) provides a detailed overview of the Marian apparitions of the nineteenth century. Jean-Emmanuel Drochon gives a comprehensive idea of the number of pilgrimage sites and their value for late nineteenth-century believers in *Histoire illustrée des pèlerinages* (Paris: Plon, 1890).

66. See the graph by Georges Bertrin of pilgrimages to Lourdes reproduced in Thomas Kselman. *Miracles and Prophecies in Nineteenth-Century France* (New Brunswick, NJ: Rutgers University Press, 1983): 165.

67. For more about the attempt to "sell" the Lourdes experience as a neome-dieval pilgrimage, see Elizabeth Emery, "The Nineteenth-Century Struggle for the Soul of Lourdes: A Modern Pilgrimage" (*The Year's Work in Medievalism,* 1999): 103–114.

68. Ruth Harris has determined that by 1900 Lasserre's work had been translated into at least eighty languages and had sold over a million copies. The 1869 historical work could thus be called "the greatest bestseller of the nineteenth century," 180.

69. OC VII, 345.

70. OC VII, 223–24.

71. The return to "primitive" medieval Christianity is one of the themes of predilection for the Catholic revival. See Gugelot, 387–390.

72. Cited in William Berg. *The Visual Novel: Emile Zola and the Art of his Times* (University Park, PA: The Pennsylvania State University Press, 1992): 149. A number of scholars, including Lewis Kamm, have convincingly argued that de-scriptions of objects in Zola's work usually communicate a character's state of mind (*The Object in Zola's Rougon-Macquart.* Madrid: Ediciones José Porrua Tu-ranzas, S.A., 1978, 3, 41). Chantal Bertrand-Jennings, however, is one of the few to have explored the capital importance played by descriptions of fictional *spaces* in Zola's novels. As she points out in *Espaces Romanesques: Zola,* most critics have written them off as predetermined by characters and action, 9. She argues that places play an extremely important role in Zola's work as forces that act on char-acters as do other characters, 11.

73. RM IV, 1648.

74. These abundant documents were published by René Ternois as *Mes voy-ages. Lourdes, Rome* in 1958, and are reprinted in volume seven of Zola's *Oeuvres complètes.*

75. OC VII, 439.

76. OC VII, 312.

77. OC VII, 235–240.

78. OC VII, 431–432.

79. OC VII, 237.

80. OC VII, 307–309.

81. OC VII, 308.

82. In fact, Zola's extremely antagonistic approach to the monks does not tell the true story. For a more accurate history of Father Peyramale's role in the de-velopment of Lourdes see Ruth Harris and Suzannne K. Kaufman ("Miracles, Medicine and the Spectacle of Lourdes: Popular Religion and Modernity in Fin-de-siècle France." Ph.D. thesis, The State University of New Jersey, Rutgers: 1996).

83. OC VII, 311.

84. See, for example, the scene in *L'Education sentimentale* where Frédéric comments upon an ugly painting that portrays Christ driving a locomotive across

a pristine forest. He assumes this secularized Christ must represent either the Republic, progress, or civilization.

85. OC VII, 398.

86. RM I, 799.

87. OC VII, 996.

88. OC VII, 650.

89. OC VII, 651.

90. OC VII, 531.

91. OC VII, 536, 539.

92. Zola himself was unsuccessful in his bid to meet with the Pope, a failure that was greatly mocked by the international press. See the caricatures of a penitent Zola reproduced in volume 7 of the *Oeuvres complètes.*

93. OC VII, 934; OC, VII, 1000–1007.

94. OC VII, 1002.

95. OC VII, 1009.

96. See Elizabeth Emery, "The Power of the Pen: Zola Takes on the Sacré-Coeur Basilica." I explore the antagonism between city and church in conjunction with Zola's relationship to contemporary caricaturists.

97. OC VII, 1501.

98. OC VII, 1443.

99. Ferdinand Brunetière's scathing commentary about *Les Trois Villes* is an extremely perceptive analysis that provides good insight into contemporary reactions to Zola's theories. The critic, a member of l'Académie Française and editor of *La Revue des Deux Mondes,* reveals his frustration with the style and subject matter, thus reflecting institutional and conservative reactions to Zola's work (*La Revue des Deux Mondes* 15 April 1898: 922–934).

100. 16 May 1896. Cited in Ternois, 605–606. Referring to Zola as a modern-day M. Homais, the pretentious bourgeois pharmacist of *Madame Bovary,* conveys Giraud's antipathy to the ideology of Zola's novel.

101. In an 1896 article entitled "Les Droits du romancier," Zola claims that a novelist must embrace "the immense world." He has enormous scientific obligations because he must be familiar with history, philosophy, sciences, all professions and all pursuits; however, all of this knowledge serves as a base to build new hypotheses about the future (*Le Figaro,* 9 June 1896).

102. "Comme le roman à thèse ne cesse d'exposer les idées qu'il illustre, l'allégorie ne cesse de faire signifier ses déterminations narratives, en disant une chose pour en parler ouvertement d'une autre," 137. Zola's emphasis on Manichean values conforms to Susan Suleiman's definition of the "roman à thèse" and its "exemplary narratives," 25–61.

103. From Zola's notebooks for *Rome.* Cited in Ternois, 407.

104. *Zola et les genres,* 146.

105. *Notre-Dame de Paris.* OC IV, 95.

106. RM IV, 815.

107. 2 May 1860, letter 17 to Baille: 153.

108. Adolphe Brisson used these terms to criticize *Lourdes* in the *Annales politiques et littéraires* (5 August, 1894, 92–93. Cited in Ternois, 364).

109. In his notebooks he calls him "Un saint . . . Il est pauvre, il donne tout. Il est humble, il donne des conseils miraculeux à tous" (Aix MS 1590, fol 15).

110. OC VII, 1272.

111. OC VII, 1563.

112. Although Pierre quotes these sources, René Ternois shows that Zola's influences also included Vogüé, Renan, Lamennais, and Littré. See D. G. Charlton's *Secular Religions in France* and Paul Bénichou's *Le temps des prophètes: doctrines de l'âge romantique* (Paris: Gallimard, 1977) for more about the "secular religions" of nineteenth-century social philosophers and theologians.

113. OC VII, 1559

114. OC VII, 1000.

115. "He gathered up most of the antireligious themes that had circulated for two centuries and expressed them with a cogency and passion unmatched by any major writer [. . .] None of his important literary successors concentrated on religion with his intensity" (Joseph Moody. *The Church as Enemy.* Washington: Corpus Books, 1968, 155–222): 221. Similarly, Micheline Tison-Braun notes, "L'attaque de Zola est la plus violente et la plus systématique que le catholicisme ait essuyé depuis la publication du *Pape* de Victor Hugo" (*La Crise de l'humanisme: Le conflit de l'individu et de la société dans la littérature française moderne.* Paris: Librairie Nizet, 1958): 307. See Philip Walker for discussion of the similarities among Zola, Michelet, and Vico (*Germinal* 23–26).

116. In order to get to these basic values, however, Zola matter-of-factly dismisses the hierarchical structure of Christianity.

117. His creed is based heavily on ideas taken from Renan's *L'Avenir de la science.* The litany of "je crois" mimics the tone of church ceremonies: "Je crois que l'avenir de l'humanité est dans le progrès de la raison par la science. Je crois que la poursuite de la vérité par la science est l'idéal divin que l'homme doit se proposer. Je crois que tout est illusion et vanité, en dehors du trésor des vérités lentement acquises et qui ne se perdront jamais plus" (RM, V, 953).

118. In *Le Romancier et la machine,* Jacques Noiray points out the importance Zola gave to language to prove his theories: "L'analyse socio-économique, la réflexion politique, font place à un simple acte de foi, dont la répétition continuelle prend valeur de démonstration. . . Il faut souligner le caractère magique d'un tel procédé: la réconciliation avec la machine que traduit à partir de *Paris* l'inversion de son image littéraire repose sur une croyance purement subjective et sur le langage qui l'exprime. Constamment associés à des termes vagues comme 'bonheur,' 'justice,' 'paix,' 'harmonie,' etc., dont la répétition prend valeur incantatoire, les mots de 'travail,' de 'science,' de 'progrès,' 'd'électricité' surtout, au-delà de

toute signification précise, annoncent et révèlent, par le seul fait qu'ils sont dits, l'exaucement miraculeux de tous les voeux de l'imagination," 232.

119. OC VII, 1561–1562

120. Aix MS1590, fol 20–21.

121. Eric Rabkin, "Atavism and Utopia." *No Place Else: Explorations in Utopian and Dystopian Fiction* (Ed. Eric S. Rabkin, Martin H. Greenberg, and Joseph D. Olander. Carbondale, IL: Southern Illinois University Press, 1983, 1–10): 1.

122. See Susan Buck-Morss, *The Dialectics of Seeing* (Cambridge, MA: The MIT Press, 1993), especially chapter 5, "Mythic Nature: Wish Image" for an analysis of Benjamin's theories about the relationship between art and technology, past and future.

123. OC VII, 1567.

124. See Jean Chevalier and Alain Gheerbrant, *The Penguin Dictionary of Symbols,* for an analysis of the symbolic resonance of wheat for life, sustenance, rebirth, and of gold for sunlight (fertility, prosperity, wealth, generosity), knowledge, and power (trans. John Buchanan-Brown. London: Penguin Books, 1996): 1097–1099 and 439–442.

125. *Le Docteur Pascal* ended similarly, but while Clotilde's incestuous child has a dubious future, Marie's child, Jean, is assured a seat at the foundation of the new world order.

126. There is a high concentration of biblical references, notably at the end of the Rougon-Macquart series. In *La Débâcle,* Jean Macquart (Saint John) foresees the Apocalypse and the second coming (RM V, 911–912). In *Le Docteur Pascal,* Pascal Rougon (repeatedly compared to the Old Testament King David), also predicts that a "new messiah" will come to redeem the Rougon-Macquarts and save them from degeneration: the new child born after his death will be free from the family's hereditary flaws (RM V, 1017–1019). See Philip Walker, "Prophetic Myths in Zola," 444–452 and *Germinal and Zola's Philosophical and Religious Thought* for elaborations on biblical myths and the prevalence of the Apocalypse in Zola's work.

127. See Elizabeth Emery, "Zola and the Tree of Jesse." For a reading of the symbolic importance of trees—one of the most important symbols in Zola's work—see David Baguley, *Fécondité d'Emile Zola: roman à thèse, evangile, mythe,* 203–204, and note 34 (109–110) of Walker's *Germinal and Zola's Philosophical and Religious Thought.* Roger Ripoll's "Le symbolisme végétal dans *La Faute de l'abbé Mouret*" also discusses the importance of this motif (*Les Cahiers naturalistes* 31:1966): 11–22.

128. See the poster that announced the publication of *Fécondité,* reproduced in Baguley, *Fécondité* 148.

129. See, notably, the artwork for the month of June, in which villagers harvest wheat under the watchful eye of the Sainte Chapelle.

130. In a 15 March 1897 critique of the play, Camille Bellaigue categorizes it as "agricole, social, industriel, anarchiste, nihiliste . . ." "Revue musicale" (*Revue des Deux Mondes,* 448).

131. 20 Februrary 1897. This piece is reproduced in OC XV, 584–592.

132. Acte III, OC XV, 565–567. Zola intended this scene for the middle of the play, but he was forced to place it at the beginning for technical reasons.

133. The lyric prose of *Messidor* (and notably the prevalent theme of stolen gold) drew many comparisons to Wagner and the Ring cycle. Zola responded by praising Wagner's "formula" and recommending a French version of it. See Guieu 74–87 and 147–154 and Lawson A. Carter (*Zola and the Theater.* Westport, CT: Greenwood Press, Publishers, 1963): 181–191. The influence of Wagner on Zola's late prose and dramatic works is a rich topic that merits further study.

134. Camille Bellaigue in *La Revue des Deux Mondes.* 15 March 1897: 448. Zola explained his objectives, which I have summarized here, in the *Figaro* article reprinted in OC XV, 586.

135. Cited in Guieu, 123.

136. "*Messidor* expliqué par ses auteurs" (OC XV, 585). Guieu, 122–123.

137. It is true that had the cathedral scene been placed in its original position (just before the destruction of the machine), the audience might have more willingly interpreted it as a product of Véronique's vision, but the power of representing such a space on stage makes it much more real than a legend should be.

138. This conclusion also sheds light on the play's title, *Messidor*—the tenth month of the Revolutionary calendar—which corresponded to our June and July. It is the beginning of summer and the year's first harvest.

139. OC XV, 586

140. "Revue musicale." *La Revue des Deux Mondes.* 15 March 1897: 450.

141. *The Anatomy of Criticism* (Princeton: Princeton University Press, 1957): 90–91.

142. The Charpentier-Fasquelle press published 88,000 copies of each of the *Trois Villes* in their first printing. The paper *Gil Blas* paid dearly (50,000 francs) for the right to publish *Lourdes* in serial form, and the book itself sold 121,000 copies in its first two months of publication (Noiray, "Notice." *Lourdes.* Paris: Editions Gallimard, 1995, 597–610): 608. The typical author of the time was lucky to sell 1,500 copies.

143. See *Zola et son temps,* where Ternois excerpts some of the polemic surrounding the novels and lists books Zola's innovative topics inspired. *Lourdes* (368–378); *Rome* (603–612); *Paris* (670–675).

144. 15 September 1894. Cited in Ternois 365.

145. Letter 136 to Arij Prins, 20 October 1894: 268.

146. See Emile Baumann's *L'Immolé,* Francis Jammes's *Pomme d'Anis* and *Ma Fille Bernadette,* or Georges Bonnamour's *Heure de Dieu.* Huysmans also wrote a scathing essay entitled *Les Foules de Lourdes.* For similarities between his text and

that of Zola, see Thierry Lescuyer, "Huysmans et Zola: Lourdes en question." (*Huysmans*. Ed. Pierre Brunel and André Guyaux. Paris: Editions de l'Herne, 1985): 324–332.

147. Huysmans, for one, was not impressed by l'abbé Peyramale's church. See *Les Foules de Lourdes*.

148. "Le bal mystique." *Le Courrier français*. 25 January 1891: 4. The pages of this periodical are full of neomedieval artwork and odes to the cathedral.

149. *New York* (Paris: Flammarion, 1981): 49.

150. Zola bestows significant names on all of the Froments. Luc, one of the "four Evangelists" of Zola's *Quatre Evangiles,* represents the Evangelist Luke, but his name also signifies *lux* or light. One of the principle goals of *Travail,* is to harness the power of solar energy. For more about Luc's charisma, see Brian Nelson's "Zola and the Ideology of Messianism" (*Orbis Litterarum* 37: 1982): 70–82.

151. OC VIII, 682–83

152. *L'Allégorie du patrimoine,* 117.

153. See Choay, 98. By analyzing Viollet's attitudes to modern architecture (especially those expressed in *Entretiens sur l'architecture*), she explains that he saw innovation in French architecture as nearly extinct and hoped to renew it through the imitation of thirteenth-century models. Gabriele Fahr-Becker traces the impact of Viollet-le-Duc's theories, especially those about the "enormous and delicate" effects possible with iron and glass, on architects and on the design used in buildings, metro signs, and interior decoration. She also shows the importance the "Gothic" played as an inspiration for this new style (*Art Nouveau*. Cologne: Könemann Verlagsgesellschaft mbH, 1997): 75–84, 136–147, 195–197.

154. *L'Allégorie du patrimoine,* 117–118.

155. See the eighth *Entretien* and Choay, 141. Jacques Noiray believes that Zola was influenced by Viollet-le-Duc's *Entretiens sur l'Architecture,* which were published in 1872, at the same time as Zola was writing *Le Ventre de Paris.* In his essays, Viollet-le-Duc uses Les Halles as an example of the ideal new architecture, which mixes art and science, architecture and engineering, 238–239.

156. See Agnès Peysson-Zeiss, "Zola, l'échec définitif," chapter four of *Littérature et Architecture.* While Peysson-Zeiss gives an interesting and nuanced reading of Zola's fascination for stone and iron structures, I disagree with her conclusion: that Zola's embrace of modernity reflects the nineteenth century's diminishing interest in medieval architecture and themes. In fact, *Le Ventre de Paris* was published in 1871, twenty years before the renewed interest in cathedrals that Zola clearly displays in *Germinal, Le Rêve, Les Trois Villes,* and *Messidor.* While he is fascinated by new forms of architecture that use iron and glass, he constantly evokes and praises their underlying medieval models, much as does Viollet-le-Duc, by evoking the new in terms of the old.

157. RM III, 596, RM III, 611–612. John Frey's reading of this passage demonstrates how Zola replaces traditional Christian values with the cult of money

in this new cathedral (*The Aesthetics of the Rougon-Macquart*. Madrid: Ediciones José Porrua Turanzas, S.A., 1978: 290). Once again, Zola vests an old system with a new, secularized (and sacrilegious) meaning.

158. See Evelyne Cosset, *Les Quatre Evangiles d'Emile Zola: Espace, Temps, Personnages* (Genève: Librairie Droz S.A., 1990, 38–40), for more about the depiction of ideal spaces in *Les Quatre Evangiles*, and see Noiray, 237–244 for more about Zola's fascination with modern architecture.

159. "Histoire de la paroisse." Brochure distributed by the Parish of Notre-Dame du Travail.

160. It continued appearing in *Le Journal* until February 9, 1898 and was sold in its entirety beginning on March 1.

161. Corr. IX, 134. See "L'introduction biographique," "Chronologie de l'Affaire Dreyfus," and "Zola et l'Affaire Dreyfus," in volume 9 of Zola's *Correspondance* for a detailed analysis of the role he played in the Affair.

162. Léon Blum later argued that it was thanks to Zola's accusations, which raised central questions about social beliefs, that France was able to begin the healing process. Cited in Owen Morgan and Alain Pagès. "Introduction Biographique" (*Emile Zola: Correspondance*. Ed. B. H. Bakker. Montreal: Les Presses de l'Université de Montréal, 1993): 31.

3. *"The Soul of Arches"*

1. Cited in Griffiths, 254–255.

2. In this article, which discusses a "bal mystique" inspired by *Là-Bas*, he added that mysticism was "grafted" upon religion, but was not a "synonym." *Le Courrier français* (22 February 1891).

3. See De Certeau. *The Mystic Fable*, vol. 1 (Trans. Michael B. Smith. Chicago: University of Chicago Press, 1992): 76. In chapters two and three, he defines the fifteenth-century concept of the mystic sciences as a *modus loquendi* that evolved into a "new science" in the sixteenth and seventeenth centuries.

4. *Maison d'un Artiste*, vol. 1 (Paris: Flammarion, 1881): 8–9. But he also created a term—*bricabracomania*—to describe the sickness resulting from this escape. See Emery, "Bricabracomania," and Rae Beth Gordon (*Ornament, Fantasy, and Desire in Nineteenth-Century French Literature*. Princeton, NJ: Princeton University Press, 1992) for an analysis of the links between ornament and psychology at the time.

5. OC VII, 12.

6. See Stephen Bann, "Poetics of the Museum: Lenoir and Du Sommerard," chapter 4 of *The Clothing of Clio: A Study of the Representation of History in Nineteenth-Century Britain and France*. Cambridge: Cambridge University Press, 1984) for a comparison of the differences in these two men's vision of the museum.

7. Emile Deschamps, a visitor to the Musée de Cluny. Cited in Bann, 82.

Debra Silverman focuses on these three restoration projects in *Art Nouveau in Fin-de-Siècle France: Politics, Psychology, and Style* (Berkeley: University of California Press, 1989).

8. Watson, 22–23.

9. Strikingly, although many churches and abbeys fell prey to post-Revolutionary excesses, only three cathedrals, all on the northern border of France, were destroyed. See Vauchez, 37.

10. "Introduction," lxxxviii.

11. OC VII, 118–20

12. *Marthe* and *Les Soeurs Vatard* also include artists or characters who reflect on medieval art and architecture.

13. Proust and Barrès would later evoke the soul of religious architecture in "La Mort des cathédrales" (1904), and *La Grande pitié des églises de France* (1913), respectively. See chapter 3.

14. An 1884 letter to Bloy reflects Huysmans's irritation with living in Zola's shadow: "Vous êtes un Sous-Veuillot et moi un Sous-Zola. L'étiquette est collée; nous la porterons notre vie durant" (22 June 1884, quoted in Suwala, "Huysmans et Zola, ou l'amitié rompue." *Huysmans: Une esthétique de la décadence. Actes du colloque de Bâle, Mulhouse et Colmar des 5, 6, et 7 novembre 1984.* Ed. André Guyaux, Christian Heck and Robert Kopp. Geneva: Editions Slatkine, 1987, 95–102): 98.

15. Zayed defines the concept of Huysmans as a painter by illustrating the importance he gave to representing reality in his work: unlike other novelists, who use description to situate characters and plot, Huysmans described for the pleasure of describing: "Il décrit pour décrire, pour son propre plaisir, sans autre préoccupation que de rendre fidèlement ce qui lui tombait sous les yeux. Comme les vrais peintres, il emportait son calepin, flânait dans les rues, errait dans les quartiers pittoresques en quête d'un site, d'une scène, d'un motif, curieux de couleur locale, attentif aux détails originaux," xvi.

16. His grandfathers were painters, his father was a lithographer and miniaturist, and his uncles collected Dutch art. Christopher Lloyd called the first chapter of *Huysmans and the Fin-de-siècle Novel*, "Word-Painting," and succinctly and clearly develops and probes the problems inherent in attempting to "paint" with words. As he remarks, literature is not a visual medium, and any attempt to equate the two can be done only on a metaphorical level. Lloyd compares Huysmans's notion of word painting to that of the Goncourt's "écriture artiste," and Baudelaire's system of *correspondances* to show the importance Huysmans attached both to style and to metaphor, 19–54.

17. Zola OC XIV, 582. It is telling that in his 1877 defense of Zola's *L'Assommoir* Huysmans prized description above all: the passages he glorifies in Zola's work are extended descriptions such as those of Les Halles in *Le Ventre de Paris* or of Le Paradou in *La Faute de l'abbé Mouret* (OC II, 151–192).

18. See Antosh, *Reality,* 7 for these categories. Huysmans had always seen himself as an outsider to the literary cliques of the fin de siècle. He was considered a naturalist by his contemporaries because of his friendship and collaboration with Zola and the Goncourt brothers, yet he was also friends with Mallarmé, Verlaine, and Villiers de l'Isle Adam. He denied membership in any school. A letter to Jules Destrée, expressing disappointment at the media's attempts to classify *A rebours* by genre is particularly indicative of this aversion; he includes and disqualifies himself from each of the literary movements (22 November 1884, letter 1: 32–33, 34).

19. A notable exception is Annette Weissenstein's 1981 dissertation "The Influence of the Visual Arts in the Work of J.-K. Huysmans" (Columbia University, 1981).

20. Some of the works not often mentioned in Huysmans studies are: *Le Drageoir aux épices* (1874), *Croquis parisiens* (1880), *L'Art moderne* (1883), *Certains* (1889), *La Bièvre et Saint-Séverin* (1898), *La Magie en Poitou: Gilles de Rais* (1899), *La Bièvre, Les Gobelins, Saint-Séverin* (1901), *De Tout* (1902), *Esquisse biographique sur Dom Bosco* (1902), *Trois Primitifs* (1905), *Le Quartier Notre-Dame* (1905), *Trois Eglises et Trois Primitifs* (1908).

21. See Baldick, 203–205 and 223–239, and Issacharoff, 95 for more biographical details about the conversion. Richard Griffiths, in *The Reactionary Revolution* gives a persuasive reading about the legitimacy of Huysmans's conversion, while Gugelot's study of the converts of 1885–1935 returns again and again to the importance young Catholics attached to Huysmans as mentor and role model.

22. See Gugelot, 10–12 and 328–335.

23. Hegel, *Aesthetics.* Cited in Hatzenberger, 32.

24. "La Symbolique de Notre-Dame" OC XI, 173.

25. A. E. Carter says: "No Romantic poet, flying to sheety lakes or maisons du berger was more of an escapist than the former naturalist, the one-time disciple of Zola." Madeline Ortoleva similarly dismissed Huysmans's fascination for the Middle Ages as "nostalgia" for a golden age (100–104), while Richard Griffiths describes Huysmans's medievalism as an ideal for what nineteenth-century society should be, 240.

26. *Le Milieu et l'individu dans la trilogie de Joris-Karl Huysmans,* 35–43.

27. See the end of *Là-Bas* and most of *Sainte-Lydwine de Schiedam.* He admires the fact that religion played a greater role in medieval life, but he was not interested in going back.

28. The painting appears in OC XII, 1, 121–122. See Ruth B. Antosh, "The Role of Paintings in Three Novels by J.-K. Huysmans."

29. While Robert Baldick's seminal biography, *The Life of J.-K. Huysmans,* gives a detailed account of Huysmans's life, the author often refers to the Durtal cycle as "autobiographical" and uses Durtal's experiences to describe Huysmans's. He also borrows liberally from literary works to describe the author's childhood, of which little is known. Most subsequent biographers have used Baldick's work extensively.

30. "Durtal et Huysmans: le jeu du montré et du caché," 181–82.

31. Cited in Lloyd, 10. See Baldick's biography for examples of Huysmans's kindness. Despite his outward grumpiness, he supported many people, both materially and psychologically. Christopher Lloyd sketches one of the most accurate and complex pictures of Huysmans's life in the first chapter of *Huysmans and the Fin-de-Siècle Novel*, 1–18.

32. In 1886 Huysmans was promoted to "sous-chef" in the Director's office of the Sûreté générale. He was in charge of expulsing immigrants and administering the pension plans of coup d'état victims. His correspondence with Arij Prins often evokes the effects political and social troubles had on his job. Pierre Froment's visit to the Ministry of Finance in *Paris* gives an impression of the hectic atmosphere of such an environment.

33. Almost every letter from Huysmans to Hannon, Destrée, Prins or Goncourt focuses on Zola's absence, and emphasizes Huysmans's jealousy of his situation. The persistent myth about Zola's social activism developed in the 1890s when Zola threw himself into the Dreyfus Affair.

34. Letters to Arij Prins. 27 April 1891 (letter 108): 219; 23 May 1891 (letter 109): 222.

35. Madeleine Ortoleva summarizes the transformations of this project (22–40).

36. Examples of Huysmans's tendency to follow his character include his conversion, Durtal's research on Sainte Lydwine de Schiedam (which Huysmans would publish in 1901) and Durtal's desire to become a Benedictine oblate (Huysmans would do so in 1899).

37. *La Faiblesse de croire*, 8–9.

38. Gugelot, 227–268.

39. Cited in Descaves, "Notice," OC VII, 351–52.

40. Huysmans did not generally attach a great deal of importance to character names: he tended to use the names of places he had seen in train timetables. Durtal's name was special. When a friend mentioned Durtal as the name of a town, Huysmans latched on its northern etymologies, then used the word to name Durtal. See Baldick, 165, for this story. See also Viegnes, *Le Milieu*, 140–41, for a reading of the "door" symbolism in Durtal's name.

41. Although Michel Viegnes has written two very good chapters about Durtal's penchant for Gothic and Romanesque sanctuaries in *Le Milieu et l'individu dans la triologie de Joris-Karl Huysmans*, he considers them all on the same level. He does not explore Durtal's changing perception of these spaces throughout his quest. Durtal is progressively able to loosen his fixation on their material values in favor of the spiritual.

42. *Certains*, OC X, 8–9.

43. Durtal explains that a King Cômor was the true model for Perrault's tale, but regional legends continued to link Gilles de Rais's butchery of small children to the Bluebeard story (OC, XII, 2, 30).

44. OC XII, 1, 29.

45. OC XII, 1, 76–78

46. OC XII, 1, 124–137; OC XII, 2, 26–29; OC XII, 1, 177–187.

47. OC XII, 2, 14

48. See Baldick for the genesis of the novel as well as for various acquaintances Huysmans praised and mocked through Des Esseintes, 78–81.

49. OC XII, 2, 198.

50. OC XII, 2, 141. He is similarly impressed by the crowd's forgiveness before Gilles de Rais's execution (OC XII, 2, 232). This is, of course, a grossly idealized vision of medieval action, but Durtal's fascination with the positive aspects of the crowd is interesting for a character who is also so passionately interested in evil.

51. "Ils s'empliront les tripes et vidangeront l'âme par le bas-ventre" (OC XII, 2, 235). Thanks to Anthony Taylor Rischard for translation suggestions.

52. Nearly every letter from this period emphasizes the glee with which Huysmans anticipated the outrage of naturalists, mystics, Catholics, and those who practiced the occult sciences. See especially the correspondence with Arij Prins, letters 93–105.

53. See Baldick, 166, Issacharoff, 82–91, and Weber, 32–35.

54. 12 February 1893, letter 122 to Prins: 249.

55. OC XIII, 1, 54–55.

56. OC XIII, 1, 47.

57. OC XIII, 1, 44.

58. OC XIII, 1, 58.

59. See Issacharoff, 98–118. There were more commentaries related to Huysmans's conversion than critiques of the book itself.

60. OC XIII, 1, 5–8.

61. OC XIII, 1, 10.

62. OC XIII, 1, 58.

63. OC XIII, 1, 57.

64. In an 1891 preconversion essay Huysmans compared art to a substitute for religion: ". . .Dans le domaine du Rêve, l'art demeure seul, en ces temps dont les faims d'âmes sont suffisamment assouvies par l'ingestion des théories des Moritz Wagner et des Darwin" (*Certains* OC X, 138).

65. OC XIII, 1, 53–54.

66. OC XIII, 1, 20. In *Là-Bas,* he had similarly lambasted Saint-Sulpice as a poor imitation of the facade of Notre-Dame de Paris because the church's profusion of columns and towers evoked a train station (OC XII, 2, 119–20).

67. Huysmans's condemnation of religious architecture based on form occurred throughout his early art historical writings. In *L'Art moderne,* a collection of essays about modern art written from 1879–1883, Huysmans similarly condemns l'église de la Trinité as secular because of its form. Inside, its "fumoir," "sopha," and "boudoir" link it to a theater or a private home, spaces no longer defined by worship.

68. OC XIII, 1, 53–54.
69. OC XIII, 1, 148 and OC XIII, 1, 20–21.
70. See Baldick 224. Goncourt, for example, praised *En Route* for its style, while criticizing the religious elements (15 March 1895, III: 1110).
71. See March-April 1895 letters to abbé Ferret, 45–47.
72. He may have sold this many in 1895 alone. Sales figures come from Issacharoff, 96 and 136.
73. "C'est une correspondance infinie, je suis passé à l'état de vague confesseur et des 4 bouts du monde, on me consulte sur son âme!!" (13 May 1895, letter 140: 274). See Baldick, 226–231, for more about these individual correspondents and Huysmans's continued relationship with them.
74. See Baldick, 262–268, 318–320.
75. *Dream Worlds*, 12.
76. Michael B. Miller. *The Bon Marché. Bourgeois Culture and the Department Store, 1869–1920* (Princeton, NJ: Princeton University Press, 1981): 166–189.
77. 22 May 1897 interview with *La Vérité*. Cited in Issacharoff, 97.
78. See Issacharoff, 97.
79. See Baldick, 206 and Issacharoff, 98.
80. See Gugelot, 75–111.
81. OC XIII 2, 153–154.
82. Issacharoff shows that reaction to the Durtal books stemmed primarily from whether the critic believed in the authenticity of Huysmans's conversion. He excerpts many of the Church's criticisms of these books.
83. Gugelot has shown that abbeys became the center of heated correspondence and journalistic inquiry; the public was fascinated by the novelty of living in a monastery, 344–346.
84. "J.-K. Huysmans" (*D'autres et moi*. Ed. Keith Goesch. Paris: Editions Bernard Grasset, 1966: 180–91): 186.
85. OC XIV, 1, 215–216.
86. See Georges Duby, "God is Light." *The Age of the Cathedrals*, 97–135.
87. These are the terms Huysmans used to describe his first encounter with the cathedral in a letter to Arij Prins. 26 December 1893. Letter 129: 260.
88. Huysmans was obsessed by the battle between body and soul after his conversion. *En Route* was, in fact, entitled "La bataille charnelle" at one time; the battle between body and soul that punctuates the book appears at the beginning with the medal of Saint Benedict he reproduces. Female flesh was always problematic for Huysmans and he was a great misogynist. See Renée Kingcaid, "Piety and Pourriture: Huysmans's Women Terrorists." (In John T. Booker-John and Allan H. Pasco, ed. *The Play of Terror in Nineteenth-Century France*. Newark, DE: University of Delaware Press, 1997: 170–186) and Charles Bernheimer. "Huysmans Writing against (Female) Nature" (*Poetics Today* 61–62: 311–324).
89. OC XIV, 2, 293–294 and OC XIV, 1, 218.

90. OC XIV, 2, 294–295.

91. OC XIV, 2, 294–295.

92. OC XIV, 1, 139.

93. OC XIV, 1, 113.

94. OC XIV, 1, 111.

95. OC XIV, 1, 162.

96. I borrow the interpretation of the image proposed by Alain Erlande-Brandenburg in *Quand les cathédrales étaient peintes* (Paris: Découvertes Gallimard, 1993).

97. OC XIV, 1, 111–113.

98. 8 March 1896, letter 143 to Arij Prins: 282.

99. This project also harks to romantic historiography as it echoes Michelet's enthusiasm for reanimating the past through books.

100. June 1897 letter to Cécile Bruyère. Cited in Baldick 249. Letter of 22 February 1897 to l'abbé Ferret, 111.

101. See Issacharoff, 136–138. Huysmans expresses dismay at the clergy of Chartres for "imploring" him not to come, primarily because the locals were angry with him for having portrayed them unfavorably in the novel. Letter to Ferret. 18 December 1897: 116.

102. François Mauriac. "J.-K. Huysmans." *(D'autres et moi.* Ed. Keith Goesch. Paris: Editions Bernard Grasset, 1966: 180–91): 181.

103. Gugelot, 65. The lists of articles published in Jan van der Meulen's indispensable critical bibliography of the cathedral, *Chartres: Sources and Literary Interpretation,* provides an excellent idea of the wealth of works consecrated to Chartres after 1898.

104. OC XIV, 2, 107.

105. OC XIV, 1, 156.

106. OC XIV, 1, 157. He also establishes a parallel between Saint Augustine and Mallarmé's definitions of symbolism, though grossly misrepresenting Mallarmé in the process.

107. OC XIV, 1, 159–60.

108. Jean-Luc Steinmetz. "Pour une incantation critique (à propos de la Cathédrale)" (*Huysmans.* Ed. Pierre Brunel and André Guyaux. Paris: Editions de l'Herne, 1985: 224–234): 226. For an extremely thorough and interesting study of the links between cathedral, book, and illustration in the nineteenth century, see Le Men, *La Cathédrale illustrée.*

109. *The Mystic Fable,* vol. 1 (Trans. Michael B. Smith. Chicago: University of Chicago Press, 1992): 50–51.

110. See especially A. E. Carter, "J. K. Huysmans and the Middle Ages," who calls *La Cathédrale* "less a novel than a guide, an enthusiastic Baedecker," 32.

111. *La Bonne Souffrance* (*Oeuvres Completes,* vol. 9. Paris, Lemerre, 1904): 165.

112. From his *Carnet de Notes,* volume one. Cited in Gugelot, 66.

113. John Ruskin's commentaries about Gothic architecture were only just beginning to be discussed in France. Proust was the first translator of the *Bible d'Amiens* (1904) and Robert Sizeraine had published a book about Ruskin (*Ruskin et la religion de la beauté,* 1897) only a few years earlier.

114. 2 February 1897, letter 154 to Prins: 298–299. An 1895 letter had evoked Huysmans drowning in manuscripts: "Je suis avec cela très-embêté, plongé dans un travail sans issue, sans renseignements précis: sur la science de la symbolique catholique, au Moyen-âge. Je suis noyé dans de vieux in-folios, d'où rien ne sort. Il y en a pour des années de travail, là-dessus" (5 October 1895, letter 142: 280).

115. XIV, 1, 161–67.

116. XIV, 1, 167–174; XIV, 1, 175–177.

117. XIV, 1, 231–249; XIV, 1, 260–271; XIV, 2, 17–51; XIV, 2, 197–217, 227–236; XIV, 2, 219–227.

118. Mâle defended his doctoral thesis, *L'Art religieux du XIIIe siècle en France,* in 1898. It was published at the end of the year and Huysmans was invited to review it. Although his criticism of Mâle's readings of a few medieval texts smack of the jealousy of sharing a topic, Huysmans praised Mâle for addressing both body and soul of the cathedral. He retracts his previous complaint about the lack of works devoted to medieval symbolism: "now this work exists, at least for the thirteenth century." Article reproduced in *Huysmans* (Ed. Pierre Brunel and André Guyaux. Paris: Editions de l'Herne. 347–348). Huysmans's last article about symbolism, "La Symbolique de Notre-Dame," also acknowledges Mâle's fine work, which combines body and soul of the cathedral (OC XI, 173). There is very little information available about the relationship between Huysmans and Mâle: we do not know if they ever met, nor do we know the extent to which Mâle may have been influenced by Huysmans's previous writings about art history. Did he read *Là-Bas* and *En Route?*

119. It is interesting to note that Huysmans, who had written dozens of articles about medieval art and architecture in addition to his fictional production, was considered as much a scholar as Mâle. Proust's critical footnotes to his 1904 translation of Ruskin's *The Bible of Amiens* consider Huysmans as much an expert as Viollet-le-Duc, Ruskin, and Mâle.

120. OC XIV, 2, 287; OC XIV, 1, 313.

121. OC XIV, 2, 279–288.

122. Vauchez, 43–45.

123. OC XIV, 2, 278.

124. He often attacked modern architects and the structures they built, such as the Eiffel Tower, which he referred to as "le clocher de la nouvelle église dans laquelle se célèbre [. . .] le service divin de la haute Banque" (*Certains,* X, 159–160). Durtal criticizes architects in *La Cathédrale* (XIV, 1, 117).

125. Huysmans was pressured to the point that he was essentially forced into early retirement. See letter 164 to Arij Prins (28 February 1898, 312–313). Gugelot discusses Claudel's situation, 320. Both Griffiths and Gugelot discuss at length intellectuals' desire to defend the Church.

126. OC XVII, 2, 149–50.

127. See Richard Griffiths, 229–239. Other anticlerical Catholics included Péguy, Bloy, and Drumont. Both Griffiths and Gugelot reveal the extent to which most of the intellectual converts to Catholicism at the end of the century were estranged from mainstream Catholicism. See especially the chapter of Griffiths entitled "Traditionalism and the Social Question," 258–287. Baldick and Issacharoff describe the reaction of the clergy to the publication of each of Huysmans's books.

128. *L'Oblat* was the most autobiographical of Huysmans's novels and is based on the years he spent as an oblate at Ligugé. See Baldick, 267–289.

129. OC XVII, 2, 139–140.

130. See Baldick, 219–223, 233–238, 273–276 for a detailed presentation of Huysmans's correspondence with groups who encouraged him to come and begin such a project with them. Gugelot has shown that such groups did eventually succeed, but not until after his death, 351, 470–471.

131. *La Faiblesse de croire,* 9–10.

132. "J.-K. Huysmans." (*D'autres et moi.* Ed. Keith Goesch. Paris: Editions Bernard Grasset, 1966: 180–91): 186 and "Allocution (11 mai 1957)." (*Huysmans.* Ed. Pierre Brunel and André Guyaux. Paris: Editions de l'Herne, 1985, 265–269): 266.

133. —". . . la grande forme de l'art moderne est là . . . la seule voie à prendre pour arriver aujourd'hui" (13 December 1879, letter 65 to Hannon: 210).

134. Pierre Brunel. "Huysmans." (*Dictionnaire des littératures de langue française.* Ed. J. P. Beaumarchais, D. Couty and A. Rey. Paris: Bordas, 1984): 1076–1081.

135. "Sur l'Oblat" (*Huysmans.* Ed. Pierre Brunel and André Guyaux. Paris: Editions de l'Herne, 1985, 258–261): 259.

136. It is astonishing that Huysmans is absent from Victor Brombert's *The Intellectual Hero* as Huysmans consistently featured characters who struggled with questions germane to this study.

137. 13 December 1879 letter 65 to Hannon: 210.

138. Cited in Baldick, 316 (his translation).

139. OC XIV, 1, 157.

140. OC XIV, 2, 57.

141. OC XIV, 2, 62.

142. Huysmans, in his 1903 preface to *A rebours,* argued that books like *Là-Bas* had helped improve society's faith. He admitted that he would have presented *Là-Bas* differently had he converted before writing it, yet he believed that it had reformed society's morals by discouraging vice (OC VII, xvii, xviii).

143. Watson 140.

144. "Durtal." First printed in *Le Mercure de France* (March 1898) and reprinted as the preface to *Le Roman de Durtal* (Paris: Bartillat, 1999): 9–19.

145. *La Faiblesse de croire,* 193.

146. 13 April 1898 letter to Charles Brun. Cited in Lloyd, 138.

147. "Durtal." First printed in *Le Mercure de France* (March 1898) and reprinted as the preface to *Le Roman de Durtal* (Paris: Bartillat, 1999): 19.

148. "Allocution (11 mai 1957)." (*Huysmans.* Ed. Pierre Brunel and André Guyaux. Paris: Editions de l'Herne, 1985: 265–69): 269.

149. OC XIV, 1, 308.

150. XIV, 2, 278–279.

151. Gourmont published this essay in *L'Image* in Februrary 1897, yet it is nearly certain that he was inspired by Huysmans, with whom he worked to collect notes for *La Cathédrale.*

152. CSB 146–147.

153. Daniel Rops. *Trois images de grandeur.* Paris. La Colombe. 1944, 18–19.

154. "J.-K. Huysmans." (*D'autres et moi.* Ed. Keith Goesch. Paris: Editions Bernard Grasset, 1966: 180–91): 186. Huysmans's correspondence to abbé Ferret seems to confirm this. In a letter from 1895 he discusses the fact that he has not been able to write a non-Catholic work since his conversion, 51.

4. *"Perpetual Adoration"*

1. His translation of *La Bible d'Amiens* received laudatory praise by members of the literary and intellectual elite (CSB 720–721). Proust knew he was an excellent scholar and admitted that he would have made a very good professor. Cited in de Botton, 177. He chose, instead, to continue devoting himself to literature. Those who have discussed Proust's passion for medieval art and architecture extensively are Jean Autret, Richard Bales, Luc Fraisse, and Theodore Johnson, Jr.

2. See Tadié, *Marcel Proust,* 426–431.

3. *Lettres à une amie* (II, 5 Dec. 1899): 5–6. Cited in CSB 719.

4. *Lettres à une amie,* 19. Cited in Bales, 25.

5. See Bales, *Proust and the Middle Ages,* for a list of these trips, 27.

6. See Richard Bales, "Proust et Emile Mâle," for a detailed study of the relationship between the two men. This article is particularly useful because little remains of the correspondence between the two: Bales interviewed Mâle's daughter, who remembered Proust's visits.

7. CSB 144.

8. The special issue of *La Revue musicale* dedicated to *Wagner et la France* in 1923 gives an excellent idea of the kind of cult status enjoyed by Wagner in late nineteenth-century France. Henri Lichtenberger, "Wagner et l'opinion contem-

poraine," employs religious vocabulary to refer to admiration of Wagner (Paris, Editions de la nouvelle revue française, 1923): 79–87. In *Opera, State, and Society in the Third Republic, 1875–1914,* André Michael Spies shows that the attraction to Wagner was so strong that France attempted to renovate its own operatic tradition in order to compete (New York: Peter Lang Publishing, 1998): 124–125, 214.

9. In 1903, Proust mentioned the hostile climate to his friend, Georges de Lauris. 29 July 1903, letter 7: III, 61–71.

10. See the notes about this article for a description of its publication history and its influence on Barrès (CSB 770–772). The two met in 1892, but became better acquainted when Barrès began a relationship with Proust's friend, Anna de Noailles, in 1903. After both *La Bible d'Amiens* and "La Mort des cathédrales," Barrès wrote Proust congratulatory letters. The title, "La Mort des cathédrales," echoes that of Barrès's *La Mort de Venise,* published in 1902. Proust responded by encouraging Barrès to write something like *La Mort de Venise* in praise of the cathedral of Vézelay (20 August 1904, letter 122: IV, 220). Barrès would evoke Proust's title in 1913 when he wrote the essays defending churches from the secular backlash that followed the 1905 separation of Church and State.

11. Proust's character has no name, though he is called Marcel twice during *La Recherche:* both times in *La Prisonnière,* in passages that Proust certainly would have eliminated if he had had the time to correct them. See Tadié, *Proust et le roman,* for a list of other such manuscript references to Marcel that Proust had systematically eliminated (30). I thus use the term "hero" to refer to the "je" whose perspective changes throughout the novel. See Marcel Muller, *Les Voix narratives dans A la recherche du temps perdu* (Geneva: Droz, 1965). The hero should be distinguished from the narrator, who is the middle-aged hero who begins telling the story in "Combray." In the time of the novel, "Combray" corresponds to the opening pages of *Le Temps retrouvé.* The narrator and the hero are thus at the same developmental stage in *Le Temps retrouvé.* Until this point, however, the narrator understands the experiences of the hero (himself at a younger age), and periodically imposes his vision on that of the hero in order to interpret events.

12. CSB 725.

13. See Tadié, *Marcel Proust* (413–425) for an excellent examination of the texts that influenced Proust in his theory of "alternative realities." Anne Henry, in *Théories pour une esthétique,* paints a broad picture of Proust's familiarity with all the major philosophical ideas of the time, yet also illustrates the originality he managed to bring to his own aesthetic theories. See especially the chapter entitled "La Révélation d'une philosophie de l'art," 45–97. Autret, 90–97, discusses the similarities between Proust and Ruskin's conception of perception.

14. "John Ruskin," CSB 132.

15. The title of this chapter comes from *The Art Spirit,* the title of a book of letters and aphorisms that Robert Henri, leader of the Ashcan school of paint-

ing, proposed to his students. His theories are strikingly similar to those of Proust (New York: Harper & Row Publishers, 1984).

16. Pissarro, *Monet's Cathedral,* 22. Monet, along with Turner, Ruskin, and Mâle served as a model for the painter Elstir in *La Recherche.* See Autret, *L'Influence* (144–151) and Bales, *Middle Ages* (66–67).

17. Proust identified this painting as one of his eight favorites in an interview shortly before his death. Mentioned in Alain de Botton, 143.

18. "Journées de Pelèrinage," CSB 89. The final section is from the same essay (CSB 104). This article was part of Proust's preface to *La Bible d'Amiens,* but he also published this section separately in *Le Mercure de France,* April 1900. Note the reference to Emerson.

19. See Tadié, *Marcel Proust,* 421. Shattuck argues that much of Proust's belief in the importance of memory and impression derives from Henri Bergson's *Matter and Memory,* which was published in 1896. *Proust's Way,* 114–115.

20. See Pierre-Louis Rey and Brian Rogers's "Notice" to *Le Temps retrouvé* for an analysis of the genesis of Proust's aesthetic theories and for a description of the content of his Cahiers. See also Jean-Yves Tadié's *Marcel Proust* for a description of "Adoration perpétuelle" and "Le Bal des têtes" 671–76.

21. "John Ruskin," CSB 109–110.

22. ARTP IV, 458.

23. "Jean had not been raised in the Church [. . .] literature was his only belief." *Jean Santeuil,* 239. Barbara Bucknall's *The Religion of Art in Proust* convincingly illustrates that in the 1890s Proust closely associated his belief in Christianity, his dislike of materialism, and his belief in an idealistic philosophy. Although his mother was Jewish, Proust was raised as a Catholic. He practiced Catholicism, yet as he matured, he transferred his belief in the religious values of Christianity to art because he felt that art was a means to spiritual salvation and an afterlife. Like Bucknall, I use the term *religion* broadly, to indicate the transcendent beliefs to which Proust's hero came to dedicate himself, but only because it is Proust, himself, who drew attention to the spiritual nature of his hero's beliefs.

24. Cited in Autret, 101. This concept returns throughout his work, and culminates in the hero's discussion of style in *Le Temps retrouvé,* which repeats this statement nearly verbatim (ARTP IV, 461, 474).

25. Proust defines metaphor in terms that evoke the etymology of the word symbol—sym (together) + ballein (to throw): "[. . .] la vérité ne commencera qu'au moment où l'écrivain prendra deux objets différents, posera leur rapport, analogue dans le monde de l'art à celui qu'est le rapport unique de la loi causale dans le monde de la science, et les enfermera dans les anneaux nécessaires d'un beau style. Même, ainsi que la vie, quand en rapprochant une qualité commune à deux sensations, il dégagera leur essence commune en les réunissant l'une et l'autre pour les soustraire aux contingences du temps, dans une métaphore," TR IV, 468.

26. "Contre Sainte-Beuve," CSB 216.

27. "John Ruskin," CSB 137.

28. Letter 49, I: 171–172 to Robert Dreyfus as a response to his friend's article, "La situation en littérature." Philip Kolb has dated this letter as 1 July 1892, although it is dated only "vendredi" in the manuscript.

29. ARTP IV, 460–461 (my emphasis). Proust did not criticize Zola and Huysmans specifically in *La Recherche*. He did, however, take aim against "realists" and the "literature of notation" through the pastiche of Edmond de Goncourt that appears at the beginning of *Le Temps retrouvé*. Proust's main target in this passage is Romain Rolland, who had rejected the concept of a pure literature: he wanted to dispense with art in order to produce texts that would treat historical and social concerns. See Compagnon, "Literature in the classroom." *A New History of French Literature* (Ed. Denis Hollier. Cambridge, MA: Harvard University Press, 1989): 820.

30. ARTP IV, 461.

31. ARTP IV, 474, 498.

32. Letter to Alfred Vallette, editor of *Le Mercure de France,* mid-August 1909, letter 78: ix. At this point, the novel was still entitled *Contre Sainte-Beuve, Souvenir d'une matinée.*

33. Antoine Compagnon, "Proust's Remembrance of Things Past," II: 219.

34. *Le Temps retrouvé.* ARTP IV, 610. This passage is repeated nearly verbatim earlier in *Le Temps retrouvé* (ARTP, 489–490). It is obvious that Proust wanted to make sure to incorporate the idea.

35. ARTP II, 219.

36. A number of scholars, including Yves Clogenson, in "Le Thème de la cathédrale dans Proust" (1964), Richard Bales, in *Proust and the Middle Ages* (1975), Kay Bourlier, in *Marcel Proust et l'architecture* (1980), and Luc Fraisse, who presents *L'Oeuvre Cathédrale: Proust et l'architecture médiévale* (1990) as a "Dictionnaire raisonné de l'architecture médiévale chez Proust," have traced and categorized the numerous apparitions of religious architecture throughout *La Recherche.* None of them, however, has commented on the ways in which the descriptions of the cathedral in Proust's series reflect the hero's growing spiritual response to art. While both Bales and Bourlier comment on passages Proust dedicated to the churches of Combray, Balbec, and Venice, neither of them mentions that the hero's increasing fondness for Gothic architecture is more than a result of his growing knowledge about it. Within the didactic system that is *La Recherche,* the cathedral marks the hero's spiritual progression along the path to developing his aesthetic beliefs.

37. ARTP I, 60–61.

38. The story of Sigebert is loosely adapted from Augustin Thierry, *Récits des temps mérovingiens.* See Bales for a discussion of Thierry's prominent role as a source for the Merovingian stories read by the hero in early drafts of *La Recherche* (*Middle Ages,* 44).

39. *Middle Ages,* 36–40.

40. At the end of *Le Temps retrouvé*, he realizes that the feeling of "premonition" in his youth was really an urge to write (ARTP IV, 622).

41. ARTP I, 149; ARTP II, 703. Françoise is, as her name would suggest, French, an incarnation of the French peasant tradition.

42. Ruskin, *Lectures on Art. Collected Works,* 20:66. Proust's translation: "le fait de servir avec le meilleur de nos coeurs et de nos esprits quelque chère ou triste image que nous nous sommes créée, pendant que nous désobéissons à l'appel présent du Maître, qui n'est pas mort, qui ne défaille pas en ce moment sous sa croix, mais nous ordonne de porter la nôtre," CSB 129.

43. CSB 69, 71.

44. Sainte-Beuve's theories had become popular again after the posthumous publication (1894) of Taine's *Derniers essais de critique et d'histoire* in which he praised his precursor for being a great initiator who had practically invented the Tainian method of scientific analysis. The article was originally published on 17 October 1869. See CSB 832, note 3.

45. CSB 219.

46. "La mort des cathédrales," published on August 16, 1904 in *Le Figaro* (CSB 147).

47. CSB 147.

48. ARTP II, 19.

49. ARTP II, 19–20.

50. ARTP II, 21.

51. ARTP II, 21.

52. See Bales, *Middle Ages,* 54–55.

53. CSB 240–241.

54. CSB 241.

55. A note in a cahier from 1916 links Mâle to Elstir: "l'opinion d'Elstir (Mâle) sur les bonnes et mauvaises restaurations" (Cited in Bales, "Proust et Mâle," 1933). See Autret, *L'Influence,* 144–151, and Bales, *Proust and the Middle Ages,* 66–67. For a summary of Proust's exchanges with Mâle during the summer of 1907, when Proust went to Normandy, see Bales, "Proust et Emile Mâle." All of his letters ask about the important architectural sites of the region, and Proust followed Mâle's recommendations seriously: he went to Caen, Bayeux, Balleroy, Dives et Evreux. In 1908 he visited Pont-Audemer, Caudebec, Saint-Wandrille et Jumièges, following Mâle's suggestions (Autret 130–31). See also Bales, *Proust and the Middle Ages,* 29–31, and Tadié, *Marcel Proust,* 431–47, 449–451, 586–598.

56. CSB 726. He had borrowed his friend, Robert de Billy's copy, and when he returned it, some four years later, Billy described its dilapidated condition: "il n'avait ni couverture ni page de garde et portait les marques de toutes les disgrâces qui peuvent assaillir un livre, lu au lit, dans le voisinage des remèdes" (*Marcel Proust: Lettres et conversations.* Paris: Editions des Portiques, 1930), 111.

57. See Bales, "Proust et Emile Mâle," 1931–1935; Autret, *L'Influence de Ruskin*, 138–157. Autret also traces Proust's debts to Viollet-le-Duc's *Dictionnaire d'architecture raisonné*.

58. Proust's last extant letter to Mâle dates from 1921, only a year before Proust's death. In addition, Proust's correspondence, especially to Reynaldo Hahn, his companion on some of his "pèlerinages," reveal his familiarity with Gothic symbolism and composition. He knew allegories and saints' lives well enough to produce clever satirical cartoons that depict Marcel and Reynaldo as comic characters imitating the actions of characters in the various stained-glass windows and royal portals of the cathedrals of France. See *Lettres à Reynaldo Hahn*, ed. P. Kolb (Paris: Gallimard, 1956) and Bales, *Proust and the Middle Ages* (145–146) for a discussion of these drawings.

59. *The Gothic Image,* 399.

60. *The Gothic Image* (Trans. Dora Nussey), 396–397.

61. ARTP II, 198.

62. ARTP II, 196.

63. ARTP IV 459.

64. ARTP II, 196–197.

65. CSB 304.

66. ARTP IV, 202.

67. ARTP IV, 224.

68. Notre-Dame de Paris and Chartres, La Sainte-Chapelle, Saint-Augustin and a number of other churches are mentioned in passing, but are not described in *La Recherche*.

69. See Bales and Autret for Proust's borrowings from Viollet-le-Duc and Emile Mâle (Saint-Hilaire). See Jo Yoshida, "Métamorphose de l'église de Balbec: Un aperçu génétique du 'Voyage au nord,'" for Bayeux, Amiens, and Dives as models for the Balbec church.

70. ARTP IV, 612.

71. Cited in Tadié, *Marcel Proust,* 442–443.

72. *La Venise intérieure: Proust et la poétique de la traduction* (Boudry-Neuchâtel, Switzerland: Editions de la Baconnière, 1991): 163–192.

73. ARTP IV, 445.

74. Gérard Genette has referred to this moment of renewal as a *mise en abyme,* in which the hero becomes Christ, while the running water of the canals outside the basilica evokes the Jordan River. "Métonymie chez Proust." *Figures III* (Paris: Editions du Seuil, 1972: 41–63): 48–49. Jean-Pierre Richard also notes this parallel, while proposing the hero as the Christ child, who, by a secular twist, is redeemed by art. Ruskin, he adds, appears as a prophetic figure since the hero carries *Saint Mark's Rest* into the church with him. *Proust et le monde sensible* (Paris: Editions du Seuil, 1974): 161–163, 171–175. Peter Collier has expanded on these remarks in "Born Again, Marcel's Mosaic," by showing how Saint Mark's fore-

shadows the rebirth of the hero as a literary figure. "L'Adoration perpétuelle" thus follows the hero's "resurrection" of Venice, and outlines his new faith: he will achieve salvation by depicting, through art, the time he had thought to have lost. *Proust and Venice* (Cambridge: Cambridge University Press, 1989): 116–141.

75. ARTP I, 179.

76. ARTP I, 179.

77. ARTP I, 464.

78. ARTP I, 444.

79. ARTP III, 693.

80. ARTP IV, 610.

81. "John Ruskin," CSB 126.

82. He argues that Proust's book is itself a *lieu de mémoire* because history lives on within it, 245–246.

83. ARTP I, 58.

84. ARTP IV, 224–225.

85. "Journées de lecture," CSB 176.

86. See Antoine de Compagnon, "Proust's Remembrance of Things Past." His clever (and often tongue-in-cheek) article exposes many of the ways in which the twentieth-century reception of Proust has transformed him into a literary deity and name brand. Richard Shattuck has recently attempted to correct the notion that *La Recherche* is essentially about memory (a belief stemming from the madeleine episode). *Proust's Way*, xiv–xv.

87. *Proust's Way*, 227–231.

88. Proust measured Zola's novel, counted its lines, and sent it to Grasset as a model for his own work. Although Proust has come to be known as a writer's writer, he intended his book for all readers, and felt that Zola's *Travail* would give an example of the length and format he wanted. See Philip Kolb's introduction to volume 12 of the *Correspondance générale* x, and letter 34, 98–100. He later abandoned the project when his friends told him that only Zola could have persuaded the public to buy such a huge book as *Travail*.

89. See Jean-Yves Tadié's "Introduction générale" to *La Recherche*, lvi–cvii, for a detailed explanation of the modifications Proust's initial plan took as a result of the interruption in publication and as Proust's corpus grew. The most significant addition is Albertine, whom Proust envisioned only in May 1913, and whose creation modified the form of the entire novel.

90. Proust's brother cobbled together the volumes we know as *La Prisonnière* and *Albertine disparue* after Proust's death so that the public would not realize the extent to which his brother's work was incomplete. Proust had intended to put these two volumes into a larger volume, *Sodome et Gomorrhe III*, and had also planned a *Sodome et Gomorrhe IV*. See the introductions to Nathalie Mauriac and Jean Milly's editions of the new manuscript (*Albertine Disparue*. Paris: Livre de poche, 1993).

91. His correspondence to Jacques Rivière, director of *La Nouvelle Revue Française*, provides a privileged view of Proust's architectural vision of his work. He often discusses his work in terms of cathedral-building and envisions his novel as a giant building, with "des substructions et des étagements divers" (*Correspondance avec Jacques Rivière*, 114). For more about Proust's conception of the term *construction*, see Fraisse, 197.

92. In "Marcel Proust and Architecture: Some Thoughts on the Cathedral-Novel," J. Theodore Johnson, Jr. outlines Proust's concept of the writer as architect and compares *La Recherche* to medieval *specula*, didactic encyclopedias intended to teach about the world and appropriate behaviors. He points out the various "mirrors" identified by Mâle and applies them to characters and descriptions of Proust's book. This is an extremely rich essay that reveals Proust's substantial understanding of medieval symbolism while making a persuasive case for reading *La Recherche* as a cathedral. Here and in other articles, Johnson acknowledges that *La Recherche*'s resemblance to a cathedral derives primarily from its allegorical foundation and not from its outward organization.

93. Luc Fraisse's *L'oeuvre cathédrale* is, perhaps, the best example of this, though he does not attempt to read the novel as a cathedral; rather, he anthologizes and comments on the prevalence of information about medieval religious architecture in the novel. George Cattaui, in "L'Oeuvre de Proust: son architecture, son orchestration, sa symbolique" (1958) and Dominique Jullien, in "La Cathédrale Romanesque" (1990), have explored the tenuous metaphor connecting the cathedral to the novel. Jullien begins her article with the assumption that *La Recherche* is built like a cathedral (43). She reads the novel through Hugo, Ruskin, and Mâle, showing how the cathedral appealed to Proust as a symbolic model for his work because it was legible (through its art) and represented time. Yet Jullien also shows that the architectural metaphor evoked by the term *bâtir* also embraces other arts: it implies construction in building terms, yet in the vocabulary of sewing "bâtir" implies the pattern set up before definitive stitching, 57.

94. Letter 198, 1 August 1919 to Comte Jean de Gaigneron: VIII, 359. The title of Jean-Yves Tadié's *Proust: La cathédrale du temps* (Paris: Gallimard, 2000) suggests the link, but the book does not comment on it.

95. Cited in Dushan Bresky. *Cathedral or Symphony: Essays on Jean-Christophe* (Bern: Herbert Lang, 1973): 30–31.

96. "Romain Rolland," CSB, 307–310. Proust repeated much of this passage in *Le Temps retrouvé* (notably the passage about the price tag) without identifying Rolland specifically. See *Le Temps retrouvé* IV, 1261, note 2.

97. Richard Shattuck has pointed out the importance of Françoise as an admirable figure of an unpretentious artist, someone able to blend both instinct and intelligence. *Proust's Way*, 222.

98. Cahiers 57 and 58, the 1908–1909 notebooks that contain these first drafts, reveal Proust's sharp focus on literary criticism: the passages begin with the

hero's reactions to his friend Bloch's superficial attitude toward literature, a doctrine that echoes the beliefs of Sainte-Beuve, Taine, Bourget, and Rolland. Bloch wants to eliminate style in order to represent life exactly as his intelligence perceives it. See the esquisses from these *Cahiers* included in the Pléiade edition of *Le Temps retrouvé,* notably Esquisse XXIV, where the hero's discussion of aesthetics comes in response to the criticism of Bloch, who dismisses style in favor of subject matter (ARTP IV, 800).

99. "Idleness or doubt or powerlessness hiding in incertitude about the art form. Should I write a novel, a philosophical study, am I a novelist?" *Le Carnet de 1908,* 61. See also Anthony R. Pugh, *The Birth of A la recherche du temps perdu* (Lexington, KY: French Forum, 1987): 32. He hesitated about choosing the novel as a form even in *Jean Santeuil,* his project for a novel. His notes for a preface question the manuscript's form: "Puis-je appeler ce livre un roman?" (181).

100. In *Théories pour une esthétique,* Anne Henry argues that Proust's success in creating a viable fictional form in *La Recherche* developed from his abortive attempts at didacticism in *Jean Santeuil.* In the first work, each episode revealed a philosophical law, discussed by the third-person narrator. She insists that Proust's success came from abandoning the analysis and commentary of *Jean Santeuil,* 98–165.

101. Letter 43, XIII: 99.

102. His correspondence shows how much he would have liked to defend his compositional strategy; he knew that he would be attacked. Shortly before publishing the first volume of *La Recherche, Du côté de chez Swann,* which appeared in November 1913, Proust began drawing his friends' attention to the work's architectural construction. He feared that, because of its complex composition, it would seem fragmented until all of the books were published: "quant à ce livre-ci, c'est au contraire un tout très composé, quoique d'une composition si complexe que je crains que personne ne le perçoive et qu'il apparaisse comme une suite de digressions. C'est tout le contraire" (20 February 1913, letter 26 to René Blum: XII, 82). Proust outlined the novel's blueprint to Jacques-Emile Blanche, and he described the Montjouvain episode, where the hero watches Mlle Vinteuil defile her father's photograph, as the "pierre angulaire" of the work.

103. CSB 142.

Conclusion

1. "Symbolic Studies" (*Annual Review of Anthropology* 1975, 145–161): 150–151, 154.

2. "Introduction," xxi.

3. "Introduction," l. He sees the cathedral as an "un lieu religieux, un lieu social, un lieu artistique," xxi, and he particularly admires the cathedral for its "majestic symphonic unity," lxxxi.

4. *The Archaeology of Knowledge.* Trans. A. M. Sheridan Smith. (New York: Pantheon Books, 1972): 6–13.

5. "Introduction," lxvii.

6. Ibid., lxxx. Other contemporary publications treating cathedrals include Robida's *Les Cathédrales de France* (1917) and Eugène Atget's albums of photographs taken inside Parisian churches (1910).

7. This is the small sculpture of two barely touching right hands, vertically joined in a striking visual homage to Gothic architecture and the community spirit it represents. The work is on display at the Rodin Museum in Paris.

8. "Introduction," cvi–cvii.

9. *Les Cathédrales de France,* 61, 68.

10. 48–49, 61, 107, 159, 161, 177. The expression was originated by Viollet-le-Duc (see Chapter 1).

11. In his introduction to Rodin's book, Charles Morice expresses shock at the incorrect theories about the Gothic style that circulated into the 1840s and 1850s (xviii–xx). Although there were a number of nineteenth-century French works devoted to the cathedral, concentrated scholarly interest in it dates primarily from the 1890s when monographs were dedicated to nearly every French cathedral. Other publications included Emile Mâle's work on Reims and German and French medieval art, Camille Martin and Enlart's *L'art gothique en France* (1925), André Michel's *Histoire de l'art* (1905), and Camille Enlart's *Architecture religieuse* (1920).

12. *Les Cathédrales,* 214.

13. Barrès. *Mes Cahiers,* Vol. 9, 1911–1912 (Paris, Plon, 1929–1957): 411.

14. *Les Cathédrales,* 63–64.

15. *Oeuvres Poétiques Complètes* (Ed. F. Porche. Paris: Gallimard, 1941): 522–525.

16. Joan of Arc was beatified in 1909 and canonized in 1920. The scholarship devoted to her "rehabilitation" as French symbol during this time is weighty. For a succinct summary, see Michel Winock, "Joan of Arc" (Trans. Goldhammer, Arthur. *Realms of Memory: The Construction of the French Past,* vol. 3. Eds. Pierre Nora and Lawrence D. Kritzman. New York: Columbia University Press, 1997): 433–482.

17. See Réau for shocking examples of the vandalism that followed the separation of church and state, 813–817. See also Georges Grosjean, *Pour l'art contre les vandales* (1910), which gives a contemporary account of such abuses.

18. See George Robinson's introduction to *The George Grey Barnard Collection* (New York: Robinson Galleries): 1941. Réau's *L'Histoire du vandalisme* abounds with such stories.

19. (lxxxvii). According to George Robinson, in 1903 there were almost no examples of Gothic and Romanesque art available in New York for art student consultation (*The George Grey Barnard Collection.* New York: Robinson Galleries:

1941). The early years of the century were the most active for American collectors like J. P. Morgan.

20. Cited in Réau, 816.

21. See Philippe Boutry, "Le Clocher," and Alain Corbin, *Les cloches de la terre*. The latter dwells on the importance churches and especially their bells played as a symbol of pride and identity in rural France.

22. 13, 15, 63, 117, 193.

23. 135.

24. For details about these and other bombings of churches during World War I see Réau, 842–850. The cathedral of Soissons was cut in half by bombs (847), while l'église Saint-Gervais in Paris had its vaulting crushed by a bomb during Good Friday services in 1918. Notre-Dame d'Amiens, too, was touched by the bombing (848).

25. "Le Vandalisme allemand," reprinted in *L'Art allemand et l'art français du Moyen Age* (Paris, 1917). Cited in Réau, 844.

26. "La Cathédrale de Reims," in *Gazette des beaux-arts,* 1921. Cited in Réau, 844.

27. "The Mediaeval Synthesis," in *The Substance of Gothic,* 149–150.

28. See *Le Temps retrouvé* (ARTP IV 374–375), in which Charlus evokes this debate.

29. According to Vauchez, 63.

30. *Choix de poésies* (Paris: Bibliothèque Charpentier, 1925): 101. The last lines of the poem read: "Rendons grâce—attendu qu'il nous manquait encor/D'avoir ce qu'ont les Grecs sur la colline d'or:/Le Symbole du Beau consacré par l'insulte!—/Rendons grâce aux pointeurs du stupide canon,/Puisque de leur adresse allemande il résulte/Une Honte pour eux, pour nous un Parthénon!"

31. Rolland wrote this in an article entitled "Pro aris." Cited in the notes to *Le Temps retrouvé,* ARTP IV, note 2, 1232.

32. ARTP IV, 374.

33. *Chronique de la Grande Guerre* (Club de l'honnête homme I): 241–242.

34. "Introduction," iii. He insisted on the role of artists in publicizing the cathedral's importance, lxxxiii.

35. Cited in Vauchez, 64–66. For other examples of such attachment to the cathedral in our century, see Vauchez, 38, 67–68, and Réau, *Histoire du vandalisme*.

36. The differences in the two cultures' conception of the style can be seen in the fact that despite Viollet-le-Duc's attempts to champion Gothic style as a way of renewing French architecture, very few new structures were built with it in France; new structures would seem shoddy imitations of the originals. America, on the other hand, which had no original Gothic architecture, experienced a flood of new building based on Gothic models, especially at the beginning of the twentieth century.

37. See Ernest Samuels, *Henry Adams: The Major Phase* (Cambridge: Harvard University Press, 1964: 542) for a discussion about the prevalence of this belief.

38. Robert Mane, *Henry Adams on the Road to Chartres* (Cambridge: Harvard University Press, 1971): 116–152.

39. In fact, various kinds of Gothic revival had occurred throughout the history of the United States, including the Renaissance Revival that inspired Trinity Church in Boston, but it was Cram who made a distinction between the preceding waves of interest in medieval architecture—which he accused of being interested in form alone—and his goals of renewing the spiritual and theoretical links with the Middle Ages. Cram was extremely harsh on early Romanesque revival buildings in New York and Boston (see especially *My Life in Architecture*). For an overview of the Gothic Revival in America, see Calder Loth and Julius Trousdale Sadler, Jr. *The Only Proper Style: Gothic Architecture in America* (Boston: New York Graphic Society, 1975).

40. "The Gothic Restoration." *The Ministry of Art* (Cambridge: Houghton Mifflin, 1914): 47.

41. He speaks of "Gothic propaganda" as well as about form and function in *My Life in Architecture* (Boston: Little, Brown, and Company, 1936): 96, 275. Douglass Shand Tucci's *Ralph Adams Cram, American Medievalist* gives a very concise overview of the importance of Cram and his prolific writing and research for American medievalism (Boston: Boston Public Library, 1975).

42. See *The Only Proper Style: Gothic Architecture in America* (Boston: New York Graphic Society, 1975): 155.

43. *Mont Saint-Michel and Chartres* (Boston: Houghton Mifflin Company, 1933): v–vi.

44. Calder Loth and Julius Trousdale Sadler, Jr., *The Only Proper Style: Gothic Architecture in America* (Boston: New York Graphic Society, 1975): 154.

45. Cited in Samuels, 540–541.

SELECTED BIBLIOGRAPHY

Primary Sources

Barrès, Maurice. *L'Oeuvre de Maurice Barrès*. Paris: Au Club de l'Honnête Homme, 1966.

Bourget, Paul. *Nouveaux essais de psychologie contemporaine*. Paris: Alphonse Lemerre, 1886.

Cram, Ralph Adams. *The Substance of Gothic*. Boston: Marshall Jones Company, 1917.

Fustel de Coulanges, Numa Denis. "L'organisation de la Justice dans l'antiquité et les temps modernes. III. La Justice royale au Moyen Age." *La Revue des Deux Mondes* 94 (1 August 1871): 536–557.

Gautier, Théophile. *Les Jeunes France*. Paris: Flammarion (Nouvelle Bibliothèque Romantique), 1974.

Goncourt, Edmond et Jules. *Journal: Mémoires de la vie littéraire*. Robert Laffont. Paris: Fasquelle and Flammarion, 1956.

Hegel, G. W. F. *Aesthetics: Lectures on Fine Art*, vol. 2. Trans. T. M. Knox. Oxford: Clarendon Press, 1975.

Hugo, Victor. *Oeuvres complètes*. Ed. Jean Massin. Paris: Le Club français du livre, 1967.

Huret, Jules. *Enquête sur l'évolution littéraire*. Vanves: Les Editions Thot, 1984.

Huysmans, J.-K. "Bouqins: A propos de Barbey d'Aurevilly, Hello, Dom Legeay et Emile Mâle." *Huysmans*. Ed. Pierre Brunel and André Guyaux. Paris: Editions de l'Herne, 1985. 345–49.

———. *Lettres à Théodore Hannon (1876–1886)*. Ed. Pierre Cogny and Christian Berg. Saint-Cyr-sur-Loire: Christian Pirot, 1985.

———. *Lettres inédites à l'abbé Ferret (Une étape de la vie de Joris-Karl Huysmans)*. Ed. Elisabeth Bourget-Besnier. Paris: A. G. Nizet, 1973.

———. *Lettres inédites à Arij Prins*. Annotated by Louis Gillet. Geneva: Librairie Droz, 1977.

———. *Lettres inédites à Camille Lemonnier*. Ed. Gustave Wanwelkenhuyzen. Textes Littéraires Français. Geneva: Librairie Droz, 1957.

———. *Lettre inédites à Edmond de Goncourt*. Ed. Pierre Lambert and Pierre Cogny. Paris: Librairie Nizet, 1956.

————. *Lettres inédites à Emile Zola.* Ed. Pierre Lambert and Pierre Cogny. Textes Littéraires Françaises. Geneva: Librairie Droz, 1953.

————. *Lettres inédites à Jules Destrée.* Ed. Gustave Wanwelkenhuyzen. Textes Littéraires Français. Geneva: Librairie Droz, 1967.

————. *Oeuvres complètes de J.-K. Huysmans.* Ed. Lucien Descaves. Geneva: Slatkine Reprints, 1972.

Larousse, Pierre. *Grand dictionnaire universel du XIXe siecle: francais, historique, géographique, mythologique, bibliographique, litteraire, artistique, scientifique, etc.* Geneva: Slatkine, 1982.

Mâle, Emile. *The Gothic Image: Religious Art in France of the Thirteenth Century.* Trans. Dora Nussey. New York: Harper & Row, Publishers, 1950.

Michelet, Jules. *Bible de l'humanité.* Paris: Chamerot, 1864.

————. *Histoire de France.* Paris: Hachette, 1835–1945.

————. *Histoire de France: Renaissance et Réforme.* Paris: Editions Robert Laffont, S.A., 1982.

Morice, Charles. "Introduction." *Les Cathédrales de France.* Paris: Librairie Armand, Colin, 1914.

Proust, Marcel. *Contre Sainte-Beuve: précédé de Pastiches et melanges et suivi de Essais et articles.* Etablie par Pierre Clarac avec la collaboration d'Yves Sandre. Paris: Gallimard, 1971.

————. *Correspondance.* Texte etabli, presenté et annoté par Philip Kolb. Paris: Plon, 1970–1993.

————. *Correspondance avec Jacques Rivière.* Paris: Gallimard, 1976.

————. *Jean Santeuil. Précédé de Les plaisirs et les jours.* Etabli par Pierre Clarac avec la collaboration d'Yves Sandre. Paris: Gallimard, 1971.

————. *A la recherche du temps perdu,* 4 vols. Ed. Jean-Yves Tadié. Paris: Gallimard (Bibliothèque de la Pléiade), 1988.

Renan, Ernest. "L'Art du moyen âge et les causes de sa décadence." *La Revue des Deux Mondes* 40 (1 July 1862): 203–228.

Rodin, Auguste. *Les Cathédrales de France.* Paris: Librairie Armand Colin, 1921.

Ruskin, John. *La Bible d'Amiens.* 10/18. Trans. Marcel Proust. Paris: Union Générale d'Editions, 1986.

————. *Sésame et les lys.* Le Regard littéraire. Trans. Marcel Proust. Brussels: Editions Complexe, 1987.

Vitet, Ludovic (Louis). "Une Nouvelle Histoire de France, de M. Guizot." *La Revue des Deux Mondes* 95 (15 May 1872): 439–449.

Zola, Emile. *Contes et nouvelles.* Bibliothèque de la Pléiade. Ed. Roger Ripoll. Paris: Gallimard, 1976.

————. *Correspondance.* Ed. B. H. Bakker and et al. Montreal and Paris: Les Presses de l'Université de Montréal and Editions du Centre National de la Recherche Scientifique, 1978–1995.

————. Manuscripts for *Les Trois Villes* (1590, 1608). La Bibliothèque Méjanes, Aix-en-Provence, France.

————. *Oeuvres complètes.* Cercle du livre précieux. Ed. Henri Mitterand. Paris: Fasquelle, 1966–1970.

————. *Les Rougon-Macquart.* Bibliothèque de la Pléiade. Ed. Henri Mitterand and Armand Lanoux. Vol. 1–5. Paris: Gallimard, 1960–1967.

Secondary Sources

Amalvi, Christian. *Le Goût du Moyen Age.* Paris: Plon, 1996.

Antosh, Ruth B. *Reality and Illusion in the Novels of J.-K. Huysmans.* Amsterdam: Rodopi, 1986.

————. "The Role of Paintings in Three Novels by J.-K. Huysmans." *Nineteenth-Century French Studies* 1984 (Summer-Fall 12–13:4–1): 131–46.

Aubert, Marcel. "Le Romantisme et le moyen âge." *Le Romantisme et l'art.* Paris: Laurens, 1928.

Autret, Jean. *L'Influence de Ruskin sur la vie, les idées et l'oeuvre de M. Proust.* Geneva: Droz et Giard, 1955.

Baguley, David. *Fécondité d'Émile Zola; roman à thèse, évangile, mythe.* Toronto: University of Toronto Press, 1973.

————. *Zola et les genres.* Somerset: University of Glasgow French and German Publications, 1993.

Baldick, Robert. *The Life of J.-K. Huysmans.* Oxford: Clarendon Press, 1955.

Bales, Richard. *Proust and the Middle Ages.* Geneva: Droz, 1975.

————. "Proust et Emile Mâle." *Bulletin de la Société des amis de Marcel Proust et des amis de Combray* 24 (1974): 1925–1936.

Bergdoll, Barry. "The Ideal of the Gothic Cathedral in 1852." *A. W. N. Pugin: Master of the Gothic Revival* (New Haven: Yale University Press, 1996): 103–135.

Bergeron, Katherine. *Decadent Enchantments: The Revival of Gregorian Chant at Solesmes.* Berkeley: The University of California Press, 1998.

Bertrand-Jennings, Chantal. *Espaces Romanesques: Zola.* Sherbrooke: Editions Naaman, 1987.

Bizzarro, Tina Waldeier. *Romanesque Architectural Criticism. A Prehistory.* Cambridge: Cambridge University Press, 1992.

Bourlier, Kay. *Marcel Proust et l'architecture.* Montreal: Les Presses de l'Université de Montréal, 1990.

Boutry, Philippe. "Le Clocher." *Les Lieux de mémoire.* Ed. Pierre Nora. Paris: Editions Gallimard, 1986. II: 57–77.

Brown, Frederick. *Zola: A Life.* New York: Farrar Straus Giroux, 1995.

Bucknall, Barbara J. *The Religion of Art in Proust.* Urbana, IL: University of Illinois Press, 1969.

Carter, A. E. "J.-K. Huysmans and the Middle Ages." *Medieval Studies in Honor of Robert White Linker.* Ed. Brian Dutton, J. Woodrow Hassell, Jr. and John E. Keller. Valencia: Artes Graficas Soler, S.A., 1973: 18–53.

Cattaui, Georges. "L'Oeuvre de Proust: son architecture, son orchestration, sa symbolique." *Critique* March 1958: 197–213.

Charlton, D. G. *Secular Religions in France: 1815–1870.* London: Oxford University Press, 1963.

Choay, Françoise. *L'Allégorie du patrimoine.* Paris: Seuil, 1999.

Clark, Kenneth. *The Gothic Revival.* London: Constable, 1950.

Clogenson, Yves. "Le thème de la cathédrale dans Proust." *Bulletin de la Société des amis de Marcel Proust et des amis de Combray* 14 (1964): 152–159.

Compagnon, Antoine. "Proust's Remembrance of Things Past." *Realms of Memory.* Ed. Pierra Nora. Trans. Arthur Goldhammer. New York: Columbia University Press, 1997. II: 210–246.

Corbin, Alain. *Les Cloches de la terre: Paysage sonore et culture sensible dans les campagnes au XIXe siècle.* Paris: Albin Michel, 1994.

Dakyns, Janine R. *The Middle Ages in French Literature 1851–1900.* London: Oxford University Press, 1973.

De Botton, Alain. *How Proust Can Change Your Life.* New York: Pantheon Books, 1997.

De Certeau, Michel. *La Faiblesse de Croire.* Paris: Editions du Seuil, 1987.

Deleuze, Gilles. *Proust et les signes.* Paris: Presses universitaires de France, 1971.

Duby, Georges. *The Age of the Cathedrals. Art and Society, 980–1420.* Trans. Eleanor Levieux and Barbara Thompson. Chicago: University of Chicago Press, 1981.

Emery, Elizabeth. "Bricabracomania: Zola's Romantic Instinct." *Excavatio* 12 (1999): 107–115.

———. "The Power of the Pen: Emile Zola Takes on the Sacré-Coeur Basilica." *The Documentary Impulse and French Literature,* vol. XXVIII of *French Literature Studies.* Amsterdam: Rodopi, 2001.

———. "The 'Truth' About the Middle Ages: *La Revue des Deux Mondes* and Late Nineteenth-Century French Medievalism." *Prose Studies,* vol. 23: 2.

———. "Zola and the Tree of Jesse." *Excavatio* 11 (1998): 74–80.

Engelbert, Edward. "The Displaced Cathedral in Flaubert, James, Lawrence, and Kafka." *Arcadia: Zeitschrift für Vergleichende Literaturwissenschaft.* 21:3 (1986): 245–262.

Erlande-Brandenburg, Alain. *The Cathedral.* Trans. Martin Thom. Cambridge: Cambridge University Press, 1989.

Fraisse, Luc. *L'oeuvre cathédrale.* Paris: José Corti, 1990.

Frankl, Paul. *The Gothic: Literary Sources and Interpretations Through Eight Centuries.* Princeton, NJ: Princeton University Press, 1960.

Germann, Georg. *Gothic Revival in Europe and Britain: Sources, Influences, and Ideas.* Cambridge, MA: MIT Press, 1973.

Griffiths, Richard. *The Reactionary Revolution. The Catholic Revival in French Literature, 1870–1914.* New York: Frederick Ungar Publishing Co., 1965.

Gugelot, Frédéric. *La Conversion des intellectuels au catholicisme en France 1885–1935.* Paris: CNRS Editions, 1998.

Guieu, Jean-Max. *Le Théâtre lyrique d'Emile Zola.* Paris: Fischbacher, 1983.

Hamon, Philippe. *Expositions: Literature and Architecture in Nineteenth-Century France.* Trans. Katia Sainson-Frank and Lisa Maguire. Berkeley: University of California Press, 1992.

Harris, Ruth. *Lourdes: Body and Spirit in the Secular Age.* New York: Viking, 1999.

Harvey, David. "Monument and Myth: The Building of the Sacré-Coeur." *Consciousness and the Urban Experience.* Baltimore: Johns Hopkins University Press, 1985.

Hatzenberger, Antoine. *L'Esthétique de la cathédrale gothique.* Paris: Harmattan, 1999.

Henry, Anne. *Marcel Proust: theories pour une esthetique.* Paris: Klincksieck, 1981.

Issacharoff, Michael. *J.-K. Huysmans devant la critique en France.* Paris: Editions Klincksieck, 1970.

Johnson, J. Theodore, Jr. "Marcel Proust and Architecture: Some Thoughts on the Cathedral-Novel." *Critical Essays on Marcel Proust.* Ed. Barbara J. Bucknall. Boston: G.K. Hall & Co., 1987. 133–180.

———. "Proust and Giotto: Foundations for an Allegorical Interpretation of *A la recherche du temps perdu.*" *Marcel Proust: A Critical Panorama.* Ed. Larkin B. Price. Urbana: University of Illinois Press, 1973. 168–205.

———. "Proust, Ruskin, et la petite figure au portail des libraires à la Cathédrale de Rouen." *Bulletin de la Société des amis de Marcel Proust et des amis de Combray* 23 (1973): 1721–1736.

Jonas, Raymond A. *France and the Cult of the Sacred Heart.* Berkeley: University of California Press, 2000.

———. "Monument as Ex-Voto, Monument as Historiosophy: The Basilica of the Sacré-Coeur." *French Historical Studies* 18:2 (Fall 1993): 482–502.

Jullien, Dominique. "La Cathédrale Romanesque." *Bulletin Marcel Proust* 40 (1990): 43–57.

Le Men, Ségolène. *La Cathédrale illustrée de Hugo à Monet.* Paris: CNRS Editions, 1998.

Leniaud, Jean-Michel. *Les Cathédrales au XIXe siècle.* Paris: Economica, 1993.

Lloyd, Christopher. *Huysmans and the Fin-de-siècle Novel.* Edinburgh: Edinburgh University Press, 1990.

Mallion, Jean. *Victor Hugo et l'art architectural.* Paris: Presses universitaires de France, 1962.

Moore, Stephanie. "Reviving the Medieval Model: The Cathedrals of Claude Monet, Joris-Karl Huysmans and Claude Debussy." *Interart Poetics: Essays on the Interrelations of the Arts and Media*. Amsterdam: Rodopi, 1997. 195–207.

Morowitz, Laura. "Consuming the Past: The Nabis and French Medieval Art" (Ph.D. dissertation, New York University 1996).

———. "Zola's *Le Rêve:* Naturalism, Symbolism and Medievalism in the Fin-de-siècle." *Excavatio* 9 (1997): 92–102.

Noiray, Jacques. *Le Romancier et la machine*. Paris: Librairie José Corti, 1981.

Ortoleva, Madeleine Y. *Joris-Karl Huysmans: Romancier du Salut*. Sherbrooke, Québec: Editions Naaman, 1981.

Peysson-Zeiss, Agnès. *Littérature et architecture. Le dix-neuvième siècle*. Lanham, MD: University Press of America, 1998.

Pommier, Jean. "Michelet et l'architecture gothique." *Etudes de lettres* 26 (Dec. 1954): 17–35.

Pissarro. *Monet's Cathedral*. New York: Alred A. Knopf, 1990.

Raimond, Michel. *La Crise du roman*. Paris: José Corti, 1966.

Réau, Louis. *Histoire du vandalisme*. Edition augmentée par Michel Fleury et Guy-Michel Leproux. Paris: Editions Robert Laffont, 1994.

Richer, Laurence. *La Cathédrale du feu. Le Moyen Age de Michelet, de l'histoire au mythe*. Nimes: Editions Palaam, 1995.

Riegl, Aloïs. *Le culte moderne des monuments*. Trans. Daniel Wieczorek. Paris: Editions du Seuil, 1984.

Saisselin, Rémy. *The Bourgeois and the Bibelot*. New Brunswick: Rutgers University Press, 1984.

Shattuck, Richard. *Proust's Way: A Field Guide to* In Search of Lost Time. New York: W. W. Norton & Company, 2000.

Suleiman, Susan Robin. *Authoritarian Fictions: The Ideological Novel as a Literary Genre*. Princeton: Princeton University Press, 1993.

Tadié, Jean-Yves. *Marcel Proust: Biographie*. Paris: Editions Gallimard (NRF), 1996.

———. *Proust et le roman: Essai sur les formes et techniques du roman dans A la recherche du temps perdu*. Paris: Gallimard, 1971.

Ternois, René. *Zola et son temps: Lourdes, Rome, Paris*. Paris: Société Les Belles Lettres, 1961.

Vachon, Stéphane. "Construction d'une cathédrale de papier." *Les Travaux et les jours de Honoré de Balzac*. Paris: Presses du CNRS, 1992. 15–41.

Van der Meulen, Jan. *Chartres: Sources and Literary Interpretation*. Boston: G. K. Hall & Co., 1989.

Vauchez, André. "La Cathédrale." *Les Lieux de mémoire*. Ed. Pierre Nora. Paris: Editions Gallimard, 1986. 91–127.

Viegnes, Michel J. *Le Milieu et l'individu dans la trilogie de Joris-Karl Huysmans.* Paris: A. G. Nizet, 1986.

Walker, Philip. *Germinal and Zola's Philosophical and Religious Thought.* Amsterdam: John Benjamins Publishing Company, 1984.

———. "Prophetic Myths in Zola." *PMLA* 74 (1959): 444–452.

Watson, Janell. *Literature and Material Culture from Balzac to Proust: The Collection and Consumption of Curiosities.* Cambridge: Cambridge University Press, 1999.

Weber, Eugen. *France Fin de Siècle.* Cambridge, MA: The Belknap Press of Harvard University Press, 1986.

Williams, Rosalind H. *Dream Worlds: Mass Consumption in Late Nineteenth-Century France.* Berkeley: University of California Press, 1982.

Yoshida, Jo. "Métamorphose de l'Eglise de Balbec: Un aperçu génétique du 'Voyage au Nord.'" *Bulletin d'Informations Proustiennes* 14 (1983): 41–61.

Zayed, Fernande. *Huysmans, peintre de son epoque.* Paris: A. G. Nizet, 1973.

Zumthor, Paul. "Le Moyen âge de Victor Hugo." *Oeuvres complètes de Victor Hugo.* Paris: Le Club français du livre, 1967. x–xxxi.

INDEX